REACHING INSIDE

50
Acclaimed Authors on
100
Unforgettable Short Stories

REACHING INSIDE

Edited and Introduced by
ANDRE DUBUS III

Boston | GODINE | 2023

Published in 2023 by
GODINE
Boston, Massachusetts

LIBRARY OF CONGRESS CATALOGING-IN-PUBLICATION DATA
Names: Dubus, Andre, III 1959- editor.
Title: Reaching inside : 50 essential authors on 100 unforgettable short
    stories / edited & introduced by Andre Dubus III.
Description: Boston : Godine, 2023. | Includes bibliographical references
    and index. |
Identifiers: LCCN 2022036552 (print) | LCCN 2022036553 (ebook) | ISBN
    9781567927696 (hardcover) | ISBN 9781567927702 (ebook)
Subjects: LCSH: Short story. | Authors, American--Books and reading. |
    Authorship--Psychological aspects. | LCGFT: Essays.
Classification: LCC PN3373 .R35 2023 (print) | LCC PN3373 (ebook) | DDC
    809.3/1--dc23/eng/20220831
LC record available at https://lccn.loc.gov/2022036552
LC ebook record available at https://lccn.loc.gov/2022036553

First Printing, 2023
Printed in the United States of America

*This book is dedicated to all the wonderful
students I've had the honor of teaching over the
years at various universities, but most especially
at the University of Massachusetts Lowell.*

✦ CONTENTS ✦

INTRODUCTION

✦ ✦ ✦ ✦ ✦ ✦ ✦

Andre Dubus III

L ATE ON A COLD night quite a few years ago, I stood on a
 Boston sidewalk with the celebrated American novelist Tim
O'Brien, who, miraculously, had become my friend. I say "miraculously" because he was a deservedly famous writer—a winner of
the National Book Award for his 1979 novel *Going After Cacciato*;
the author of the widely read and critically acclaimed *The Things
They Carried*, a book many discerning readers have called a perfectly executed work; and the author of two other novels and a
memoir and what was then his latest, *In the Lake of the Woods*.

I was in my early thirties at the time, and to support my own
writing, I worked as a self-employed carpenter and part-time creative writing instructor. In the past five years, I had published
two books that very few people had bought or read, though this
fact did not bother me too much; I am the son of the master short
story writer Andre Dubus, whose books had never sold well, and
I believed that that was just how it went. I was also hard at work
on what I hoped would become my second published novel, and
I was in Boston that night to take my fiction writing class from
Emerson College to hear Tim O'Brien read from his new book.

I first met O'Brien at a party at my father's house several years earlier. I was shy around him, this man whose work I revered, until he told me that he wanted to get into better physical shape and could I put him on a weight-training program. Using my father's bench and weights, I spent the next half hour showing Tim various exercises and how to do them and when and for how long. A few months later, he was invited to read at the MFA program I was enrolled in up in Vermont, and after his reading to hundreds of people, after he'd signed dozens and dozens of books, we went to a bar where, over a pitcher of beer, we planned to work out together early the next morning before his master class, which we did for nearly two hours.

And so, at that bookstore that night in Boston, Tim and I treated each other like the friends we'd become. But in front of my writing students, all of whom admired O'Brien's work as much as I did, I felt mildly embarrassed about this for I never would have met O'Brien if my father had not also been a writer accomplished enough to have Tim O'Brien come to his house. The overwhelming majority of my students did not come from families with writers in them. Plumbers maybe. Waitresses (many of them single mothers) for certain. Truck drivers or electricians or accountants. But few of them had ever met a "famous author," let alone seen him or her in one of their homes.

After Tim's reading, I tried to introduce him to as many of my students as I could. He had a full crowd that night, and after it was over, my newly inspired students walking back to their city campus, Tim and I stood on the sidewalk talking about our workouts when a taxi pulled to the curb. But I'd forgotten to have Tim sign my copy of his new novel, and just as he was about to leave I asked if he would mind signing one more, and he took out his pen, opened his book, and inscribed something on the title page before we hugged and then he was gone.

Under the nearest streetlight I read what he'd written: *Andre, I hope this reaches inside.—Tim.*

I read the line three times. It was like walking by an open window and hearing music you didn't know you'd been trying to play your entire life. *Reach inside.* Isn't that what I'd been trying to do daily for years? To capture on the page human truths, large or small, that may then gather the power to reach inside another? I wanted to chase down Tim's taxi, and I wanted to thank him for that line.

I TELL THIS STORY about Tim O'Brien because within it lies the underpinnings for this anthology: that writers, even the most accomplished among us, are no different from the rest of us, and that many of them, if not all, share O'Brien's wish that their work will go deeply enough into its subject for it to reach inside the reader.

Nearly ten years after that evening with Tim and my students, writing daily and nightly and failing far more than succeeding, I found myself the author of a novel that rose to the top of the bestseller lists, that put me on TV shows and in awards ceremonies, that sent me down the red carpet of a Hollywood premiere, that made me and my young family some real money, something that I and the people I came from had never known. I was invited to travel the country to read from the novel at universities and bookstores, libraries and literary festivals, from coast to coast. And the strangest part of all this is that I found myself regularly in the company of my literary heroes, women and men whose work I'd been reading and trying to emulate for years. Along the way, I have discovered something: as I huddled with my literary heroes in pubs or restaurants or shared a cab on the way to an airport or sat around the dinner table at one of their homes, the overwhelming majority of them spend a lot of time talking about what they're reading or have just read or are getting ready to finally read.

The idea for Reaching Inside rose from these conversations, past and present. It became clear to me again and again that no matter how celebrated these writers had become, the overwhelming majority of them had come from childhoods with no writers in them, and what had put them on their artistic paths was reading just the sort of work that Tim O'Brien had inscribed to me, writing that entered them and their dream worlds, had maybe even altered their view of life and their place in it, writing that, ultimately, made them want to write something substantial themselves.

So why not ask writers to write about *that*? For each of them to choose two short stories that had done *that* to them?

I sent out letters of invitation to fifty of the finest writers in the country and asked each of them to choose two short stories—one canonical and perhaps one that is lesser known—that have fed them in some way, that have kept that artistic flame lit or sparked it for the very first time, and then to write one brief essay about both stories. The results of those invitations are what you have here before you. In a time of so many digital distractions, of short attention spans and cluttered thinking, this anthology is simple in its approach and design: fifty compelling essays about one hundred accomplished short stories by fifty distinguished living writers.

Here, we have Mary Gordon on works by Tillie Olson and Katherine Anne Porter: "Without these two stories, I would not have written fiction . . . it felt like a blow, shattering the last of my resistance to writing prose." In Tobias Wolff's exploration of Hawthorne's "Wakefield" and Joyce Carol Oates's widely anthologized masterpiece "Where Are You Going, Where Have You Been?" Wolff asks: "[W]hat are the consequences, over time, of this habit of holding oneself apart and looking in? Can you, once you've taken the backward step, ever reclaim your place in the living stream?"

We have Joyce Carol Oates herself studying the choice of two verb tenses used in John Updike's "A & P": "Is this an error on the author's part or a shrewd decision? When we write/read/think in the present tense, we are literally not yet in possession of what comes next . . ." We also have Anna Quindlen's deeply personal and moving description of how her "literary education is like the strata of the earth. When you dig down, you can see the layers . . . first you need to learn about storytelling, and then you need to learn about life, in all its complications and contradictions."

In Junot Díaz's insightful essay on stories by Edwidge Danticat and Octavia Butler, two completely different writers, he draws compelling parallels between Danticat's poverty-stricken Haiti and Butler's bleak dystopian dreamscape: "It's as hellish a scenario as it sounds and for those of us descended from enslaved Africans, all too believable."

Here, too, Michael Cunningham argues: "Every story, whatever its nature, is by definition a single writer's attempt to tell some section of a story too vast to be told." He then goes on to focus on the masterful endings of two short stories, comparing James Joyce's "The Dead" to "Work" by Denis Johnson.

In Julia Glass's essay, she confronts the question: "By what false certainties do all of us live, trivial or grand, God-fearing or profane?" And in his exploration of two John Cheever stories, Paul Harding discovers this: "Repression and concealment are arguably Cheever's artistic preoccupations . . . they are the sources of his stories' sublime beauties . . ." Sue Miller takes on Tim O'Brien's "The Things They Carried" and Edward P. Jones's "Spanish in the Morning," parting the curtain on their individual shapes, "on the improbable way (each) is made." And Richard Russo, in an essay that is as personal as it is instructive, examines how stories change as we, their readers, age and change. His focus here is on "Builders," by Richard Yates, and Shirley Jackson's "The Lottery," and he delves into each with his characteristic humor, rigor, and compassion.

THERE ARE MORE ESSAYS, of course, each as beautifully written as another, each inspiring and edifying in its own specificity of voice and vision. In gathering these compelling pieces, I was reminded of a line from Willa Cather: "A writer is at his best only when writing within the character and range of his deepest sympathies." In other words, we must *care* about our writing subjects and, often, it is the writing itself that leads us to discovering just what that is. These passionately written essays are inspiring and instructive, and therefore infectious: readers are bound to find themselves finishing an essay, then reaching immediately for the short story they've just read about.

But more than any of this, what we have here in this lovely, moving, and, frankly, powerful anthology is an open invitation to its readers that they too are invited to this grand circus that is the writing life, that no matter whether someone has won the Pulitzer Prize or the National Book Award, as many of these contributors have, whether you began life on blue-collar back streets or in white-collar comfort, whether you've ever met a published writer or believed the authors of famous books were all dead, everyone is welcome here, everyone is encouraged to open this book and to take in these masterful essays that reach inside us, and, as Tolstoy reminds us, transfer feeling from one heart to another.

—Andre Dubus III

REACHING INSIDE

ANN PATCHETT

✦ ✦ ✦ ✦ ✦ ✦ ✦

SONNY'S BLUES
James Baldwin

THE LONG-DISTANCE RUNNER
Grace Paley

✦ ✦ ✦ ✦ ✦ ✦ ✦

I N THE SPRING OF 1985, I got a letter from the University of Iowa
telling me I had been accepted to the Writers' Workshop. The
teaching assistantship I had been awarded consisted of a little bit
of money and, more important, in-state tuition. All I had to do
was teach an undergraduate course called Introduction to Literature that would comprise two novels, two plays (one Shakespeare,
one contemporary), a selection of poetry, and some short stories.
I was twenty-one years old, and in those days I cared about short
stories more than anything else. I received a free desk copy of *The
Norton Anthology of Short Fiction*, and the summer before I drove to
the Midwest to be a writer, I read the whole thing. As far as I was
concerned, there was nothing in it that touched James Baldwin's
"Sonny's Blues."

I rented half a duplex in Iowa City with Lucy Grealy, a friend
from college. Lucy and I had the same financial-aid package, and
the same deep feeling for "Sonny's Blues." It was the single thing
that made us look forward to teaching. Again and again we went
over the story, sitting at our fragile kitchen table. The narrator's
love for his brother Sonny was well intentioned but so filled with

misunderstanding. How could anyone who didn't live for art fully comprehend the suffering of someone who did? As we were about to begin our lives as writers, the story made us feel we were poised to face the same dangers Sonny faced—our own tortured souls, a break from all who loved us and could never understand us, even the heroin seemed possible. "All I know about music is that not many people ever really hear it," Sonny's brother tells us. "And even then, on the rare occasions when something opens within, and the music enters, what we mainly hear, or hear corroborated, are personal, private, vanishing evocations. But the man who creates the music is hearing something else, is dealing with the roar rising from the void and imposing order on it as it hits the air." James Baldwin understood that even as we prepared to give our lives to art, we faced the very real risk that no one would listen. It didn't matter though, we couldn't stop ourselves. We were doing the thing we were called to do.

I included "Sonny's Blues" in just about every literature or creative writing class I ever taught, but I haven't taught one in a very long time. When I went back to my *Norton Anthology* all these years later, I found that I had underlined more sentences than I left alone, writing notes of explanation to myself in the margin, adding stars for emphasis. I also found that in the intervening years, I had become something of a postmodern reader; I wasn't as comfortable with such a straightforward story of suffering and grief as I had once been. Baldwin does nothing to soften the blows: the death of the boy's uncle, the death of the beloved only daughter, the deathly struggle of Sonny, who, we are led to believe, may make it through his addiction but very possibly will not. I soon remembered everything I had loved in the unflinching telling. When Lucy and I had first read the story, in graduate school, we thought the message was that art is unimaginably hard. Now I can see that Baldwin was telling us that *life* is hard, and that art, however difficult, is for the lucky ones. In art at least the pain could be put to use.

THIS TIME AROUND, READING "Sonny's Blues" made me think of another story I loved: "The Long-Distance Runner," by Grace Paley. She too had something to say about the past, about being pulled to what is no longer there, to what is there, to what we love and are afraid of. She does it in a way that I'm more comfortable with now, a slightly surrealistic vision of the world where the things we'd rather not admit about ourselves are laced with a dose of palliative humor. Paley's alter-ego Faith puts on her running shorts and jogs back to her old neighborhood. She finds it crumbling, trash strewn, and completely African American.

"'I used to live here,' I said."

"'Oh, yes,' they said, 'in the white old days. That time too bad to last.'"

When Faith is charged by an angry mob, she runs to seek shelter in her childhood apartment. There she is taken in by Mrs. Luddy, who lives with her son Donald and three baby girls in foster care. Every time Faith starts to leave, she can't quite make it. "I'd get to the door and then I'd hear voices. I'm ashamed to say I'd become fearful. Despite my wide geographical love of mankind, I would be attacked by local fears." From her perch at Mrs. Luddy's window, which had once been her own window, Faith gives us a larger view of the world: the tiresome routines and sweet pleasures of motherhood, the lifesaving value of a woman's friendship, the change and the sameness of the view over time. Like all Grace Paley stories, this one feels as if it were meant to be read aloud, or possibly sung. In its cartoon reality, it feels oddly like something that might have happened, and that the truth of the actual events was perhaps stretched out by too much telling.

Grace Paley was born in the Bronx in 1922, and it is the Bronx Faith goes back to when she runs. James Baldwin was born in Harlem in 1924, and that's where Sonny goes when he gets out of prison. None of this necessarily provides the two stories with a connection to each other; still, they make a comfortable fit. If Faith did run home after Mrs. Luddy pushed her out, she may well have gone through Harlem. She may have run all the way to Greenwich Village, where Sonny played jazz in a club with the people who understood him and were truly his family. Had they met somewhere along the way, Sonny and Faith, despite whatever differences there were between them, I believe they would have understood each other perfectly.

MARY GORDON

✦ ✦ ✦ ✦ ✦ ✦ ✦

I STAND HERE IRONING
Tillie Olsen

PALE HORSE, PALE RIDER
Katherine Anne Porter

✦ ✦ ✦ ✦ ✦ ✦ ✦

WITHOUT THESE TWO WRITERS, I could not have written fiction. I mean these words literally and not metaphorically.

It was 1972. I was in graduate school, getting an MFA. I believed I was a poet. There were poets I could look to: Plath, Sexton, Rich. Particularly for me, Denise Levertov. But I couldn't find women fiction writers doing what I wanted to do: to write lyrically, and to include the large issues. Life, death, identity, heartbreak: the world. I had been enlivened by Lessing's *The Golden Notebook* and revved up by Mary McCarthy's *The Company She Keeps*. But both lacked the lyric touch, and this was central to what was most important to me.

My first reading of "I Stand Here Ironing" was a reading through tears. Forty-two years later, I read it through tears. But that first reading: a revelation. It was what I was looking for: fiction that was unabashedly unironic, uncool ... unmale. This was a story about a mother and a daughter. It contained details like swollen breasts and the hysteria of getting children dressed in the morning. The language flowed with a breathtaking immediacy; there was a hint of "not made in America" in the cadence. And among many

astonishments: the inclusion in so brief a story of the political realities of the larger world. Mentioned just briefly, but studding the
surface like red nails on a white wall, are the Depression, the War
. . . most importantly the abiding fear of nuclear annihilation.

The specificity of her details seared images into my brain.
Unbearable, the clarity of the scene at the convalescent home,
where the sick child is sent to be fattened up because her mother has been told by experts that she cannot provide the proper
nourishment.

"High up on the balconies of each cottage the children stand,
the girls in their red bows and white dresses, the boys in white
suits and giant red ties. The parents stand below shrieking up to
be heard and the children shriek down to be heard."

And how deft the evocation of those paradoxically paradisal
days when the child, sickish but not sick, stays home with the
mother in a cocoon of unreal safety.

"Mostly Emily had asthma, and her breathing, harsh and la-
bored, would fill the house with a curiously tranquil sound. I
would bring the two old dresser mirrors and her boxes of collections to her bed. She would select beads and single earrings,
bottle tops and shells, dried flowers and pebbles, old postcards
and scraps, all sorts of oddments."

Perhaps the most heartbreaking aspect of the story is the
mother's guilty acknowledgment of her failures—none the less
real because there was no choice.

"She was a beautiful baby . . . You did not know her all those
years she was thought homely, or see her poring over her baby
pictures, making me tell her over and over how beautiful she had
been—and would be, I would tell her—and was now, to the seeing
eye. But the seeing eyes were few or nonexistent. Including mine."

THAT SAME YEAR, 1972, and quite by chance, I discovered Katherine Anne Porter in an anthology that we graduate students

who were teaching Freshman Composition were required to use. I read "Pale Horse, Pale Rider" and it felt like a blow, shattering the last of my resistance to writing prose. She was doing it, what I thought could not be done. She was writing about death and love and war with an imagistic richness and a radiant, demanding narrative line.

The story must take its place in the outstanding literature of the First World War, but its contribution is singular. It is, after all the story of the War at Home, and from a Woman's point of view. And it is the story of the Spanish Influenza Epidemic, which dealt as many deaths as the War Itself.

The rooms Porter created were as real to me as my living room but she was fearlessly using the large words that—post-Hemingway—we had been told (but I was yearning for them) we were not allowed to use. In this story I found a sentence that I still find miraculous, impossible: it should not work, but it is the sentence of all sentences that I most admire: "Death is death and for the dead it has no attributes."

It begins in a dream and moves to a newspaper office where Miranda, the heroine, encounters patriotic bullying and the hazards of being a working woman in a male domain. Two Liberty bond salesmen are waiting for her, suggesting that if she doesn't buy a bond, her job will be in danger. The older is drawn with a few, masterful strokes. "He might be anything at all: advance agent for a road show, promoter of a wildcat oil company, a former saloon keeper announcing the opening of a new cabaret, an automobile salesman—any follower of any one of the crafty, haphazard callings."

I still remember the hair standing up on the back of my neck at the juxtaposition of the words *crafty* and haphazard.

I can only conclude that the reason Porter hasn't achieved the eminence she deserves is that her best work is in the short story, the unfavored younger sister of prose fiction. And everything she writes is from a perspective that is unabashedly and unmistakably female. When a pathetic failed hoofer confronts Miranda for giving him a bad review, she responds in a way that is all too familiar to women who are called upon to judge: "You shouldn't pay any attention at all. What does it matter what I think." And not least among the large subjects Porter treats in this story is Romantic heterosexual love from a woman's perspective. "He was tall and heavily muscled in the shoulders, narrow in the waist and flanks, and he was infinitely buttoned, strapped, harnessed into a uniform as tough and unyielding in cut as a straight jacket, though the cloth was fine and supple."

Adam is hardly a standard-issue he-man; part of his allure is that he is maternal: he even holds his beloved's head when she vomits—the real definition of manning up.

Miranda returns from her brush with death to discover that her lover has died of the flu, most probably contracted through her. She can face the world only with the aid of makeup, provided by her woman friend and fellow reporter. "One lipstick, medium . . . a box of apricot powder . . . I don't need eye shadow, do I? No one need pity this corpse if we look properly to the art of the thing."

It is not possible to read these two stories without an enlargement of our understanding of what it might mean to look properly to the art of the thing. The thing, the story, told by women, in women's voices, fearlessly poetic, passionate and grand.

MADISON SMARTT BELL

✦ ✦ ✦ ✦ ✦ ✦ ✦

KING OF THE MOUNTAIN
George Garrett

SREDNI VASHTAR
Saki

✦ ✦ ✦ ✦ ✦ ✦ ✦

T HE ONE THING I might have in common with the writer
called Saki (and I'm guessing here) is that we both developed an appetite for reading and daydreaming during long
hours laid up sick as small children. The resemblance ends
there. I had my parents and was loved and well cared for. Saki,
government name Hector Hugh Munro, lost his mother to
miscarriage when he was two years old. His father returned to
police work in the British Far East colonies, leaving the boy
and his older brother and sister in the hands of a hostile grandmother and a couple of witchy aunts who found doctors to tell
the children they were terminally ill and would not live to grow
up. Munro survived to complete his education, to write several
volumes of mordant short stories, full of Aesopian ironies but
free of moral purpose, and to enlist, in his forties, in the British
Army during World War I; he died in combat. His last words
were "Put out that bloody cigarette!" Three-on-a-match—three
people sharing a light from the same match—is bad luck because it allows the sniper in the opposite trench enough time to
sight his rifle.

I discovered Saki at age eleven, going out to milk the cow with my cousin, who was older but a less experienced dairy hand. I was happy to do all the milking as long as my cousin kept me entertained with Saki stories recited from memory. I heard the one about the cloyingly good little girl who was discovered and eaten by a wolf because her fearful trembling made her medal for Good Conduct clank against her medal for Supreme Priggishness, and the one about the cat who not only talked but also blackmailed guests at a house party, where he (the cat) was wont to stroll across the bedroom balconies at night. I probably heard "The Open Window" and "The Interlopers," and possibly "Sredni Vashtar."

The latter is, I believe, Saki's only fictional rendition of his own wretched childhood. In the story the siblings are out of the picture and the unpleasant female relatives rolled up into one, who the ostensibly invalid Conradin calls "the Woman." The story, with its japes about Anabaptist hens and such, was clearly intended to entertain adults, but at eleven I found it riveting. Conradin's despair was alien, thus fascinating to me, while the story he set by his imagination was quite familiar. "Without his imagination, which was rampant under the spur of loneliness, he would have succumbed long ago."

What if imagination could actually change the real world? The weight of the story comes from Conradin's hopeless helplessness in the hands of inimical adults, and invests the religion he invents around his hen and ferret with its rich, dark, sinister tone. To an adult audience, all that must seem pleasantly absurd, but at eleven I bought it without reservation:

> *Sredni Vashtar went forth,*
> *His thoughts were red thoughts and his teeth were white.*
> *His enemies called for peace but he brought them death.*
> *Sredni Vashtar the Beautiful.*

Do one thing for me, Sredni Vashtar . . . With Conradin I bate my breath, hoping the most improbable hope, and when instead of the Woman the deified ferret emerges from the shed, licking its bloody chops, both I and the character have what we most wanted: proof that an imagined thing, if willed fervently enough, can overturn the oppression of "necessary and disagreeable" reality.

"KING OF THE MOUNTAIN" I read when I was a good deal older, and enthralled by multiple readings of Robert Penn Warren's *All the King's Men*. George Garrett's story seemed, in my first few readings, a distilled version of the operatic exercise of Southern political power depicted in Warren's novel. I barely noticed the "boy" who's witness to everything, who has nothing in common with Saki's Conradin . . . except proximity to a sacred violence, the sacraments of blood. But Garrett's is an ordinary, healthy boy; no one has told him he's going to die young. He consents to be steered away, eyes averted from his fallen father, beaten nearly to death by the Ku Klux Klan. That boy is lively, insouciant, almost oblivious to the trouble in his household, carefree to throw stones at a mockingbird or climb a mulberry tree and look around his world, "as high and proud and lonely as the king of the mountain, and nobody, would dare to come and pull him from his perch."

I was first caught up in the big, heroic dimensions of the story: the way the lawyer-father crafts his climb to the summit of local power, first using his own body as a blood sacrifice, then the body of his dog. No, he probably didn't plan either act of violence, but he knows how to turn them both to account. And the final triumph is all the sweeter (for the lawyer, his family, and the reader) because the cause is unquestionably just.

In later readings I found the ambivalence, looking through the boy's eyes—as when he watches his father argue with his mother over the gun she's brought into the house for their protection:

"If it wasn't for the boy, I'd beat you with my cane." The boy processes the experience through unconscious analogy: "You gotta be mean to be a jaybird." As an adult (I believe Garrett's first-person frame narrator and the grown-up boy are one and the same, that the closing dialogue is an inner one), he sees the contradictions without being able to digest them: "I saw him beat a man to his knees with his cane for talking sassy to him on the street; yet I've also seen him have an Air Force sergeant jailed for browbeating the Negro bootblack in the barbershop." As a child, so studiously guided by his father, "the boy knew for the first time how close is violence to love. If you rubbed the lamp and said the right words, you could call up a giant."

Both stories deliver enormous empowerment, while showing what single-minded, ruthless determination is needed to acquire it. Though Kierkegaard could not have been thinking about such narratives when he coined the phrase, it fits: Purity of heart is to will one thing.

MEG WOLITZER

✦ ✦ ✦ ✦ ✦ ✦ ✦

CLAY

James Joyce

YOURS

Mary Robison

✦ ✦ ✦ ✦ ✦ ✦ ✦

IF, AS MARGARET ATWOOD once somewhat playfully suggested in an interview, "Novels are about time and poetry is about eternity," then what is the short story about? I'm not sure what answer Atwood would give, and of course I'd be very curious to find out, but it seems to me that certain short stories—in particular certain very short ones—are also about time, but perhaps more specifically they are about the suspension of time. This is at least partly true of two very short stories, "Clay," by James Joyce, and "Yours," by Mary Robison, both of which I have long admired. Published almost seventy years apart by two obviously very different writers, to my thinking they overlap in interesting ways. Both of them give examples of what's sometimes considered "earned" emotion in fiction, and both also traffic heavily in the unsaid. Each one relies on the held moment for much of its power. Time doesn't necessarily stay suspended for very long in these two works, but it does so for at least as long as is required to allow the moment to gather uneasiness and then, finally, something stronger.

I first encountered "Clay," one of the quiet masterpieces in James Joyce's *Dubliners*, during John Hawkes's writing workshop at Brown University. I had poked around in *Dubliners* before; my high school English class had predictably read "Araby," which was a good choice for the likes of us, we who were ourselves at the tail end of being children. "Araby" was melancholy, deftly tracing a particular kind of desperation; and most of us enjoyed taking our own emotional pulses, quietly checking on our various adolescent agonies. "The Dead," the long, leisurely, and magisterial novella that closes the book, lay right there in plain sight in the green paperback we were all given on the first day of the class, but apparently I was not ready for it until my early twenties, at which point I understood its greatness.

But bracketed between "Araby" and "The Dead" was "Clay." Its protagonist is the long unmarried Maria, who excitedly makes a journey to spend a festive evening with the family of the man who, along with his brother, she took care of when he was a boy. At Joe's house Maria takes part in a game that involves being blindfolded and choosing among various objects. Instead of choosing the ring, which would have been an encouraging symbol of marriage in her future (an unlikely prospect), Maria puts her hand in something wet and cold—the clay of the story's title. Clay suggests the ground, the grave, and death. The story reaches its heightened, held moment after Maria touches the clay: "There was a pause for a few seconds; and then a great deal of scuffling and whispering. Somebody said something about the garden, and at last Mrs. Donnelly said something very cross to one of the next-door girls and told her to throw it out at once: that was no play. Maria understood that it was wrong that time and so she had to do it over again: and this time she got the prayer-book."

After the awkwardness is dispensed with, the rest of the evening is considered "merry"—no harm done. But the secret harm done by people to other people because of casual cruelty, and the unbearable accommodations that have to be made when we can't afford to process what has really happened, are what the story actually conveys.

So many stories that I had read for school up until that point, "Araby" included, seemed to be about an event taking place in a character's life, during which he or she learns something and can never go back to the state of not-knowing, the state of innocence. But "Clay" is unusually subtle, and in its "time stands still-ish" climax, the epiphany is something of an anti-epiphany. Writers, Hawkes seemed to be telling us, didn't need to plant everything right there on the page, didn't need to be Johnny Appleseeds of metaphor and meaning. Some things could stay partly or entirely unsaid, even in an excruciatingly elongated held moment, and that didn't mean the reader would be left unaffected. "Clay" affected me powerfully, with its beauty and sub-rosal ache.

A NUMBER OF YEARS later, when I was done with college and was teaching my own fiction workshop, I taught Mary Robison's "Yours," and though I didn't realize it at the time, I now think that I meant it to be a kind of "Clay" stand-in. I didn't want to pilfer from Hawkes's syllabus; I had read the Robison story in the New Yorker not long before, and thought it was wonderful, and considered it instructive for my workshop to read. The story involves a husband and wife named Clark and Allison. He is much older than she is; his "relations up North" never approved of their marriage, once sending him a letter that read, "'You're being cruelly deceived.'" Robison continues, "There was a gift check for Clark enclosed, but it was uncashable, signed as it was, 'Jesus H. Christ.'"

On Halloween eve jack-o'-lanterns are carved and lit, and as the story continues, any preconceived ideas the reader has about this couple and their potential mortality, given their differing ages, are upended. Allison is dying right now, the reader learns, and in fact she dies before the night is through. Her death, in the middle of this very brief story, comes as a shock; it's as though we think there isn't *time* for someone to die here, and yet of course in life and in fiction, there's always time.

Like "Clay," this is a compressed story of a life, but the held moment here is quite different from Joyce's, and the related tragedy in "Yours" doesn't concern a character who refuses to take in what the reader knows. Instead, Clark feels something deeply, and feels the desire to express it, but his wife is slipping away from him: "He wanted to tell her, from the greater perspective he had, that to own only a little talent, like his, was an awful, plaguing thing; that being only a little special meant you expected too much, most of the time, and liked yourself too little. He wanted to assure her that she had missed nothing."

Robison's very short, compressed story may not hold secret corners and wings, the way apartments and houses do in dreams (or at least in my dreams). But in its depth and reach, and in its ability to pause to examine human connections and failings, it, like Joyce's "Clay" and other fine short works of fiction, contains enough space, or at least enough power, to stop time, even briefly.

DANI SHAPIRO

✦ ✦ ✦ ✦ ✦ ✦ ✦

THE CIRCULAR RUINS
Jorge Luis Borges

GETTING CLOSER
Steven Millhauser

✦ ✦ ✦ ✦ ✦ ✦ ✦

Fiction writers are able to play with elements of time in ways unavailable to artists working in any other form. Painters, sculptors, musicians, playwrights—none can directly address the way time moves in our consciousness, in our bodies, in our memories. With the rhythm, cadence, context, and meaning of language at our disposal, writers can speed time up, slow time down, collapse, contract, upend, reverse it. We are able to pass through time's infinite chambers. Is the past truly past? Is the future unspooling as we imagine it? Are we creating reality through our consciousness of it?

Because we *can* perform these high-wire feats, it has always struck me that we *should*. Not all the time, of course. Many magnificent stories hew to a kind of realism of time, moving forward at a pace that feels familiarly human. But in the case of Jorge Luis Borges's "The Circular Ruins" and Steven Millhauser's "Getting Closer," seconds, minutes, hours, days, weeks, months, years, centuries explode and are once again restored to order, and the essential question of what is permanent and real is posited without ever being asked directly. As in the best of fiction, it shimmers and eddies between the lines.

A nine-year-old boy gets ready to dip his toe into a lake on the first day of summer. This is all that actually *happens* in "Getting Closer." I've often wondered how Steven Millhauser might have described the story to a pal as he was writing it. (My guess is that he didn't let himself get roped into such a conversation.)

As his family set up their beach chairs and thermoses by a picnic table, the boy is suffused with a wordless longing that builds and builds within him as he prepares to head down the soft, crumbly slope to the water: "It's what he's been hoping for, but here at the edge of the river he doesn't want to let the waiting go. He wants to hang on with all his might." It's a sunny day, a forest floor littered with pine needles. Nothing is wrong, nothing at all, yet the boy feels with a sudden, preternatural certainty that "under the shining skin of the world, everything is dead and gone." He has "seen something he isn't supposed to see, only grownups are allowed to see it." If he dips his toe into the water, time will continue to rush ruthlessly forward. His beloved grandmother will die. His mother will grow old. *He* will grow old. All beginnings contain within them their ends. All life ends in loss. All love, sorrow.

BORGES'S BRIEF, FABLELIKE STORY might be a phantasmagoric distant cousin of Millhauser's. The protagonist—an "obscure man"—arrives on an altogether different shore, his work cut out for him: He intends to "dream a man into reality." He dreams and dreams until he makes a boy, beginning with his heart—"on the fourteenth night he touched the pulmonary artery with his finger"—and then, over the course of years, the skeleton, each eyelid, the "innumerable hair." He is determined that the dreamed-up boy, once born, never know that he is not real, but instead a mere phantom. He fears that the boy, whom he now thinks of as his son, might "discover in some way that his condition was that of a mere image. Not to be a man but to be the projection of

another man's dream, what a feeling of humiliation, of vertigo!"
Borges uses a rare exclamation point here, as if to underscore
the allegory. And the moment is tremendously moving because
within the circular ruins that form the story's center, what we
are reading about is love and fidelity, longing, regret, fear, and—
again—the loosening of the boundaries and ties of time so that
all that is left, all that is important, is the beautiful, struggling
human soul in conflict with itself and its plight.

THESE TWO STORIES DANCE together in surprising ways and,
when read in tandem, create a rich contrapuntal music. In my
own writing and reading life, I have found myself ever more
strongly drawn to work that pushes aside the scaffolding of story
and leaves behind only the architecture of what is essential. A
boy is pierced by the awareness that he will lose all he loves. A
man dreams a boy into being. Again, nothing much happens. No
earthquake, no bullets, no heartrending betrayal—in fact, hardly
an interaction between characters at all. The drama is internal.
Life, after all, is most often composed of the invisible, minute
shifts in consciousness that lead us to moments of revelation.
These revelations don't tend to present themselves with fanfare.
A moment opens up like the aperture of a camera and we see
something we recognize to be true. We build the whole of our
lives out of these moments, drawing lines, one to the next, as if
tracing a constellation in the night sky. When a work of fiction
mirrors that cosmology of consciousness back to us, it is an act—
the writing, the reading—that makes our own inner world whole
once more.

Near the end of "Getting Closer," our boy is shaking in panic
at the water's edge. "You can't live unless there's a way to hold
on to things," he thinks. But there is no way to hold on to things,
and the best a short story can do is to capture the flawed, frail,
noble human spirit as it searches for meaning, all the while being

formed, enriched, and eroded by time. Here, such stories seem to be offering a hand to the reader: *Join my shimmer and eddy. Be obscure. Dip a toe into the water. And for just this brief moment, together we will know what it is to be alive.*

ZZ PACKER

✦ ✦ ✦ ✦ ✦ ✦ ✦

PAPER LANTERN
Stuart Dybek

A SOLO SONG: FOR DOC
James Alan McPherson

✦ ✦ ✦ ✦ ✦ ✦ ✦

A T THE BEGINNING OF Stuart Dybek's quasi sci-fi "Paper Lantern," a ragtag quartet of scientists are attempting to build a time machine, without much luck: "in one direction, we'd reached the border at which clairvoyants stand gazing into the future, and in the other we'd gone backward to the zone where the present turns ghostly with memory and yet resists quite becoming the past." After this teasing whiff of Nietzschean eternal return, the scientists, work-weary and exhausted by their efforts to "measure the immeasurable," decide to break for dinner and head to their favorite spot: a Chinese laundry–cum–restaurant, its single red paper lantern "the only nod to decor."

Then there's a fire. But to reduce the story to a fire—or several—is to miss the point. Dybek, much like the Symbolists, loves to mix the profound and the profane, the mighty with the mundane. In this way, his fiction operates more like poetry whose lyrical lines have somehow wandered over to play on the grassy lawn of prose. And this is the wondrous trick that "Paper Lantern" pulls: it begins with a sly slide away from all the typical ways we tell a story, the ways in which we read a story, and the ways we typically *witness* a story.

A number of fictional conventions are deployed, only to find themselves jettisoned for more poetic ones. For example, the story opens in the epic preterit, or—in plain English—the surprisingly unjarring usage of the past tense to connote a storytelling present. "We were working late on the little time machine in the makeshift lab upstairs. The moon was stuck like the whorl of a frozen fingerprint to the skylight." All past tense, right? Yet no more than one paragraph later, the shift begins. "Down the broken escalator, out the blue-lobby past the shuttered newsstand, through the frosty fog, hungry as strays we walk, still wearing our lab coats, to the Chinese restaurant around the corner."

In other words, the story announces itself as a story by using the most conventional means possible: by employing the syntax of the storyteller, one who uses the past tense to convey that something already happened, and thus giving the instance—whether fictional or not—the quality of unassailability—of being, as it were, Calvinistically predetermined. We are receiving secondhand information, after the fact. Even so, our minds instantly deem reports given in the past tense as "real," and we proceed from there.

When Dybek *does* switch to the gnomic present—that timeless present of eternal reflection, interrogation, and memory—we hardly notice. "Paper Lantern" performs yet another sleight of hand: it exchanges the story's central metaphor for a central image. Whereas a central metaphor might warehouse multiple meanings and levels of significance within a story, or seem to serve as the core of all the story's meaning like some nuclear reactor, "Paper Lantern's" central image—fire—becomes more akin to a story essence, one that becomes more powerful than metaphor in that the central image invites and generates multiple metaphors of its own.

Images nest themselves within yet other images: the faux fire glow of the restaurant's paper lantern becomes the real fire in the laboratory, the fire in the laboratory consumes yet another fire, this one frozen in time by a photograph, the protagonist's erstwhile lover likewise frozen in the foreground. The hall-of-mirrors effect does not end there: this long-ago love and her fiery red hair ignite, in turn, yet another kind of fire. By this point, all of these conflagrations mimicking and mirroring one another achieve yet another by the magic trick: by the time you've finished reading "Paper Lantern," you have not read one short story, but rather have read six or seven interlocking prose poems.

JAMES ALAN MCPHERSON'S STORY "A Solo Song: For Doc" also operates on an additive principle, but instead of images aggregating to create a collage, "A Solo Song: For Doc" is more like a deck of cards, and the railroad dining car waiters who form a virtual brotherhood on the rails are each introduced via stats, worldview, and rituals, all of which illuminate just how each goes about undermining the prejudice and racism that conspire to undermine *them*. The eponymous "Doc" of the title is crafty Doc Craft, a sly, honorable precursor—or alternative—to the street hustler who resists the system by taking advantage of it.

> [He took] over his station and collected fat tips from his tables by telling the passenger that the Sheik had had to get off back along the line because of a heart attack. The Sheik liked that because he saw that Doc understood crackers and how they liked nothing better than knowing that a nigger had died on the job, giving them service.

When the upper echelons of railroad management assemble a manual whose byzantine conscriptions are designed to keep the waiters underpaid and overworked, our "oldhead" narrator—a veteran railroad waiter who's clocked many miles—tries to convince a summer "youngblood" that the official waiter's manual is not the all-important "big, black Bible" the railroad executives would have him believe. The true book from which the young-blood should learn is the life and times of past waiters, their styles, "pretty moves," and waiters' craft. The narrator values Doc above all because he is a "Waiter's Waiter," one who follows his own code of excellence: to be a Waiter's Waiter is to write the book, not to be rendered helpless by it.

McPherson, who died in late July 2016, was a writer, a Harvard Law graduate, and the first African American to win the Pulitzer Prize for Fiction. Yet McPherson's ultimate unsung vocation was as a folklorist of the American Experience, and his specialty was the creativity enmeshed in Blackness, and specifically how African Americans carved a world of beauty and worth out of everyday life. To strip away the beauty, grace, flash, and style of the waiters that "built the railroad" by replacing it with needless code, retribution, and penalties is a form of injustice akin to redlining: a form of redlining meant to fence in the improbable manhood and freedom Doc and African American men like him created out of whole cloth by virtue of their spunk and ingenuity.

ANN BEATTIE

✦ ✦ ✦ ✦ ✦ ✦ ✦

BLISS
Kathering Mansfield

THE PRINCE
Craig Nova

✦ ✦ ✦ ✦ ✦ ✦ ✦

THIS MASTERFUL STORY SEEMS to begin in *medias res* as it creates a little mystery: Who is this prince, and what exactly is happening regarding the sale of his last piece of property? The tone is matter-of-fact until we come to the word *turmoil*. Throughout the story, the prince's thoughts will remain impenetrable, as we intuit the words unspoken and skip over his surface formalities. Paragraph one orients us subtly to what's going on, presenting characters, perplexing us slightly with the specificity of a couple of words that set the tone for what lies under the surface: great tension. There will even be a gun. Physical violence. Images of people play-acting physical violence as well. A reference to war. But at first, our prince is merely observed, which suggests that this might be a leisurely story, a Chekhovian narration that implodes as it builds.

In the second paragraph, there's information about the main character's earlier life (the remembered situation with his father, whose attitude toward life figures strongly in the prince's life). The prince has a lot of ghosts in his life, but we don't know that yet. As we proceed and the narrative provides more information—at least about the sale of the property—a pattern is established: we observe until different, more complete information infuses our assumptions. We're spectators of the prince, who's going through the day's motions, much as the prince will soon be a spectator at the sale of his property, where his nemesis André and his family will stand watching. Eventually we learn of the physical abuse André, a seemingly minor character, inflicts on his wife. The prince is briefly, surprisingly forthcoming about his desire for André's wife, though this is not a fairy tale, and the prince won't get what he wants. What, exactly, does he want? Wouldn't anyone want his property returned, his wife and child alive again, the status quo of prince-dom? But that obviously isn't going to happen. Eventually the prince packs his gun, and we wait for it to go off (Chekhov never said such a thing, but we so wanted to believe that it's become common misinformation).

What a complex story, with its mixture of past and present, and the truly sad ending—not what we expect, but far riskier: the banal, nevertheless charged moments that precede whatever happens off the page. (As voyeurs, all we can see is white space.) Property sold—though at the last minute the auctioneer allows the prince to keep a pornographic book we heard about earlier, almost in passing, said to be his uncle's (if so, the prince has not divested himself of the "erotica"). The illustrations are sexual, but contrived, orchestrated images; among other things, they evoke the undercurrents of sexuality off the page in this story, and also the cruelty André inflicts on his wife, whom the prince—as we've come to understand—covets. This desire may not be a stunning surprise to the prince—we can't be sure, from the evenness of the tone—though it certainly surprises the reader. Through the years, Marie and the prince have only potential, but missed, moments, though she looks at the prince with "shameless intimacy."

Bristol, the prince's pseudo girlfriend (as the pornography is pseudo sex; as the prince's entire life, by extension, is a pseudo life, since what prince is this, what kingdom lost?) drives him to the airport. He tells her he'll be fine; after all, he—like Gatsby—is "an Oxford man." He boards a flight to New York, where he will disembark and . . . shoot deer. Earlier in the story, he came up with a sadly ingenious way to repel deer: human hair, gathered in bundles, suspended from the orchard's trees. When he leaves, having to choose between the fruit rotting and the deer eating it, he makes the humane decision. Off he goes—just another guy in a scarf and leather jacket, so all-purpose that he might be a hipster or (as Bristol jokes, so tellingly) a "gangster."

Again, we remember Gatsby, whose own shady past plays a role in his death. He wasn't the Great Gatsby, but rather James Gatz. We acquire our identities, which sometimes exist more for the benefit of others than for ourselves; we hide behind them, to varying degrees (leather jackets cut across class lines and are almost the perfect protective coloration).

When, at story's end, our character is in limbo on a fancy plane, leaving what is already gone (we've seen it go) and moving toward a certain yet simultaneously uncertain future, the reader intuits the ending that comes after the ending. Every subtle clue is there: even the scarf worn nonchalantly with the leather jacket has drawn attention to his neck. The "black hood" suggests the henchman's hood, dropped over a prisoner's head before death. This prince had a lot of sadness in his life. In his final moments he's served a pear (his trees, whose fruit the deer are devouring) and wine (communion?): a romantic still life. "Pear" and "deer" are also puns. And what sits before him might as well be a poisoned cup and Eve's fateful apple (not that the gun won't do). Our prince exited Paradise long before story's end. If it was ever there, in France, "about two hours from Paris by car."

KATHERINE MANSFIELD'S "BLISS" USES symbols more overtly than Craig Nova (if we were really good actors, we might be able to pantomime a passage from "The Prince," but the exact wording of Mansfield's metaphors would make that highly unlikely).

On the surface an unlikely comparison, these two stories exist deep beneath their surfaces and show us that whether the narration is done from some distance (Nova) or by inhabiting the mind of her character, their subjects can't hide from us, as we gradually figure out what's really happening.

To some extent, we read by current-day standards. In rereading this amazing story, I can't help but wonder how little time would elapse before a psychologist would understand Bertha (though no story is simply a riddle to be solved). The writer uses language beautifully, and purposefully. Her images are not only riveting; they also convey the story's subtext: the sexual significance of the phallic silver tree that seems "almost to touch the rim of the round, silver moon" gives us instant information that Bertha—who is quite good at intuiting—is only beginning to understand. What an awful evening, with the excessive poet, humorously damned by Mansfield with *italics*. And guests named "Face" and "Mug." Do we want to know these people? They seem simian, from the jungle (I speak metaphorically), whereas Miss Fulton is so silvery (significant), so dignified, by comparison.

This is a story about feelings that exceed words, yet ironically it is constructed with perfectly chosen words. But language is limited, and ultimately these words fall short (how risky for a writer) because what Bertha instinctually knows, language cannot express. We discover that her marriage is not good, and if we might have considered her husband rather neutrally, his pronouncement about his daughter ends that. This couple is not in love. Harry will move on. The silent, strong bond and desire Bertha feels toward Miss Fulton will materialize but, cruelly, as a tryst between husband and friend; we, too, see this in the hallway. As has also happened with her own child, Bertha is excluded—almost cosmically, it seems: we might as well be watching a horror movie when we see Miss Fulton's "moonbeam fingers." Those spooky fingers will never reach in Bertha's direction, any more than the tree lit by the moon will change position.

T. C. BOYLE

✦ ✦ ✦ ✦ ✦ ✦ ✦

THE BROTHER
Robert Coover

SORROWS OF THE FLESH
Isabel Huggan

✦ ✦ ✦ ✦ ✦ ✦ ✦

M Y FIRST AESTHETIC EXPERIENCE—THAT is, an apprehen-
sion of a work of art in a way that melded form, substance,
and beauty—was when I was a teenager burying myself in the
improvisations of John Coltrane and trying, mightily but fum-
blingly, to blow along with him on my saxophone. The second
was when, in my early twenties, I picked up Robert Coover's first
collection, *Pricksongs & Descants*. At the time I'd begun to think
of myself as a writer, though I did a whole lot more thinking on
the subject (fantasizing?) than actual writing, and the stories I
was attempting were often modeled as a series of fractured narratives in which paragraphs or scenes were meant to stand as
mini-chapters or building blocks of the larger story. In Coover, I
found the technique perfectly realized and I began to blow along
with him too, but in a more controlled way than with Coltrane
and on a keyboard instead of keys themselves. The story most
anthologized from Coover's first collection is "The Babysitter,"
an experiment in deconstructing a narrative and reassembling
it from multiple and often conflicting points of view. There are
other equally brilliant stories in the book that don't seem to have

come to anthologists' attention quite as often, and "The Brother," the one I've chosen here, stands as an example.

For me, it's the voice that makes this story. Coover's narrator (brother, as you will see, to one of the foundational figures of our cultural mythology) speaks in a familiar country dialect, as befits his status as a farmer, which helps humanize him and enables him to gain the reader's sympathy. The story is composed of a single long breathless sentence that propels the story forward even as the reader begins to see how Coover subtly and subversively reinterprets the biblical story and questions its ethos at the same time. Ultimately, "The Brother" stands as a challenge to received notions and a nonpareil lesson in point of view.

THE SECOND STORY I'VE chosen here, Isabel Huggan's "Sorrows of the Flesh," is a powerful evocation of a teenager's first crush and how that experience deepens into an understanding of a more mature relationship—specifically that of her stultifying parents. The opening line—"Because my father was a banker, I was never able to have any pets while I was growing up"—may be a simple statement of fact, but it resonates throughout the story on a subtextual level, affecting the narrator's notions of what love and caring really are. This piece is from Huggan's first collection, *The Elizabeth Stories*, a series of connected stories that track the narrator from childhood through adolescence. I first came to the book serendipitously—it was recommended to me by a member of the audience at a reading I was giving in support of one of my own collections in the late 1980s, and I have been a devotee ever since.

Huggan's great triumph throughout these stories is in reproducing first a child's and then a teenager's way of thinking without a false note, without condescension or the hermetic qualities a lesser writer might bring to the material. Elizabeth's uncertainty, her humiliations, her passion for her teacher, Jerry Wheeler, and her ultimate disillusionment and reassessment of her parents' relationship comprise her rite of passage, the sorrows of the flesh we all must live through. And with. As many times as I've read this story, it still manages to affect me deeply and take me back to a place I've long moved beyond but that will nonetheless always remain present in me. That's what a great story can do. Live with Elizabeth—and Noah's brother too—and see what I mean.

ANTHONY DOERR

✦ ✦ ✦ ✦ ✦ ✦ ✦

THE GARDEN OF FORKING PATHS
Jorge Luis Borges

CONTINUITY OF PARKS
Julio Cortázar

✦ ✦ ✦ ✦ ✦ ✦ ✦

IN 1996 I MOVED to New Zealand with a backpack, a fly rod, and a three-pound, 1,600-page short story anthology. The anthology contained 115 stories, arranged alphabetically by their writers' surnames, and during my first week in the southern hemisphere I happily disappeared into fiction by writers such as Margaret Atwood, James Baldwin, and Ambrose Bierce.

Then I hit the first three paragraphs of Jorge Luis Borges's "The Garden of Forking Paths."

Ugh. Dates cluttered his first paragraph; his second carried about as much narrative energy as a legal deposition. A page number, some unrecognizable names, an "insignificant" delay, and a footnote? This was his opening? Was Borges, I wondered, *intentionally* thwarting my interest? Why?

I flipped ahead to "This Way for the Gas, Ladies and Gentlemen," and Tadeusz Borowski's devastating first sentence, "All of us walk around naked," promptly sank the hook of narrative back through my lip.

On I went. I finished the whole anthology and never went back to Borges.

Years passed. Years! In graduate school, friends enthused about his work; professors described him as a major influence on Barth and Pynchon and Carlos Fuentes.

I'd think: Borges? The guy who wrote that klutzy opening?

Twice more I dragged that three-pound tome off its shelf and retried "The Garden of Forking Paths." Twice more I gave up after the first few paragraphs.

Who knew what my problem was? Maybe I just needed to grow up.

Then, one rainy night not so long ago, I opened the anthology and tried again. I crawled through the thickets of Borges's opening frame and something new happened: I found myself ensnared. Here was the spy Yu Tsun, operating undercover for the Germans in Britain, with a secret to convey and no way to convey it. His partner was down; his resources were nil; his revolver had one bullet left. *Aha*, I thought. *Now I see what "The Garden of Forking Paths" is: an old-fashioned spy story.*

But then Yu Tsun gets off the train in Ashgrove, descends a forking road through "confused meadows," and meditates on a maze that an ancestor may or may not have built, a lost labyrinth (which, one thinks, is strange because labyrinths are meant to get people lost, not to get lost themselves), and I became very aware that these ruminations on mazes occurred inside a text that in itself felt very much like a maze, a labyrinth through which I was continually struggling to find my way, and I started thinking about the phone book Yu Tsun had just pored through, and about the alphabetical arrangement of the anthology I was holding, about order and disorder, West vs. East, then vs. now.

The story and the maze, I realized, were one and the same.

By the time I reached the part where Stephen Albert reads from Ts'ui Pén's novel—an imaginary novel embedded inside an imaginary letter embedded inside an imagined story embedded inside a 1,600-page book—I considered my mind sufficiently blown. The spy story had become secondary, form eclipsed content, and the whole piece began to vibrate with meaning.

Why was the boy reading Tacitus on the train? Why was the town named Ashgrove? Why does Stephen Albert die in the same manner as Ts'ui Pén? With each pass through the text, a dozen possibilities came to the surface, and I began to see that Borges's intention was not to impede his reader's progress, as I had originally presumed, but to continually redirect it, precisely as the corridors of a labyrinth sometimes send you scurrying back the way you came.

You turn left, then left again; you become both bewildered and delighted, winding always toward the center, where a minotaur just might be waiting to devour you.

Julio Cortázar's "Continuity of the Parks," published twenty-six years after "The Garden of Forking Paths," sends similar sensations snaking through the shrubbery of the reader's soul. Here a businessman sits in a velvet armchair and falls into a novel, detaching himself "line by line from the things around him." When he is fully rapt, the point of view pivots to the characters in the novel, who are about to execute the murder of guess who? The businessman himself. Subject becomes object, witness becomes victim, and Cortázar's story turns in a circle like the Greek Ouroboros and eats its own tail.

Both stories bring to mind the French phrase *mise-en-abyme*— "placed in abyss." People who study heraldry use the expression to talk about little shields drawn inside of larger shields, art historians use it to talk about little paintings inside of larger paintings, and film critics use it to talk about little movies embedded inside larger ones.

I'm drawn to the phrase because for me it captures the sensation of reading itself—not only metafictional stories like Borges's and Cortázar's, but *all* stories. When we open a work of fiction, we fall into its sentences and slip momentarily out of our lives; we leave *our* now to enter *its* now. I might be in an armchair in Boise, but I'm simultaneously on a raft floating down the Mississippi. I might be on a flight from Chicago to Buffalo, but I'm also riding a whaling ship through the South Seas. The two timelines transubstantiate. And what's so incredible about reading is that when we close a good book and the normal Newtonian progress of time resumes its march, we feel that the ribbon of our own personal timeline has thickened somehow. We feel something like the "invisible, intangible swarming" Yu Tsun feels as the variations of his own life spiral around him.

In other words, we have been placed in abyss.

As readers we get to live through a multiplicity of eras; we occupy, to borrow Borges's phrase, "a growing, dizzying net of divergent, convergent, and parallel times." This is an incredible, dangerous, and breathtaking superpower. And I think Borges and Cortázar are intent on reminding us of this.

At the beginning of "The Garden of Forking Paths," Yu Tsun wonders, "Was I—now—going to die?"

Yes, Yu Tsun, by the end of your story, you will die. So will the businessman at the end of Cortázar's. So will all of us. Time always wins. But through the labyrinths of stories we can escape—however temporarily—the prisons of absolute time, and fracture our own terrible isolation.

GISH JEN

BARN BURNING
William Faulkner

BARTLEBY, THE SCRIVENER
Herman Melville

+ + + + + + +

"**B**ARN BURNING" AND "BARTLEBY." I've always thought of them together—all those Bs. Do not they beg to be used in a joke? Bartle B. Burning the Barn! Or: Barn, Burning, and Bartleby. And though in fact "Barn Burning" was written in 1939 and "Bartleby" in 1853, I always think of "Barn Burning" first and "Bartleby" second, in part because of the ages of the protagonists. "Barn Burning" is about a boy, after all; it's a coming-of-age story. "Bartleby" is about a man; it's a coming-to-terms story.

But also Faulkner's South seems distinctly Old World—a timeless, codified world with clear class distinctions, rituals, and rules. The courtroom seems to have been there forever—that big white house, too. As for the De Spains, who live in the house, they always have and always will; the Snopeses never have and never will.

Melville's Wall Street, in contrast, seems a far more modern place—a commerce-driven world. His is an America making itself up as it goes, an America where people can come from nowhere and know no one. This is an America so like our own that it seems only fitting that Bartleby's refrain should have made it onto Apple's iPhone. (If you ask Siri, "Read me a haiku?" Siri will answer: "Sometimes I wonder / What it would be like to say / 'I'd prefer not to.'")

And yet at heart, "Barn Burning" and "Bartleby" have something in common. They're both about impossible, unsocialized men; and they're about someone who does not know what to do with them.

In "Barn Burning," it is the father who is the problem—the proud, unswerving, lawless Abner Snopes. That he goes and plants his dirty foot on the De Spains' white rug is no surprise. He is titanic, bigger than life; he is defiance itself. Does the son get his perverse integrity, does he get the fiery rage behind it—the rage that the great white house was built, as his father says, "with nigger sweat"? And what about us? Are we sympathetic or not to Snopes's refusal to contribute his own sweat to the white house and all for which it stands? And even if we are—another burning. Can we condone it?

What should the boy do? Abner Snopes is not exactly a man who can learn from experience. Indeed, he reminds the English major in me of Satan on the heath in Milton's *Paradise Lost*—a Satan who even when thrown down to hell by God remains unbowed. Snopes is destruction itself, but there is something preternatural about him, too; his steps are the steps of a giant. It's no small thing for his son to muster the strength to break away.

We see Snopes in the figure of Bartleby, too. Bartleby sets nothing on fire. He leaves no footprints on a rug. But he has his refusenik refrain: "I'd prefer not to." In a world of orders coming in and orders completed, he is a nonparticipant. In a world of motion, he is stillness. A young man in need of job training, we might almost think, except that because this is Melville writing, Bartleby is much more than that: He is a raiser of an enormous question mark. Would we rather, too, at some level, "prefer not to"? Do we even know, really, what we'd prefer? Are we finally just senders of letters that will end in a Dead Letters Office? In his passive resistance, Bartleby interestingly anticipates the Occupy

Wall Street movement of 2011. His beef with society is so much larger than that of the protesters, though—not just with income inequality, but also with the whole order of things. Is this why, wan and exhausted though he is, there is something preternatural—something Snopesian—about him, too?

In both stories there is a choice to be made: Should the boy in "Barn Burning" remain with the father? Should the narrator in "Bartleby" let the clerk stay? Faulkner, in his Nobel address, called the essence of story "the human heart in conflict with itself." And indeed, in both these stories, there is a central figure who must finally, somehow, draw a line, and for whom I have the deepest sympathy.

But why? you may ask. I am not from the South. I am not a boy. I have never known anyone to step on a rug like that. Nor am I a lawyer or a law clerk. I am, rather, a law-abiding daughter of Chinese immigrants who has never taken to squatting in an office, much less torching a barn.

At the same time, I know how that house looks to the Snopes family. I know how shut its doors, how off-limits its rooms. And I know, too, how meaningless some work can be. I know what questions life can raise, and how strangely two people can be connected.

What's more, these stories seem to me to be about something very close to choosing—or refusing—to assimilate. So many immigrant characters in literature are anxious to get with the program in their new country, but not all: When I look at my own story, "In the American Society," for example, I see a refusenik father character a bit like Abner Snopes and Bartleby.

What is it in a person that says no? So often this is a thing we admire—even a form of wisdom. Still, it is a thing with a cost; and though I did not realize it when I first read either "Barn Burning" or "Bartleby," I realize today why it is these stories have stayed with me all these years. It's that cost—and for the protagonist who must choose another way, a haunted freedom.

STEWART O'NAN

✦ ✦ ✦ ✦ ✦ ✦ ✦

WINTER DREAMS
F. Scott Fitzgerald

BOYS
Rick Moody

✦ ✦ ✦ ✦ ✦ ✦ ✦

A CTION IS CHARACTER. THOUGH it sounds Aristotelian, this deathless axiom was tossed off by F. Scott Fitzgerald from his sickbed in Hollywood while jotting down notes for the never-to-be-finished *The Last Tycoon*. Then, it wasn't the Zen nugget of wisdom we now accept it as, but rather a marginal reminder to himself. The screenwriting gigs he'd taken to pay his debts and buy time to work on the novel forced him to learn a new dramatic language. Because movies don't use deep point of view, only the objective eye of the camera, and scripts don't afford the writer the luxury of detailing a character's history, he had to ditch his normally rich interiors for broader gestures indicating for a mass audience who his people were. Now, as he prepared to braid his plotlines in *The Last Tycoon*'s final sections, including violent strikebreakers, a jealous husband, a contract killing. and a plane crash, he may have been reassuring himself that, as in *Gatsby*, the rising action wasn't all just movie melodrama; it followed naturally as an expression of his characters' true selves, as well as the strange world of Hollywood—that the movement of the novel was surprising yet inevitable, as John Gardner says.

Character is action, or, in character we see the potential for action and change, whether a change of fortune or a change of heart. In "Winter Dreams," often cited as the seed of *Gatsby*, Fitzgerald cleaves to this more literary notion, letting us know who Dexter Green is from the start so that once the action begins, we understand why he does what he does. His pedigree is there in the very first line, neither rich nor poor, son of the second-best grocer in Black Bear, mingling, as a casual kind of servant, with the wealthy. Before any real drama occurs, Fitzgerald gives himself a page to establish Dexter's romantic sensibility, even handing us his dreams of victory and acceptance. We know, well before Dexter himself, what he wants, and so aren't surprised when he does what he does to get it. Like Chekhov's shotgun on the wall, the potential has been there from act one.

When this story first appeared, in 1922, Fitzgerald was famous for chronicling the wildness of the new flaming youth, especially the modern woman, and the derangements and complications of love. Here he adds the yearning of the outsider or commoner to rise to the highest possible station in American society, the leisure class. As with his portraits of the callow, aimless young, Fitzgerald frames this desire both earnestly and ironically, recognizing at once its appeal and its worthlessness. Even as Dexter achieves his dream of joining the foursome at the golf club, he has the sense of being a trespasser. Later, just before he meets Judy Jones in the middle of the lake, he's lost in nostalgia for a night he stood listening to dance music outside a prom because he couldn't afford to go inside. In the end he's a success, but without Judy an empty one, and, on hearing of her fate, though it's commonplace, his disillusionment is complete. His dreams and his ideal are gone, and both he and the world are poorer.

When writing of loss, the author has to make what is lost present and precious. Conventionally, if an element is important to the story, it needs to be shown dramatically, in scenes, so the reader can feel it, rather than simply being told by the author. Character in action, using dialogue and image, hitting all five senses. Across the six discrete sections of "Winter Dreams," spanning more than a dozen years, Fitzgerald gives us Dexter and Judy fully. In the major scenes—their first meeting on the golf course, their night on the lake, their petulant dinner, their reunion at the University Club—Fitzgerald delivers Dexter's irresistible attraction to Judy and her world, heightening the romance through setting with music, weather, and lighting effects. Beyond the sheer beauty of his writing, highlighted by his sense of metaphor and ear for speech ("It's awful cold," she shouted), he's a genius at mood, even with the singsong, fairy tale–like refrain of "There was a fish jumping and a star shining and the lights around the lake were gleaming." After our lovers get back together, at the end of Section IV, we never see Judy again, yet Fitzgerald has made her so present that, like Dexter, in the final two sections we miss her, and feel his sorrow.

"This story is not his biography," Fitzgerald reminds us at the beginning of the very last section, only the story of this one love, the author narrowing his scope, focusing to show us character in action and action working on character, every element carefully chosen to illuminate Dexter's loss of innocence.

IN A STRANGE, COMPELLING way, Rick Moody's "Boys" *is* a biography of its titular characters. Employing a unique, almost pointillist approach, Moody takes one sentence and reloads it over and over to show the passage of time and its effect on one anonymous middle-class American family. The rhetorical device of repetition lends momentum to the piece, giving it the feel of an incantation. Structured as a single, relentless paragraph, with some sentences running on for more than a hundred words, including parenthetical asides and a jokey use of italics, "Boys" inundates the reader with a profusion of details and events that, while seeming generic and random, gradually gather emotional weight and significance.

Like a core sample, "Boys" tells the history of a family. The action isn't a plot that relies on its characters' unique personalities or situations; instead, it's the boys' coming of age—the passage of time and the natural shocks we all face. Changes of fortune, changes of heart. While the story is unconventional in the extreme, like Fitzgerald, Moody makes present and precious what is lost, though, with the strictures he's put on himself, his sentences have to contain or at least evoke whole scenes. It's a bravura performance, lyrical and comic, a blend of the high ("ideas leaden, reductive, inflexible") and the low ("one striking the other with a rubberized hot dog"), the density and pacing of the piece thrilling. In the end, for all its nostalgia, like "Winter Dreams"—like any great story—"Boys" leaves us bereft and devastated, with a keener appreciation for all we've lost and all we still have.

TOBIAS WOLFF

+ + + + + + +

WAKEFIELD
Nathaniel Hawthorne

WHERE ARE YOU GOING WHERE HAVE YOU BEEN?
Joyce Carol Oates

+ + + + + + +

I FIRST READ "WAKEFIELD" some forty years ago, and it has haunted me ever since. The premise itself is odd, and oddly disturbing, revealing as it does a possibility vaguely felt but never so sharply recognized: the notion of stepping out of one's life, as if out of a parade, and watching it pass by. What would it be like to renounce all the circumstances that define us—family, work, routine, our daily obligations and rewards, even the bonds of love and friendship we had thought foundational? And how would things proceed without us?

That is just what Hawthorne's "Wakefield" does. He kisses his wife of ten years goodbye one evening, on the pretext of leaving for a short business trip, but instead takes a room in the next street. He has no firm intention of staying away, indeed he has no firm intention of any kind. He acts on a whim, and before long that whim has authority over him; it becomes the defining power of his life. The day stretches into another day, and then a week, and a month, and so on. Without ever meaning to, he absents himself from his home, and the widow his poor wife believes herself to be, for twenty years. And then, with no clearer purpose than before, he returns home.

45

Hawthorne tells this story in a strikingly artful way. He begins with the claim of having read something like it "in some old magazine or newspaper." This rhetorical move—appealing to a documentary source—is meant to attach a sense of authenticity to the fiction that follows, and thus lure the reader into that unguarded receptivity any imaginative writer hopes to create in the reader. Hawthorne plays his hand brilliantly by pretending not to know who this man really is, and what he's like—why he would do such a thing. He invites us to join him in "shaping our own idea" of Wakefield's character from scratch, and, while maintaining the fiction that we are collaborators in Wakefield's creation, proceeds to delineate him in such vivid and suggestive detail that by the end of this brief story we feel as if we know him: indeed, know him better than he knows himself—for we can detect in Hawthorne's subtle portrait the selfishness, whimsy, and cold curiosity that might lead a man to do what Wakefield does, and a moral laziness that would have him shrink from the rigors of self-scrutiny, and give the promptings of a whim such terrible, enduring power.

No explanation is given of Wakefield's background, or work, or position in society, or how he comes by the money that allows him to sustain his shadow existence as a mere observer, solitary, disembodied. The result, despite the opening claim of "authenticity," is that the story takes on the atmosphere of a dream, a sleepwalking dream wherein we are made captive to Wakefield's paralysis of the soul and forced to look on life through his eyes, always from the outside.

This parable of the dangers lurking in our smallest fancies is also, it seems to me, a cautionary allegory of the artist's life—the moral peril of stepping back, as artists must, to get a view of the whole parade. What are the consequences, over time, of this habit of holding oneself apart and looking on? Can you, once you've taken that backward step, ever reclaim your place in the living stream?

Joyce Carol Oates's "Where Are You Going, Where Have You Been?" turns Hawthorne's question on its head. Here the living stream is not only a source of vitality, of sensual fulfillment and engagement, but also a dark current of mystery and danger. Connie begins as "Wakefield" ends, cushioned from life, solitary, a religious devotee of the shopping mall and the movie theater and the drive-in restaurant. *Religious* is not too strong a word. As Connie and her girlfriend enter a restaurant, "their faces were pleased and expectant as if they were entering a sacred building that loomed out of the night to give them what haven and what blessing they yearned for." From the tower of her beauty and ignorance and self-satisfaction, Connie looks down on everyone—on her sister, on her parents, on the friend she uses as an alibi when she sneaks off with boys. She is, in other words, an American teenager.

Into this paradise of thoughtless self-regard comes the serpent, the wonderfully named Arnold Friend. Everything about him is wrong: He's older than he pretends to be, his slang forced and dated; he keeps promising not to hurt Connie, when she has not accused him of any such intention; and there are hints that he is not entirely human. Arnold Friend stands on the porch of Connie's house, talking to her through the screen door, intent on luring her outside, at first to take a ride, then with the promise of becoming her "lover." He is at once seductive and repulsive, and unmistakably menacing.

And here the story takes its great turn, for instead of Arnold Friend simply pushing his way inside and abducting Connie, as in a conventional narrative, he puts the privilege and burden of choice on her: she must decide whether to remain inside or come to him—to all the possibilities and perils that wait outside her family home and the safe, dependable, painless existence she has taken for granted—our American version of innocence.

Connie chooses what all our children must choose: that is, to leave us, to embrace uncertainty and risk, even mortal risk. They must come to understand, as Connie does, that at a certain point our protections will be worse than useless; they'll become a kind of prison. I read this story as a writer, struck with admiration for its mastery and seriousness, its capturing of that last tremulous moment of childhood. But I also read it as a father, watching with a certain pang as this girl opens the door and steps out into the world.

JESS WALTER

✦ ✦ ✦ ✦ ✦ ✦ ✦

THE SCHOOL
Donald Barthelme

BULLET IN THE BRAIN
Tobias Wolff

✦ ✦ ✦ ✦ ✦ ✦ ✦

I ONCE HAD A story rejected for being "too funny." In fairness, I can't say that particular story was anything *but funny*. But the rejection (which arrived during a long dry season of them) sparked some deep reflection in me over humor's place in fiction. Was it something to be modulated, a spice that easily overwhelms? Could a story be great—not in spite of being funny but *because* of it?

When in doubt (and writers are *always* in doubt), go back to what you love. Most writers can conjure up a dozen or two short stories they think are truly great. For me, Donald Barthelme's "The School" and Tobias Wolff's "Bullet in the Brain" are two of these—near-perfect examples of compression, movement, innovation, audacity, play, and, most important perhaps, transcendence.

And look: both are *funny*. Subversively, disturbingly funny. Funny in the way that only death can be funny, which is the other thing they have in common. They are not about death in an allegorical or metaphorical way. These stories walk right up to death and laugh in its endless black face.

49

The first thing you notice about "The School" is the voice. First published in 1976, "The School" begins in rattled insecurity, a sentence featuring eight commas, two ellipses, and a spray of false starts and hems and haws.

> Well, we had all these children out planting trees, see, because we figured that . . . that was part of their education, to see how, you know, the root systems . . . and also the sense of responsibility, taking care of things, being individually responsible.

The teacher will never be named or described but we *see* his character immediately: the averting gaze, the shuffling feet. We're not even out of the first paragraph and things are dying. "They were orange trees. I don't know why they died, they just died."

The pattern creates the humor. Amid other problems (a strike, trouble with the boiler), death accretes in this classroom like falling snow (snake, mice, gerbil) until we laugh in expectation: "We weren't even supposed to have a puppy."

Five paragraphs in, the puppy's a goner and note the precision of detail: the Gristedes truck, the knapsack, even the dog's name. Donald Barthelme was a master of *metafiction* (see the postmodern wing of literature, alongside magical realism and fabulism). Metafiction offered a playful awareness of language and storytelling that cut hard against that other big movement of its time, the dirty realism of Raymond Carver, Jayne Anne Phillips and Richard Ford.

But there's a lesson in the way writers like Barthelme and Robert Coover (and, for that matter, Gabriel García Márquez and Aimee Bender) wield their vivid imaginations: the absurd is grounded in the concrete, as real as any realist.

This is the secret to comic writing, too. Precision sets up exaggeration: "And then there was this Korean orphan that the class adopted through the Help the Children program."

Every story exists first in its genre (comic, romantic, domestic, suspenseful . . .) but great stories transcend genre in a way that can seem inexplicable, even magical. "The School" does it with a thrilling and sudden shift in tone.

> One day, we had a discussion in class. They asked me, where did they go? The trees, the salamander, the trop- ical fish, Edgar, the poppas and the mommas . . . And they said, is death that which gives meaning to life? And I said no, life is that which gives meaning to life . . .

This shift begins musically, with a slowing of tempo ("One day"), a lowering of tone ("They asked me"), and that incredible turn, to a moment of hilarious, lucid *searching*. (". . . is death that which gives meaning to life?").

The story has gone from "merely funny" to a weirdly pro- found disquisition on mortality and meaning. When the students inquire about "the taken-for-granted mundanity of the everyday" and ask their teacher to have sex with his teaching assistant so "we can see how it is done," there's a wistful ache of truth in the absurdity. The story ends as it began, with the blithe acceptance of new life ("I opened the door, and the new gerbil walked in") and we laugh again. But our laughter is different now—knowing, winsome, black as night.

The "turn" is even more remarkable in Tobias Wolff's incredi- ble "Bullet in the Brain"—a complete shift of point of view, voice, and tone, a display of perfect control and audacity.

The story, first published in 1995, starts in close third person. Anders, a critic "known for the weary, elegant savagery with which he dispatched almost everything," is in line at the bank behind two women "whose loud, stupid conversation put him in a murderous temper."

Then, two bank robbers come in, yelling that if people don't cooperate they will be "dead meat." The critic is upset more by the cliché than the danger.

"Oh, bravo," Anders said. "Dead meat." He turned to
the woman in front of him. "Great script, eh?"

At this point, you might think Wolff is writing pure satire, a
sendup of critics. When the bank robbers threaten Anders, he
can't even summon normal human fear, only more aesthetic disappointment in the bank robbers.

"Fuck with me again, you're history. *Capiche?*"
Anders burst out laughing. . . . "*Capiche*—oh, God,
capiche," and at that the man with the pistol shot Anders right in the head.

Go on. Tell me you saw that coming. No redemption, no lesson learned, no moment of reflection typical of American fiction.
Just: bang, dead. Writers are urged to "kill your darlings" but really, who kills his protagonist?

And funny? This is a very different sort of humor, an edgy
burst of laughter that comes from profound disbelief. *Did he really
just do that?* It's as the bullet smashes into Anders skull that the
story makes its incredible pivot.

. . . the first appearance of the bullet in the cerebrum set
off a crackling chain of ion transports and neurotrans-
missions . . . flukishly calling to life a summer afternoon
some forty years past, and long since lost to memory.

All along, Wolff has played audaciously with cliché. Now, the
speed of the brain's synapses enables Anders to "contemplate the
scene that, in a phrase he would have abhorred, 'passed before
his eyes.'"

Again, Wolff surprises us, by not going to the "summer afternoon" but instead giving us "what Anders did not remember,"

his first lover, his wife, his daughter. In all that Anders *does not remember*, Wolff gives us the fully realized character he avoided in his satirical opening.

As with Barthelme, there's great musicality to Wolff's writing. "He did not remember" becomes the story's melody ("He did not remember shouting, 'Lord have mercy!' He did not remember deliberately crashing his father's car . . ."). And once again, a comic story reveals its serious intent: the question of what makes a life. When he finally gets to the moment when Anders *did remember*, Wolff slows the pace with short sentences. "Heat. A baseball field. Yellow grass . . ." The clock is ticking, the bullet making its way through all of our brains.

What is at the core of a human being? What memory, what insecurity, what truth? On that long-forgotten summer day, two boys arrive to play baseball and one of them is asked what position he wants to play.

> "Shortstop," the boy says. "Short's the best position they is." Anders turns and looks at him . . . strangely roused, elated by those final two words, their pure unexpectedness and their music.

Is this the birth of a critic, railing against language that once elated him? Or is it more universal than that? Do we each unknowingly spend our lives denying that which moves us?

In Anders's and the story's final moments ("The bullet is already in the brain; it won't be outrun forever . . .") Wolff writes one of the loveliest last paragraphs I know, an ending of pure, elegiac *grace*. Reading it, we—like Anders—are at once destroyed and somehow redeemed.

KIRSTIN VALDEZ QUADE

✦ ✦ ✦ ✦ ✦ ✦ ✦

LOVE
William Maxwell

DANCE OF THE HAPPY SHADES
Alice Munro

✦ ✦ ✦ ✦ ✦ ✦ ✦

A LICE MUNRO AND WILLIAM Maxwell are among the writers who have most influenced my thinking about story.
Even a casual reader of their work knows that whether the
subject in question is the loss of a mother or a decapitation in
a sawmill, their real concern is always the act of storytelling,
how we frame and reframe and attempt to make meaning of the
events of our lives.

Both writers return again and again to the experiences of
childhood. Children, at the mercy of a huge and wondrous and
menacing world, must be savvy and observant and must take
their power where they can get it: in passing judgment on those
around them, in seeking and sneaking, in creating private, invi-
olable worlds. No one writes about childhood as movingly, as
attentively—and as unflinchingly—as Maxwell and Munro.

What immediately stands out about Munro's "Dance of the
Happy Shades" is the oddness of the point of view. This is a
present-tense story, told from the first-person perspective of a
girl on the brink of adolescence, who has almost, but not quite,
outgrown piano lessons. And yet her voice has the maturity of a

retrospective adult—and, more than that, the omniscience of an author. Over and over, she delivers information she could not have access to: she hears both sides of her mother's telephone conversations, she reports on not just her mother's unspoken thoughts, but also on the thoughts of the other mothers as they grudgingly attend old Miss Marsalles's party for her piano students. The narrator interacts in scene only once, eight pages in, when, looking around at the gathered guests, she complains to her mother, "I am the oldest girl here."

The party goes as one might expect: it's hot and tedious, the children's performances dull. The mothers regard the proceedings and all of Miss Marsalles's efforts with pity, condescension, and disgust.

Enter the children from the Greenhill School, children with developmental disabilities who—surprise!—are to play alongside Miss Marsalles's other pupils. The mothers, acutely and claustrophobically attuned to propriety, are taken aback: " . . . there is nowhere to look. For it is a matter of politeness surely not to look closely at such children, and yet where else can you look during a piano performance but at the performer?" They're offended, one suspects, that the Greenhill children have also been invited to a party they've felt was their own to disparage, their own to deign to arrive at. The internal chorus of the mothers turns from polite uneasiness into hysteria: "WHAT KIND OF PARTY IS THIS?"

And then Dolores Boyle, the oldest Greenhill student, takes her place at the piano and, against all odds, plays *music*.

"Aha!" the reader thinks with glee, as the music, "fragile, courtly, and gay," surrounds the mothers. "Someone's about to learn a lesson!"

Munro might easily have ended the story here: The narrator and the mothers would come to confront their pettiness and prejudice, see the hypocrisy of their good taste, would finally recognize the value of Miss Marsalles's generosity and educational methods and sentimental faith in children. The mothers would acknowledge and be edified—elevated, even—by the musical gifts of this overlooked child, and would come away better.

Munro, however, doesn't allow for easy epiphanies. Instead, as the song fills the room, the mothers retreat still deeper into their prejudices: " . . . the performance begins to seem, in spite of its innocence, like a trick—a very successful and diverting one, of course, but perhaps—how can it be said?—perhaps not altogether *in good taste*."

And then we get the real surprise: our narrator, the observant child who is blessed with omniscience and who seems on the verge of passing judgment on the mothers, who might separate herself from them and their pettiness, doesn't. Instead, she becomes entirely absorbed into their way of thinking, and in the last paragraph, the point of view slips into the first-person plural, even as it acknowledges that they leave the party changed: "But then driving home . . . . why is it that we are unable to say—as we must have expected to say—Poor Miss Marsalles?"

WILLIAM MAXWELL'S "LOVE," ANOTHER story about a teacher, is a more straightforward, traditional narrative: It is told from the point of view of a retrospective adult recollecting a childhood event. His subject is death, and he alerts the reader right off the bat. When the graceful, doomed Miss Brown writes her name on the blackboard in her "flawlessly oval Palmer method," we're told, "The letters might as well have been graven in stone." Not *carved*, not *engraved*, but *graven*.

The gifts the children give their adored young teacher— an apple, asters, sweet peas—are all lovely, living, perishable things. "We meant to have her for our teacher forever," the narrator tells us. "We intended to pass right up through the sixth, seventh, and eighth grades and on into high school taking her with us." It's a sweet instance of the children's unrealistic belief in permanence, which in the next line takes on a much more sinister cast, when Miss Brown is replaced, without a word, by a substitute teacher.

Miss Brown is sick, they learn, and the narrator and his friend go visit her. When the boys arrive at the door, the old aunt says, "I'll find out if she wants to see you." Their beloved teacher grants them an audience, and they discover that she is lost to them already: " . . . I was struck dumb by the fact that she didn't seem glad to see us. She didn't belong to us anymore."

Miss Brown dies, and the story shifts from the narrator's memory to his imagination, and we end in a corner of the graveyard he has never seen, alone with the old aunt—nameless and featureless—bent over her niece's grave. We end with the repetition of the gift of flowers, but this time the adoring love of the fifth-grade class is set in contrast to the more steadfast and futile love of the aunt for her dead niece. In a line that recalls Joyce's ending of "The Dead," she "arranged the flowers she had brought in such a way as to please the eye of the living and the closed eyes of the dead."

The story might have been a simple account of a child's first experience of death but for a single detail, a detail that I didn't notice in my first reading of "Love" and that I cannot now stop thinking about: Miss Brown invites the boys into her death chamber, and in doing so exposes them to TB. The story moves past this moment fairly swiftly in the only awkwardly phrased clause in the story: "The angel who watches over little boys who know but they can't say it saw to it that we didn't touch anything." The awkward syntax highlights the strangeness of the moment; a truth the boys can't quite yet access is buried there.

I can't help but linger here with Miss Brown, to wonder what she's thinking as she allows the boys to be brought to her bedside. At best, she's too ill and wasted to be thinking about contagion. At worst, there's something strangely aggressive in the gesture: why should *their* health and youth be protected? Or perhaps her desire to glimpse her old life in these boys is greater than her prudence. Miss Brown is no longer their teacher, no longer responsible for their well-being; she is now just a deeply sick, deeply frightened young person watching herself die.

This, then, is her last lesson to her students: Love will not save you. Youth will not save you. Beauty will not save you. And those adults you trust? Not only won't they save you, but they might, in fact—through menace or neglect or simple distraction—be the ones to put you in danger.

"THE FACTS ARE NOT to be reconciled," we're told as Dolores Boyle plays "Dance of the Happy Shades." And indeed they are not. This is as good as any a summation of both Munro's and Maxwell's artistic projects in general: forcing the reader—and the characters—to occupy an uncomfortable no-man's land in which facts cannot be reconciled, but only examined carefully and with clear, honest eyes. How can one reconcile the fact that the present moment, like Dolores Boyle's "fragile, courtly" music, "is in the room and then it is gone"? How can one reconcile the fact that a person as young and lovely as Miss Brown can be alive and then dead? What is "a great unemotional happiness," anyway?

I love these stories because they surprise me. Because they discomfit me. Because regardless of how many times I read them, I am not done reading them. They, like childhood itself, demand to be examined again and again.

MONA SIMPSON

✦ ✦ ✦ ✦ ✦ ✦ ✦

THE LADY WITH THE DOG
Anton Chekhov

GOOD PEOPLE
David Foster Wallace

✦ ✦ ✦ ✦ ✦ ✦ ✦

A T THE TIME I started to write this, the *Mona Lisa* was in the news for having survived yet another attempt at vandalism. The painting had already been stolen, hidden for years, and re-covered. Since the 1950s, it had been protected behind glass not only from stray attempts at destruction but also from the proximity and breath of so many fans. The price of popularity, for an oil painting on poplar, has been steep.

Unlike the *Mona Lisa*, Chekhov's "The Lady with the Dog," possibly the best-known short story in the world, did not seem to me to have suffered from fame. Its mystery and beauty survived numerous translators and a century of encounters with the reading public, perhaps because it offers the universally appealing myth of resurrection. At least I thought that until I taught the story again.

At the center of Chekhov's story, written when the author was thirty-nine and had recently fallen in love with the actress Olga Knipper, is Gurov, a man "not yet forty" but already jaded and world-weary. An urbanite, his youthful dreams have long ago been put away. Gurov studied "the Arts (philology)" at university but now works in a bank; he "trained" as an opera singer but has "given it up." He owns two houses in Moscow, takes three city newspapers (denying he reads any), goes to restaurants and clubs, attends dinner parties and anniversary celebrations, and entertains "distinguished lawyers and artists," his pleasures the consolation prizes of an affluent, settled life.

But the story opens not in Moscow but in Yalta, where Chekhov traveled with Olga Knipper in July 1899. (Chekhov wrote the story in October of that year; it was published in December. The author turned forty in January.)

Gurov no longer has any romantic feelings for his wife. He secretly (and treacherously) believes she's "unintelligent, narrow, inelegant"—a description that would hurt her acutely, if she knew of it (we're being told, in particular, that she considers herself "intellectual"). And Gurov is disloyal to her in more than his thoughts; he's been unfaithful to his wife "often," we're told, "and probably on that account, almost always spoke ill of women"—as if this were a natural consequence, chronic infidelity causing one to speak ill of women. (I can think of at least two philanderers who claim to love women.)

We're told that Gurov's womanizing follows a pattern.

> Experience often repeated, truly bitter experience, had taught him long ago that with decent people, especially Moscow people—always slow to move and irresolute— every intimacy, which at first so agreeably diversifies life and appears a light and charming adventure, inevitably grows into a regular problem of extreme intricacy, and in the long run the situation becomes unbearable. But at every fresh meeting with an interesting woman this experience seemed to slip out of his memory, and he was eager for life . . .

Bitter—a word used twice to describe Gurov's experiences with women—is not an adjective one expects to be linked to a philanderer, and this feeling of bitterness remains an enigma, as women are attracted to Gurov; "they love him even though he does not make them happy." One could easily imagine him guilty, perhaps smug, likely hard-hearted, more apt to inflict bitterness than to suffer it. What hopes had he had for these adventures that repeatedly disappoint him? Gurov's lack of romantic feeling extends beyond his marriage; his ambitions, for his work and even for his affairs, sound modestly curtailed, the liaisons are to be "light and charming," undertaken to "agreeably diversify life."

The tempo of the story's narration alternates between summaries, like the one above, in the conditional mood, and simple scenes. Short story writers, in particular, try to give readers the sense of their characters over more time than they have room to render in scenes strung together with "and then"s. Often, they establish a pattern of repeated behavior, and then show the cycle beginning again. Immediately after we've read a summary of the typical stages of Gurov's affairs, we see him *a* woman, forget everything he seemed to understand about himself, and imagine "a swift, fleeting love affair" with this new woman, whose name he did not know.

The woman whose name he did not know is another vacationer in Yalta, and Gurov's initial impressions of her are ambivalent. One night, before going to sleep, he "thinks how recently she had been in school, doing exercises, like his own daughter. He recalled the diffidence, the angularity that was still manifest in her laughter and her manner of talking with a stranger. This must have been the first time in her life she had been alone in surroundings in which she was followed, looked at, and spoken to merely from a secret motive which she could hardly fail to guess." David Magarshack translates the line as "with only one secret intention." My students had no doubts about that "one secret intention." The phrase echoes the still contemporary idiom "he's only after one thing." Gurov thinks there's something "pathetic" about the woman. By then, he's learned her name—

Anna—surely a reference to Tolstoy's famous adulteress; *Anna Karenina* was published twenty-two years earlier to enormous popularity and controversy.

But before Gurov beds Anna, Chekhov reminds the reader of Gurov's sexual history:

> From the past he preserved memories of careless, good-natured women, who *loved* cheerfully and were grateful to him for the happiness he gave them, however brief it might be; and of women like his wife who *loved* without any genuine feeling, with superfluous phrases, affectedly, hysterically, with an expression that suggested that it was not *love* nor passion, but something more significant; and of two or three others, very beautiful, cold women, on whose faces he had caught a glimpse of a rapacious expression—an obstinate desire to snatch from life more than it could give, and these were capricious, unreflecting, domineering, unintelligent women not in their first youth, and when Gurov grew cold to them their beauty excited his hatred, and the lace on their linen seemed to him like scales. [italics mine for emphasis]

Why this list? Why the generalized teams of women (the good-natured, the hysterical, the beautiful and cold). It's certainly a catalog that would have given Anna pause, had she read it. And knowing Gurov's "only one secret intention" it's interesting that the verb the narrator uses for the physical act of sex is *love*. (Anna's is "to live!")

Gurov uses the words *diffidence* and *angularity* to describe Anna's sexual manner. She had "an awkward feeling" he thinks, "a sense of consternation, as if someone had suddenly knocked at the door."

Worse even than that, afterward she feels remorseful. She becomes dejected "as though it was her fall" and begins doubting again and again that he respects her. She calls herself "a vulgar, contemptible woman" and seems to believe that she is an irredeemable sinner. Gurov finds all this drama "old-fashioned" and "inappropriate." After all, this was supposed to be a light, charming, and "fleeting" affair.

Anna doesn't let up. "It's wrong," she says. "You'll be the first to despise me now." Then Gurov cuts open a watermelon that was on the table in her room and begins to slowly eat a slice. He says nothing to contradict her and there is silence for half an hour.

Half an hour!

In a spill of emotion, Anna tells him that her husband "may be a good, honest man, but he's a flunkey." Though her desperation makes him irritated and bored, Gurov nevertheless eventually comforts her. They laugh together and late at night take a cab to Oreanda, where they sit near a church and listen to the sea. "The sea had roared like this long before there was any Yalta or Oreanda, it was roaring now, and it would go on roaring, just as indifferently and hollowly, when we had passed away." That "we" seems to issue from Gurov's thoughts, meaning himself and Anna, but also more than the two of them in what James Wood would call the authorial "stretch" in free indirect discourse. "And it may be that in this continuity, this utter indifference to life and death, lies the secret of our ultimate salvation, of the stream of life on our planet, and of its never-ceasing movement towards perfection. . . . Sitting beside a young woman who in the dawn seemed so lovely, soothed and spellbound in these magical surroundings—the sea, mountains, clouds, the open sky," Chekhov writes, "Gurov thought how in reality everything is beautiful in this world when one reflects: everything except what we think or do ourselves when we forget our human dignity and the higher aims of our existence." A man walks up to them, looks at them, and then walks away. "And this detail seemed mysterious and beautiful too."

These surprising moments of spiritual yearning in Gurov's emotional makeup—more than his work at the bank or his membership in the Moscow professional elite—distinguish him, for it's his internal life that changes in the course of the story.

WHEN GUROV AND ANNA part—her husband has called her home—they both believe it will be forever.

> This young woman whom he would never meet again had not been happy with him; he was genuinely warm and affectionate with her, but yet in his manner, his tone, and his caresses there had been a shade of light irony, the coarse condescension of a happy man who was, besides, almost twice her age.

This affair seems to have ended without the "bitterness" alluded to in the description of his habitual experience with women. Gurov returns to Moscow and at first is relieved and pleased to fall back into his predictable pattern—a cycle of banquets, clubs, restaurants, and celebrations, "the winter routine of Moscow." He discerns the poor quality of a fish one night at a restaurant, feels flattered when "well known" people visit his house and he plays cards opposite a professor.

But attentive readers know before even Gurov does that as guns placed on stages must go off by the third act, patterns announced in stories must be broken, to allow new life to begin.

Gurov expects to forget Anna, his newest conquest, in a month. Then, Chekhov surprises his character: Gurov does not forget her. Instead, his memories of her intensify.

"Had he been in love, then?" Gurov asks himself.

Chekhov seems to believe in the mystery of love. Anna is no more beautiful or talented or intelligent than the (many) women Gurov could not love. Even Gurov understands that she is "in no way remarkable." Love falls into his life unpredictably, and though he didn't "earn" this love, it changes him. Gurov's initial lack of hope had extended beyond his marriage, beyond his modest ambitions as a lady's man; one could have fairly accused him of lacking substantive hope for life.

His love for Anna restores him. We see, near the end of the story, a scene of Gurov walking his daughter to school on his way to meet Anna (Gurov's children are alluded to three times, each in connection with Anna, never in a scene with their mother); he patiently explains to the girl the nature of snow. In his calm affection, one senses Gurov's new receptivity to the world. The story offers an essentialist view of love as something mysterious, uncontrollable, even divine. Even cynical, average people can fall decently in love, it claims, and the world is born again for them, its wonder and beauty intact.

In a beautiful arc, Gurov has gone from a state of spiritual stagnation to a sense of humility and gratitude (he is alive again, part of which means being conscious of his own impending age and death). But—as my students were ever alert to—that is Gurov's arc, Gurov's love, Gurov's story. The women in the piece, Gurov's wife and, most important, Anna, are not given this same internality. Gurov is afraid of his wife. Did Chekhov make her pretentious, even phony, as he made Anna's husband a flunkey, to bind our sympathy with his protagonists, away from the wronged parties?

Anna is left—in the famously "open" ending Nabokov and many others praise—in love and crying again. Those states appear to be causal for her, the way disappointing women and then speaking ill of them were once linked for Gurov. Anna tells her husband she's going to Moscow every few months to see a specialist for female troubles. Her husband, we're told, does and does not believe her. My students enjoyed looking up translations of those "female troubles." The always-discreet Constance Garnett has Anna telling her husband "she was going to consult a doctor" about "an internal complaint." Ivy Litvinov says Anna is seeing "a specialist on female diseases." Another alludes to her "consulting a professor" about a "female disorder." Magarshack uses the term "gynaecologist."

Her husband likely thinks she's consulting a "gynaecologist" (Magarshack) because she has not yet become pregnant. The reader imagines that these visits may serve the opposite purpose—as attempts to prevent conception. "Teas" and "village sorcerers" were used at the turn of the century in Russia, and abortion was still legally homicide at the time the story was published. A few years later, the1903 Criminal Code slightly lightened penalties, sending women who performed abortions on themselves to workhouses for one to three years. Notably, the penalty was worse for married women.

Gurov's sensibility expanded with love: he's more patient with his child now, he notices nature in a fresh and grateful way; at home in his native Moscow, he's still going through the motions of his external life (the clubs, the dinner parties presumably with his wife) while his secret life grows. Anna is waiting for him in a hotel room, crying. The reader is left not knowing what the future holds for this couple, except that the affair is ongoing, a long way from any ending, and that the most difficult parts lie ahead.

Won't Anna eventually become pregnant? Then what? That, perhaps, is why she is crying.

THOUGH WE'LL NEVER KNOW what happens to Anna, we do know what happened to Chekhov and Olga. Though Chekhov, like Gurov, had once been a womanizer—more than thirty affairs have been chronicled, he frequented brothels, and he was, according to William Boyd, "the ultimate commitment-phobe," he and Olga married in 1901. They had a long-distance relationship, in their case predicated not by adultery, but by a more modern problem. Olga was in Moscow performing almost every night and

Chekhov's doctors ordered him to stay in Yalta, for his health (he was already suffering from tuberculosis). In his letters, he calls her doggie, baboon, granny, cricket, sperm whale, and little German (her parents were Germans who became Russian citizens).

Chekhov lived with his sister, Maria, who cared for him and, according to Jen Benedetti, the editor and translator of the letters, Olga Knipper was more like a mistress than a wife: she and Chekhov met rarely, and their time together was intense and passionate. At one point Maria, who resented Knipper, wrote to tell her to back off. Still, Chekhov and Knipper were trying to conceive, as they put it "a little half German."

But in 1902 Olga, experiencing severe abdominal pain, was taken to the Moscow Clinical Obstetric Institute, where the Tsarina's doctor performed surgery to remove a fetus from one of her fallopian tubes. By Boyd's account, Chekhov wrote to one of the surgeons present at the operation, asking for some clarification. The dates did not add up. According to the size of the ectopic pregnancy, Olga seemed to have conceived in January, a month she was in Moscow and Chekhov in Yalta—800 miles apart. Despite this news, Chekhov behaved with quiet restraint and dignity. After the operation, Olga became seriously ill with peritonitis and Chekhov, aware that he himself was dying, nursed her through the summer.

Chekhov left his money, his dramatic works, and his Yalta house to his sister, Maria; his house in Gurzuf and five thousand rubles to Olga; and money to his three brothers. But after his death, because the will was not notarized, the Russian probate court ruled that his estate be divided among his three brothers and his widow. His sister, as a woman, was not able to inherit. Chekhov's three brothers and Olga legally transferred everything to Maria, who turned the Yalta house into a museum for her brother and lived in it during the German occupation (the source for this is Encyclopedia.com). Olga Knipper-Chekhova never remarried and remained childless. She stayed with the Moscow Art Theatre, where, in 1943, she re-created the role of Madame Ranevskaya in *The Cherry Or-chard* on the occasion of its 300th performance.

DAVID FOSTER WALLACE's "GOOD People" is a very different kind of story. We begin with two young people in a park by a lake and immediately sense that there's trouble. They sit on top of a table, their feet on the "bench part that people sat on to picnic or fellowship together in carefree times." We are told early on that our protagonist (who, like Gurov, is named much earlier than his female counterpart) does not love his girlfriend, "not that way," in a characteristic Foster Wallace sentence:

> The girl wore a thin old checked cotton shirt with pearl-colored snaps with the long sleeves down and always smelled very good and clean, like someone you could trust and care about even if you weren't in love.

These are not just any similarly dressed young people; they're religious—they met in campus ministry at the junior college they attend. Lane is a nineteen-year-old man who, when struggling to "turn a matter over to Jesus Christ in prayer," socks a fist into the other palm as if it were a baseball glove. Not loving your girl-friend is one kind of trouble, given that Lane "had liked the way she smelled right away" and knows his mother respects her. It is spring, the season of romance and renewal, and the air, suffused with honeysuckle and lilac, is "too much" for Lane, who stays "very still and immobile."

They sit on the picnic table near the lake for the duration of the story.

Lane is stuck, "frozen." It had been a "black week." The worse he felt, "the stiller he sat."

The problem is that Sheri is pregnant. They have scheduled an appointment for an abortion this afternoon, but this morning, very early, Sheri had come to Lane's house and now they sit, talking and not talking about the decision. Lane, Wallace writes,

> so fervently wished it never happened. He felt like he knew now why it was a true sin and not just a leftover rule from past society. He felt like he had been brought low by it and humbled and now did believe that the rules were there for a reason. That the rules were concerned with him personally, as an individual. He promised God he had learned his lesson. But what if that, too, was a hollow promise, from a hypocrite who repented only after, who promised submission but really only wanted a reprieve?

He offers to delay the appointment, to give them more time to pray. He reassures Sheri (again) that he will be "there with her."

She laughs "in an unhappy way that was more just air out her nose. Her real laugh was different." She says that where he'll be is in the waiting room.

Nothing Lane says lands right. He has the terrible sense that he must act and feels incapable: "something was required of him that was not this terrible frozen care and caution, but he pretended to himself he did not know what it was that was required of him. He pretended it had no name."

If the name of what is required of Lane is "love," it is a more arduous love than Gurov's. Gurov recognizes his enduring feelings for Anna after the reader does and then, after those feelings prompt him, he goes to see her in her provincial town. Lane has to act now, without being "in love."

> All the different angles and ways they had come at the decision together did not ever include it—the word—for had he once said it, avowed that he did love her, loved Sheri Fisher, then it all would have been transformed. It

would not be a different stance or angle, but a difference in the very thing they were praying and deciding on together. . . . But he could not say he did: it was not true.

Though Lane is endlessly self-examining, he fears in the course of his ruminations on the picnic bench that he's a hypocrite and a liar, it never seems to occur to him to lie about this.

> But neither did he ever open up and tell her straight out he did not love her. This might be his *lie by omission.* This might be the frozen resistance—were he to look right at her and tell her he didn't, she would keep the appointment and go. He knew this. Something in him, though, some terrible weakness or lack of values, could not tell her.

He hopes—poor Lane—that she'll say something to "unfreeze him." Paralyzed, Lane is "desperate to be good people, to still be able to feel he was good."

Then the story takes a mysterious turn. What it is that Lane needs to do is pray and it turns out that he has been praying, all this time on the picnic bench, without fully knowing that was what he was doing. And because of his prayer, something befalls Lane too, something less romantic than the intense memories of Anna that tag Gurov in Moscow. Lane is instead given clarity to "see into Sheri's heart," and what he sees there is that this girl, whom he knows so well that he can distinguish her real laugh from this feint, whose smell he likes, is in a terrible, pitiable situation, with no out: "she can neither do this thing today, nor carry a child alone and shame her family."

Lane is "made to know what will happen" moments before it does: Sheri will tell him that she understands he does not love her, *not that way,* and that it's all right. He also understands that she will be lying.

There on the table, neither frozen not yet moving, Lane Dean, Jr., sees all this and is moved with pity, and also with something more, something without any name he knows, that is given to him in the form of a question that never once in all the long week's thinking and decision had even so much as occurred—why is he so sure he doesn't love her? Why is one kind of love any different?

Gurov's love comes from above. It's unpredictable, not answerable to summoning, a mercy, or a curse; in any case, it's destabilizing. It can make you better, deeper, more caring. It might make you both excited and a nervous wreck if you're a woman in a pre-birth-control society. It's hard to know how it will end. Lane has to work to achieve the feelings themselves, he has to act "as if" the feelings Gurov experienced had fallen whole into him too. To adopt the usage of contemporary psychology, if Gurov's love is a noun, Lane's is a verb.

Even those struck by bolts of passion may disappoint each other and perhaps the best ending possible is people who rise above their own feelings to be kind, as Chekhov was, in caring for Olga in her illness after the abortion, even with the likely knowledge that he'd been betrayed, as Olga was in reverting the inheritance of his sister, even a sister who hadn't embraced her, because that was what Chekhov wanted.

In Foster Wallace's story, pregnancy is the thing that falls into his characters' lives, unpredictably, not love. But both Sheri and Lane believe in the "it" kind of love—the bolt of lightning, the unmistakable brand (they've read their Chekhov). In fact, each imagines that if only Lane felt that way, everything could be altogether different. Sheri believes in the distinction enough so that if he definitely told her no, he didn't feel that way and couldn't, wouldn't ever, she would go ahead with the abortion she doesn't want. Each is willing to accept that a feeling should determine the rest of their lives.

But the end of Foster Wallace's story undermines that kind of tyranny. What if kindness, not the absolute imperative of enchantment that leads to Gurov's expansiveness and Anna's tears, could be a genre of love just as valuable?

RICHARD RUSSO

✦ ✦ ✦ ✦ ✦ ✦ ✦

THE LOTTERY
Shirley Jackson

BUILDERS
Richard Yates

✦ ✦ ✦ ✦ ✦ ✦ ✦

R EADING RICHARD YATES'S "BUILDERS" is a lot like viewing
The Graduate. What you get out of the experience probably
has a lot to do with how old you are. Younger viewers of the
Mike Nichols film invariable identify with Benjamin, so isolated
there on the escalator in the movie's first shot and later at the
bottom of the swimming pool, as anxious as he is clueless about
his future. Later, wanting more from their liaison than sex, he
pleads with Mrs. Robinson to talk to him, and when she refuses,
the younger viewer quickly writes her off as a cynical destroy-
er of innocence and idealism. See the same movie twenty years
later and you understand Mrs. Robinson. Because really, what
does Benjamin's callow narcissistic prattle have to do with her?
He has just the one thing she wants, the only thing any mature,
still attractive, sex-starved woman *would* want. The movie hasn't
changed; the viewer has.

The first time I read "Builders" I was in graduate school, trying
to make myself a writer and botching the job, so I immediately
identified with young Bob Prentice. A wannabe writer, he too
was married to a kind, generous, hardworking woman who was

doing more to keep them afloat than he was, though her work wasn't nearly so exalted as his own. The fact that Prentice spent so much time goofing off while pretending to write behind the trifold screen in their tiny apartment didn't trouble me particularly because writing—real, honest writing—is hard and because I occasionally goofed off too. Nor was I all that troubled by Bob's snobbery—he considers his fine writerly sensibility trump in all circumstances—or his ability to "tune out" people he considers beneath him, a skill that allows him sell people like Bernie Silver short, something his less verbally sophisticated wife steadfastly refuses to do.

Rereading "Builders" in middle age is an entirely different experience, and not just because Prentice ultimately fails to become the writer both I and he wanted so desperately to be and, in the bargain, lost the good woman he should have clung to for dear life. Rather it's because the middle-aged heart goes out to Bernie Silver, whose dreams, over a lifetime, have taken such a terrible beating. Sure, he's a name-dropper and a bit of a narcissist, always wanting to be the center of every story, but he's also totally lacking in guile, as faithful as the best dog you ever owned, and also possesses a generosity of spirit that's missing in the man he's hired to tell his stories. Bernie may have lacked opportunity, we realize, but he has as much of the artist in him as Prentice does. Seeing the photograph of the young Bernie, the cynical Prentice suspects that the bugle Bernie's playing may be "just for the photo," but by the end of the story we know better. Life may have stolen Bernie's youth and promise, but he remembers being somebody and is incapable of surrendering the possibility that he might be somebody again. He has the kind of faith you need to be an artist, lacking only the talent, whereas Prentice has the talent but not the faith.

One aspect of the story, though, was the same for me at twenty as at sixty-four. Self-consciousness—Yates makes clear—is the enemy of art. It's only when Prentice loses himself—his snobbery and ambition and disdain—that he begins to really write. He may not like the stories he writes for Bernie. He may look down on them the way he does on Bernie himself, but at least he's no longer pretending to write. And although he might make fun of Bernie's idea of "building" stories, every time he's given another assignment he dutifully digs the foundation, throws up the walls, puts a roof on, and finally allows for the possibility of illumination. And by the end he seems to understand that his failings are his own, not Bernie's; his sad wish for illumination is really a yearning for wisdom. We feel bad for him. How can we not?

But it's Bernie who haunts the mature reader. The last time Prentice sees him, Bernie, looking worn out, is dressed like the cabby he is—twill cap, cardigan sweater, change machine on his belt, his fingers gray "from handling other people's coins." This, we understand, is what life does to men like Bernie Silver, whereas Prentice has no one but himself to blame.

Back in the 1960s, when I started studying literature, my professors urged students to have "an original relationship" with every text, which I took to mean that it's not a good idea to know too much about a story or poem before you read it. Historical, cultural, and political contexts were important, but they represented the cart that shouldn't go before the literary horse. A reader who's told what he's supposed to see will likely see it whether or not it's there. Far better to come to the story or poem "clean."

THE PROBLEM WITH SHIRLEY Jackson's "The Lottery" is that such an original relationship is virtually impossible. The story has been so widely anthologized, discussed, and taught that even if you haven't read it you probably know a lot about it, including (especially) its ending. There's simply no way to reproduce the experience readers in 1949 had when they picked up the issue of the *New Yorker* that contained the story. No fiction before or since ever generated so much mail, so many canceled subscriptions, so much moral outrage. Indeed, twenty-first-century readers, their sensibilities dulled by decades of violent horror movies, may find the story quaint, its surprise ending reminiscent of O. Henry, as if "The Lottery" were intended to be read as a companion piece to "The Gift of the Magi."

Many of the outraged readers who wrote to Jackson demanded to know what the story meant, and this is almost always the wrong question to ask of any literary work. You can understand the temptation, though. Written just a few short years after the end of the Second World War, it's hard not to read "The Lottery" as a Holocaust story. Jackson seems to be dramatizing the phrase Hannah Arendt would coin a decade later when she covered the Adolf Eichmann trial: Jackson's villagers do seem the very embodiment of "the banality of evil."

Mr. Summers, who conducts the drawing, determined that every i be correctly dotted, every t be crossed, all the while ignoring the barbarity of the entire proceeding, anticipates Eichmann, another bureaucrat, who testifies that he was "just doing his job." The question on the minds of so many people after the atrocities of the death camps became known—how such a thing as the Holocaust could have happened, how so many ordinary Germans could have allowed it—is chillingly answered in Jackson's contemporary American setting.

So why does such a compelling one-to-one historical equivalency feel wrong? Even when we attempt to expand the story's context, to see it as an allegory about ritual, our blind willingness to follow even senseless, harmful traditions, the result still feels reductive. For me, the story lives most brilliantly in its smallest details. It's Mrs. Hutchinson who draws the black spot, but it might have been her boy, Little Dave, a child so small he needs help drawing his slip of paper from the black box. Jackson leaves no doubt that if the most helpless member of the community had been chosen, his own mother would have been one of the ones throwing stones. That terrible realization reminds me of the kind of nightmares most children have at one time or another—dreams in which the people who are supposed to love and protect them might, for no good reason, suddenly turn on them. It would be wrong to think of such nightmares as representing irrational fears; rather, they signify a "fear of the irrational": the possibility that beneath the thin veneer of civilization there lives something reptilian, something utterly devoid of reason and compassion, something that doesn't love us at all.

RON RASH

◆ ◆ ◆ ◆ ◆ ◆ ◆

WHERE WILL YOU GO WHEN YOUR SKIN
CANNOT CONTAIN YOU?
William Gay

A WORN PATH
Eudora Welty

◆ ◆ ◆ ◆ ◆ ◆ ◆

A GREAT SHORT STORY is always a sort of miracle, combining as it does a poem's linguistic precision and a novel's sense of a narrative fully realized. Such is the case in two of my very favorite short stories, Eudora Welty's "A Worn Path" and William Gay's "Where Will You Go When Your Skin Cannot Contain You?" Not a word feels superfluous or misplaced in either story, and at each story's conclusion the reader feels that nothing more needs to be said. Both stories are extraordinary technical achievements, including their deft use of irony. But what I admire just as much as the technical mastery is how each story ultimately transcends irony to follow Rilke's admonition that the artist should "[s]earch into the depths of things; therein irony never resides."

In Welty's story, Phoenix Jackson's trials on her journey to town are both arduous and frightening. Her eyesight is poor and her mind confused, but she is undeterred by what she imagines and the very real dog and hunter who attempt to turn her back. The journey becomes a sort of grail quest, leading to the "document that had been stamped with the gold seal and framed in the gold frame, which matched the dream that was hung up in her head." Eyesight, memory, vigor, family—all have been taken from her. Even the grandchild, whose medicine is the reason for her journey, is possibly dead.

Phoenix's name is appropriate, because she does rise out of the ashes of her whole life. All that survives is Phoenix's love for her grandchild, and that love is honored each time she walks the worn path toward town, toward the hospital where she demands the medicine she believes might heal him. With the exception of the nurse, Phoenix is perceived with either amusement or contempt by those she encounters. No one understands her quest fully, not even Phoenix, yet that fact makes her quest all the more selfless and courageous. As Welty herself said of the story, "The path is the thing that matters."

"WHERE WILL YOU GO WHEN YOUR SKIN CANNOT CONTAIN YOU?" is also the story of a quest. "The Jeepster couldn't stay still. For forty-eight hours he'd been steady on the move and no place worked for long." Unlike Phoenix Jackson, the central character in Gay's story, the Jeepster, is portrayed much less sympathetically. He is a violent, foul-mouthed drug addict who has hurt those around him, including his ex-girlfriend Aimee, a woman he had at times pimped for their drug money. When Aimee is killed by her estranged husband, the Jeepster is unable to console himself. As he tells his former drug dealer: "I never felt like this. I never knew you could feel like this." Despite his lack of sleep and his increasing drug intake, he cannot find relief.

Phoenix struggles to remember; the Jeepster struggles to forget. He is stunned by the depth of his love for Aimee and laments the role he's played in her death. He is stunned that, after all he has done to himself as well to others, he is yet human. When he is banned by Aimee's family from viewing her body at the funeral home, the Jeepster goes in anyway, pistol in hand, and takes her body by force. He drives out to a rural farmhouse, staying inside a cellar with her until a search party led by Aimee's father finds them. In one last attempt to allay his grief, The Jeepster, not unlike Rider in Faulkner's "Pantaloon in Black," rises up so that the men will beat him savagely, perhaps enough to finally free him. The story's last words are spoken by Aimee's father. "He don't know what it is to hurt, he might as well be deaf and blind. He don't feel things the rest of us does." The Jeepster's one wish throughout the story is that the outraged father's words prove true.

In "An Arundel Tomb," Philip Larkin ends his poem with the lines "Our almost-instinct, almost true: / what will survive of us is love." The undercutting of sentiment in the penultimate line is typical of Larkin, but the last line goes beyond irony. When all else is burned away, what does remain of us? What is at the core of being human? That is the question both Gay and Welty ponder in their stories, and, as different as Phoenix Jackson and the Jeepster are, their actions reveal the same answer. As Welty herself noted about "A Worn Path," the story's subject is "the deep-grained habit of love."

There was a time in my twenties when I admired cynicism and cleverness in fiction, even attempting a bit of such writing myself. There was always a self-congratulatory wink that I too could detach myself enough to view humanity as if I were a scientist studying bacteria through a microscope. Writers fear being accused of sentimentality. As I've grown older, however, I find such fiction, though at times entertaining, the literary equivalent of a Quentin Tarantino movie. The literature I go back to satisfies the head but also engages the heart. It is not sentimental, but it is filled with sentiment, which is why "A Worn Path" and "Where Will You Go When Your Skin Cannot Contain You?" remain two of my favorite short stories.

ANNA QUINDLEN

✦ ✦ ✦ ✦ ✦ ✦ ✦

THE GIFT OF THE MAGI
O. Henry

WANTS
Grace Paley

✦ ✦ ✦ ✦ ✦ ✦ ✦

A LITERARY EDUCATION IS like the strata of the earth. When you dig down, you can see the layers. For a Catholic girl like me, there were Bible stories, Noah and his ark, David and his slingshot, Jesus raising Lazarus from the dead. And there was poetry, not very good poetry, or at least conventional in its subjects and forms. Longfellow's "The Children's Hour" and Alfred Noyes's "The Highwayman" instead of Yeats and Robert Lowell. They were poems with predictable rhyme and meter, easy to memorize, which was what was required. Once I sat at a dinner with a group of people about my own age, and together we all recited Joyce Kilmer's "Trees," shouting out the last two lines in unison: "Poems are made by fools like me, / But only God can make a tree."

I'm not disdainful of this poetry; it was an early layer of my personal earth, the literary equivalent of addition, beginning the business of learning how to work with words. Then came short stories—"The Bear," by Hemingway, and "The Necklace," by Guy de Maupassant. But the one I remember best is "The Gift of the Magi," by O. Henry. Like Kilmer's poem, almost everyone my age read it and knows it so thoroughly that it has become a cliché, a shorthand for everything from selfless love to uncommon coincidence. I read it when I was twelve, and loved it.

It fulfills some of what a short story ought to be: dense, compact, with a good deal written between the lines. "One dollar and eighty-seven cents." That is how it begins, and instantly you know that someone has less money than they desire. It is also intimate in the way the best short stories are. It opens the door, invites you in. Later, when I read the work of Chekhov and Eudora Welty, I would realize there were ways to do that that were subtle. "Magi" is not a subtle story, which is also why I loved it at twelve. It invites you in this way: "While the lady of the home is slowly growing quieter, we can look at the home. Furnished rooms at a cost of $8 a week. There is little more to say about it."

Of course that observation is not what people remember about O. Henry's best-known short story. They remember the plot, which can be summed up in one sentence. She sells her hair to buy a chain for his watch and he sells his watch to buy combs for her hair. The story tells a reader that there is a symmetry to life, a satisfying circularity, and in case you are dim enough to miss this, the author steps in at the end with a kind of Aesop's-fable coda: "Of all who give gifts, these two were the most wise."

This is a good thing to learn while you are young, this idea of order. It is not true, not even remotely true, in life and therefore in prose, but it is like Picasso drawing portraits before he found cubism. You have to be able to describe an apple before you can evoke hunger. That comes later.

AND THUS IT WAS that one day I ran into a story by Grace Paley, just after I had graduated from college. The story is called "Wants," and it is a bookend to "The Gift of the Magi," a story that is unlike it in every possible way and yet in some strange fashion mirrors it because of that. It is also algebra to the arithmetic of O. Henry. It has no plot, no surprise ending, yet the cross-purposes of a woman and a man in a marriage are here, too, in much less sentimental and reassuring form.

Once again we are invited in, this time as though shot out of a cannon: "I saw my ex-husband in the street." Immediately the juxtaposition of two people working at cross-purposes begins. "Hello, my life," she says in greeting. "No life of mine," he responds. Everything that follows reinforces the sense of two people whose sensibilities never intersect. He says he always enjoyed breakfast during their married life; she remembers that all they ever had was coffee but that there was a hole in the kitchen closet that let in the smell of bacon from an adjoining apartment. He emphasizes their lack of money; she, their comforts. "We had nice red pillows and things," she says.

"He had had a habit throughout the twenty-seven years of making a narrow remark which, like a plumber's snake, could work its way through the ear down the throat, halfway to my heart," the narrator observes, poetically, unsurprising since Paley was also a poet. The ex-husband makes such a remark as he announces that he's buying the sailboat he's long desired. It is an odd accusation: "you didn't want anything."

I met Paley once, at a dinner, and intimidation made me hesitate to ask a question that had always obsessed me: Did she mean in "Want" to refer to "Magi"? After all, the first is a story about two people who in the first blush of love and marriage sacrifice to get the other what is wanted. In Paley's story the two people are far past any first blush, but one implies savagely that if the other had wanted more, if he had been able to give her something, things might have been different.

Certainly I was two different people when I read each story for the first time. When I was a girl I believed that life and love were like the O. Henry story, with a pleasing shape and a pinkish overlay of romance. That was a good place from which to begin. But when I was a young woman I had begun to understand that

that was not so, that life could be jagged, random, and uncertain, and marriage sometimes a series of misunderstandings that ended, not with a resolution, but with bitterness and schism.

This is exactly right, exactly the way the strata of a literary education should arrange themselves for someone who wants to write. First you need to learn about storytelling, and then you need to learn about life, in all its complications and contradictions. "But I do want *something*," the narrator in Paley's story says. "I want, for instance, to be a different person." The story is very short but the whole world is in it.

JAYNE ANNE PHILLIPS

+ + + + + + +

A GOOD MAN IS HARD TO FIND
Flannery O'Connor

IN DREAMS BEGIN RESPONSIBILITIES
Delmore Schwartz

+ + + + + + +

O NE COULD NOT FIND two writers more different than Flannery O'Connor and Delmore Schwartz. Schwartz, a Jewish
Marxist who was probably bipolar, found his crucible in the al-
cohol abuse that ended his life at fifty-two; O'Connor, a devout
Catholic Southerner, lived a life circumscribed by the lupus that
killed her at thirty-nine. Both writers attained their clearest visions
in the two stories you are about to read. Schwartz, a Freudian, believed in understanding the mystery of the unconscious; O'Connor said that the assumptions underlying her fiction are "those of
the central Christian mysteries." Both writers fought their demons
and triumphed on the page, blindingly and completely.

O'Connor's deadpan humor doesn't exactly obscure the violence in "A Good Man is Hard to Find," but creating sympathetic
characters is not her goal. The Baileys are mighty entertaining,
though, so we drive right along with them while the Grandmother
steers. Death, for O'Connor, "is the most significant position offered the Christian." The Grandmother, facing the Misfit alone,
"realizes, even in her limited way, that she is responsible for the
man before her and joined to him by ties of kinship . . . deep in

the mystery she has been merely prattling about so far. And at
this point, she does the right thing, she makes the right gesture."
Those are O'Connor's words, from a 1963 reading at Hollins College. Death, whether sharp and sudden or long and anguished, is
a mere passage. Grace is the point. The Misfit shoots his opportunity, but picks up the cat and says the line etched forever in
literature's big book.

DELMORE SCHWARTZ'S TITLE IS an epigraph to a book of Yeats
poems called *Responsibilities*, but Yeats claimed not to have written the line; it's ascribed to an "old tale." Perfect, for this tale, too,
is endless. Author of a perfect story at age twenty-two, Schwartz
began a brilliant academic career by skipping high school gradu-
ation for early enrollment at Harvard. He finally graduated from
NYU in philosophy but moved out of his mother's apartment
in his junior year. He found a cheap room in a boardinghouse
off Washington Square and worked twelve hours a day "to become a great poet." An isolated month later, he wrote, in a burst
of catalytic energy, "In Dreams Begin Responsibilities." A friend
reported visited Schwartz one July weekend in 1935 to find him
"ecstatic—he knew he'd written a masterpiece."

Schwartz believed that the movies in our minds demand we
acknowledge every image, construct a narrative, and accept the
burden of understanding. "Dreams" is an exaltation, a lament, a
mourning song, a comic/tragic coming-of-age. Schwartz tapped
the primal knowledge we all possess, yet seldom recognize or articulate. Inspired by the "dream" of life when Schwartz was at the
fresh zenith of his intellect and powers as a writer, "In Dreams
Begin Responsibilities" was the title piece in his first collection,
stories and poems published by New Directions on Delmore's
twenty-fifth birthday.

Schwartz published, over his lifetime, five volumes of poetry,
stories, criticism, and plays. Despite his success, he suffered des-

perate alcoholism and a midlife academic slog from one visiting professorship to another. He held forth, quoting a heavily annotated copy of *Finnegan's Wake*. Lou Reed, his student at Syracuse, led Professor Schwartz to and from obligatory literary cocktail parties and called him "my mountain." In "In Dreams Begin Responsibilities," we find Delmore Schwartz at the glorious beginning.

Schwartz once said that his subject was "the wound of consciousness." Irving Howe wrote that Schwartz "found a language for his parents' grief" but "In Dreams Begin Responsibilities" transforms history, place, and character into primal truth. His "merciless passionate ocean" with its waves "tugging strength from far back" and cracking "at the moment of somersault . . . when they arch their backs so beautifully," drowns each of us in his genius. The shining "lip of snow" remains, cold and clean, perfect, new.

EDITH PEARLMAN

✦ ✦ ✦ ✦ ✦ ✦ ✦

A LOVE MATCH
Sylvia Townsend Warner

ROMAN FEVER
Edith Wharton

✦ ✦ ✦ ✦ ✦ ✦ ✦

"BEFORE YOU WERE A writer you were a reader," says Seymour to Buddy in Salinger's *Seymour: An Introduction.* Indeed. Reading precedes writing and stimulates it. Willy-nilly we become familiar with the flexibility of language.

As a little girl I was enchanted by Kipling. My favorite character was the Elephant's Child, but I didn't feel compelled to imitate his or any other animals' transformations, to invent on my own the myth of, say, where the eagle got his beak. (Where *did* he get it, anyway?) I was inspired by the Stories—not to write them, just to read them again and again.

Some readers do become emulators, in James's happy word. Eventually, I turned into one of those. It didn't happen until high school—in the 1950s, in my case, a decade when the proper ambition for a female was love and a family, when chastity was a high personal virtue. Both of the stories which inspired me to write dealt with those themes implicitly, and they dealt also with corresponding sinful behavior—sexual treachery in "Roman Fever" and, in "A Love Match," love outside not only marriage but outside the law; and also considered outside the bounds of tasteful behavior (the story may change your mind about that).

In my proper girls' school we studied English prose style, and practiced it. We learned grammar and its usefulness not only for clarity and for precision but also for artistry. We expanded our vocabularies. We became addicted to inventing rich phrases (and eventually heeded warnings against heaping them on top of each other). There are examples of the precise and effective use of words in both my model stories. "Beauty cannot be suborned," says the narrator in "A Love Match." Before some spring day sixty-plus years ago, I did not know the meaning of *suborned*—to incite secretly. Since then I have never forgotten it. At around that time I learned the power of metaphor—Mrs. Slade in "Roman Fever" has "a small nose supported by vigorous black eyebrows" as if the brows were an architectural device.

Grammar, syntax, figures of speech, structure: these were the things we studied. We read and analyzed "Roman Fever" as a group. I read and more or less analyzed "A Love Match" by myself. What I noticed—then, or probably later—was the use of mystery. Mystery, differently employed, makes these stories useful as a pair. "Roman Fever" rests on a secret like a column on its base; the secret erupts in the single final sentence, like a Corinthian capital. And the beginning writer—for I had begun to be a writer, planting execrable handwriting in a composition book as if my prose gained vigor from its illegibility—eventually goes back to note the ways this exploded secret is prepared for—the careful thoughts of Mrs. Ansley, the unfiltered ones of Mrs. Slade. The resulting conversation offers a revelation—". . . your mother rushed you off to Florence and married you," Mrs. Slade reminds Mrs. Ansley. The concealment and hurried legitimizing of an unborn child was familiar in the fin-de-siècle setting of the reminiscence as well as in my own girlhood. Abortion was perilous and shameful; we knew that from our mothers. In our enforced virtue we were more attuned to this hint of the disgrace of pregnancy than would be a reader of today.

In "A Love Match," set during and between the two World Wars, there is no secret kept from us—the incestuous love of Justin and Celia for each other blossoms in the first section, as if the story were beginning and not ending with the acanthuses of a Corinthian column. Though unlawful, that love is marital in nature, including an infidelity (only briefly hidden), snoopy neighbors, village life, affection softening but not weakening as the principals age and the heroine gains weight. We know about the love; some villagers find out; even the choruslike air-raid rescuers get in on the secret.

But there *is* a revelation—something we weren't quite sure of. In the last paragraph this middle-aged couple, after a fatal bomb attack, are found dead and must be disentangled—an apt, thrilling verb—before they can be properly buried, separately, as if their relationship were only that of siblings. Disentangled . . . after a quarter century their passion is still vigorous—and, we are encouraged to presume—exercised nightly. In "Roman Fever" another side of passion is revealed. What we might today call a one-night stand is something that at least one of the participants would call a night not to be forgotten, not regretted, and made immortal by its issue.

These two stories of unexpected passion inspired me to make my specialty not the irresistible power of sex (though I write about that too) but instead the subject of surprising bonds and unexpected behavior—like the Elephant's Child confronting the Crocodile, or a proper virgin's nighttime whirl into dangerous Rome, or the enviable partnering of a pair of sibs. I have devoted many stories to unlikely pairings—a person with an unsuitable occupation, for instance; God-fearing religious figures' devotion to kitchen-table gambling; a woman's delight in passing as a man; the insistence of a mother passing as a wife.

A WORD ABOUT WORDS. There is an old-fashioned caution in both these stories, suitable to their era. We know before she tells us that Mrs. Ansley made love to Mr. Slade; we know it because of her grief at the loss of a letter supposedly written by him. We know that Justin and Celia are wedded, so to speak, because he calls her not Darling or its equivalent, but "Puss"—a nickname usually employed with the casual affection of a brother but here carrying the unmistakable intimacy of a husband. There is no need for explicitness in either story; in fact, we are moved by its absence. Today's writers, borrowing this reticence, might find that when the fagots of *fucks* and companion branches are removed from the fire, the sexual flames rise higher, fed by grief over a letter, grief rendered without a word squandered on the physical. Ardor burns bright, heated by that searing domestic endearment "Puss."

PETER ORNER

✦ ✦ ✦ ✦ ✦ ✦ ✦

GUESTS OF THE NATION
Frank O'Connor

WELCOME
John Edgar Wideman

✦ ✦ ✦ ✦ ✦ ✦ ✦

FRANK O'CONNOR'S *THE LONELY Voice*, first published in 1963, is the only book about short stories I've ever been able to stomach. This may be because O'Connor offers little insight on how to write stories. O'Connor knows such instruction would not only be useless; it would completely defeat the purpose. Stories are patently abnormal things. Each one is a warped and unique universe unto itself. The minute you attempt to streamline a certain methodology of telling, you limit the expression of human experience.

O'Connor knew in his bones that stories come from our most unknowable places. *The Lonely Voice* is about storywriters O'Connor reveres: Maupassant, Chekhov, Turgenev, Joyce, Mary Lavin, and J. F. Powers, and a couple he doesn't: Hemingway (innovative style triumphs over substance) and Katherine Mansfield (brilliant but forgettable). It's about the idea of being a storywriter itself, this lunatic idea of devoting your life's blood to making up stories about things that never happened and people who never existed. It's an imperfect, provocative, at times cranky book (among other things, his thoughts on Hemingway sweep too broadly and he's dead wrong about Mansfield), but I couldn't live without it. I've taped *The Lonely Voice* back together so many times that now the pages are mostly all out of order.

> For the short-story writer there is no such thing as essential form. Because his frame of reference can never be the totality of human life, he must be forever selecting the point at which he can approach it, and each selection he makes contains the possibility of a new form as well as the possibility of a complete fiasco.

I once tried to get all that tattooed on my arm, but the dude said he didn't do paragraphs. Yet doesn't this pretty much say it all? I don't know about you but I'm constantly dancing, flatfootedly, between two poles—moderate success and complete fiasco—in writing and, God knows, in life.

The Lonely Voice is also a lamentation for stories never imagined. O'Connor speaks up for stories and the people who write them—and, in doing so, the people who read them—as few ever have. Another sentence that amounts to prophesy: "The saddest thing about the short story is the eagerness with which those who write it best try to escape it."

Even today, fifty years later, for most fiction writers, and certainly for most publishers, the novel, hell or high water, remains supreme, especially in this country, where we still revere all things big for big's sake. This has always confounded me. I'm with O'Connor till the bitter end. How many good stories have been lost because writers slaved away their best years larding unnecessary words onto an unworthy novel? What truths lost? What things we needed to know that now we never will? What new forms never created? O'Connor:

> There is in the short story at its most characteristic something we do not find in the novel—an intense awareness of human loneliness.

If the novel, generally, is the more communal form, the short story is for loners, for those off to the side. O'Connor believed one of the reasons stories stand apart is that they are so often told from the perspective of an outsider, or, as he put it, "in the voice of a member of a submerged population." He acknowledged the clunkiness of the term 'submerged population' but admitted he couldn't come up with anything better. Members of a submerged population are people who, for whatever reason, either by force or by choice, have been excluded from what might be considered majority society. Characters in stories are often people utterly without influence, economic, political, or otherwise.

O'Connor knew all about being powerless. As his biographer Richard Ellman put it, "Few writers of humble circumstances have begun quite so humbly as Frank O'Connor did." His father was an abusive alcoholic who often threatened his mother with a razor. Frank, as a young kid, would try and defend her. The Civil War broke out when O'Connor was eighteen, and he left to join the Republican forces. Out of this war experience came one of his earliest stories, "Guests of the Nation," a touchstone I read whenever I need to be reminded, which is frequently, how incredibly cowardly human beings can be.

And also, sometimes, how graceful in the face of that cowardice.

"Guests of the Nation" is about two British soldiers, Belcher and Hawkins, who are being held by Irish Republican soldiers. The Irishmen include the narrator, a soldier named Bonaparte; his friend, a religious true believer named Noble (somehow O'Connor gets away with these names); and their nominal leader, Jeremiah Donovan, who is a fair hand at documents and has big farmer's feet.

From the very first sentence, it is clear that whatever separates these men, as Englishmen, as Irishmen, is nothing compared to what brings them together. "At dusk, the big Englishman Belcher would shift his long legs out of the ashes and ask, 'Well, chums, what about it?' . . ." It's what happens. You live among one an-other, you break bread, you play cards, you argue about religion. The labels fall away. No longer are they the Englishmen and us the Irishmen. We're Belcher and Hawkins and Bonaparte and Noble. Call us friends, chums.

The story seems so simple it could almost be a lesson. *Love thy neighbor.* Great stories are never lessons. They're warnings. And "Guests of the Nation" has been warning us for more than ninety years. This is what it means to be inhuman. Jeremiah Donovan receives word that the British have shot four of their men, includ-ing a sixteen year-old boy. When Donovan explains to the usually silent Belcher, just before he shoots him in the head, that he's only doing his duty, Belcher's reply always breaks my heart. "I never could make out what duty was myself," he said. "I think you're all good lads, if that's what you mean. I'm not complaining."

"Guests of the Nation" is the kind of story that is best expe-rienced rather than talked about. But I do want to add one last thing. There's no typo in the glorious last sentence of the story, which reads:

> And anything that happened me after I never felt the
> same about again.

Although many readers fill it in for themselves, there is no missing "to" before "me." The odd and perfect construction of this final line is only one of the reasons that Frank O'Connor's "Guests of the Nation" remains among the most enduring sto-ries ever about how violence feeds violence. It goes, of course, far deeper than O'Connor's mastery of the unique cadence of Irish speech. Two senseless executions so effect Bonaparte that they didn't just happen *to* him—now they *are* him. They are ours, too, as long as we keep reading this story.

AND THEN THERE ARE other stories cut so close you can only tell them in shards. Try taking on the whole thing directly and it only breaks apart on the page. You can't talk about it. You've got to talk about it. You can't talk about it. A couple of years ago I was away from my daughter for five weeks. She was about two and a half at the time, and I remember sitting in a little coffee shop in upstate New York feeling rested but guilty for all the time I was spending by myself. I took out John Edgar Wideman's *All Stories Are True*. I often carry this collection around with me. The energy of Wideman's prose is like a shot of epinephrine. His work always reminds me to get my head out of my own sand and look around. But that day I began to reread the last story in the collection, "Welcome." By the first sentence of the second paragraph—"She would be twelve now."—I realized I wasn't going to be able to finish it this time. My family would be surprised to hear that I weep. They've never seen me do it. I do it down in the garage, tearlessly. There's this welling up and I have to gulp air because I feel like I'm suffocating.

Do you remember the opening sentence of Ford Maddox Ford's *The Good Soldier? This is the saddest story I have ever heard.* Out of many contenders, the saddest story I've ever heard (and reading, I believe, is a way of listening) must be Wideman's "Welcome." That day in Essex, New York, in a coffee shop called the Pink Pig, I picked up a *People* instead. So I put down a short story. Big deal. But I remember it. How one day I couldn't endure someone else's losses on the page because I was homesick for my own kid. What does this say about my ability to endure my own losses when those losses come? As they have, as they will again. This morning, as an act of private penance, my family asleep, I returned to "Welcome," and wept. All out wept for a change. For the two lost children in the story: Njeri and Will.

It's the end of December, Christmastime—Homewood, Pittsburgh. The streets are covered with the rags and tags of snow, and the wind, known as "the hawk," blows under your clothes the moment you step outside—but still the carolers sing. And one family is grieving. Sis lost her daughter—Njeri—at just over a year old. It happened a few Decembers back but the pain remains raw, especially this time of year. Tom, her brother, has lost a teenage son to prison—a life sentence. Both losses are unassuageable and infinite. "You could lose a child like that, once and for always in an instant and walk around forever with a lump in your throat . . ."

Separate calamities, yet as in any family, grief merges.

As Sis walks the winter sidewalks on her way to buy groceries, the faces and voices of her family—the living, the dead, the gone—flood her mind. The story moves forward deep inside Sis's consciousness, with few intrusive transitions. For Wideman, thought and time refuse to be linear. They bob and flow like the unpredictable current of memory itself. The story captures, as few I know, the crazy ebb and flow of an ordinary day. As we carry our groceries, don't we also lug our devastations?

At its starkest, "Welcome" is about how we survive the unsurvivable. Tom arrives in Pittsburgh for Christmas Eve. The family is reunited for a brief time, and all the love and absence crowds together. Nothing aches more at a gathering of family than want for those who are missed. It's like there are gaping holes in the room. Everybody has to step around them. When Sis manages to steal a moment alone with Tom, he tells her how hard it is to come home, to face these familiar streets. On the one hand, it's rejuvenating, but at the same time, given what he's going through, it's a kind of living hell, too: "Like the world is washed fresh after rain, right, and when you step out in the sunshine everything is different, Sis, anything seems possible, well, just think of the opposite."

And then—and here's the part I anticipated not being able to take that day in the Pink Pig—the story takes a sharp and magnificent swerve outward into other people. "Welcome" is told, as I said, from mostly the perspective of Sis, but Wideman won't be constrained by any conventional notions of point about view.

As the grief merges, so do the voices of these two siblings. Sis and Tom become one as Tom recounts how the night before, after his flight arrived, he drove over to his old favorite place, the Woodside Barbeque, for some chicken wings. "You know how I love them salty and greasy as they are I slap on extra sauce and pop a cold Iron City." On the way, Tom tells Sis, who tells us, he sees a young father and his little boy waiting for a bus in the cold. The bus isn't coming for days, if at all, this late on a weekend.

What follows in the story is a moment of such rare grace it hurts. It's Belcher about to be shot all over again: "I think you're all good lads . . ." There are times the generosity of a fictional character bursts off the page and into our consciousness for good:

> On my way back past that same corner I see the father
> lift his son and hug him. No bus in sight and it's still
> blue cold but the kid's not fidgeting and crying anymore
> he's up in daddy's arms . . .

I don't want to get into what it might have taken John Edgar Wideman, the man, the father of a son in prison, to write this story, to create such music. This is the gift of fiction. Out of his own agony, Wideman grants his fictional father, Tom, his fictional mother, Sis—and the rest of us—deliverance. I wonder sometimes how certain writers do it, how they are able to leave, for a few moments, at the desk, their own pain behind. Because all our losses are collective. If they're not, we're truly doomed. If we can't overcome them ourselves, the very least we can do is recognize that we aren't the only ones out here trying to survive.

JOYCE CAROL OATES

+ + + + + + +

BATTLE ROYAL
Ralph Ellison

A & P
John Updike

+ + + + + + +

Could two stories by contemporary American male writers of the mid-twentieth century be more dissimilar? At least, at first glance.

John Updike's brilliantly condensed, intensely lyric homage to the voice of another American contemporary, J. D. Salinger, has long been the Updike story most anthologized, as it is likely the Updike story that is the most readily accessible to young readers. Ironically, or perhaps appropriately, in its very brevity and colloquial lyricism, "A & P" isn't characteristic of Updike's short stories, which tend to be much longer, richer in detail and background information, slower moving and analytical; this is a story told exclusively from the perspective of a teenaged boy, in the boy's mildly sardonic voice—"In walks these three girls in nothing but bathing suits."

The boy is a checkout cashier at an A & P store in the (fictitious) small town of Tarbox, Massachusetts, an old New England settlement that dates to 1634, close enough to the Atlantic Ocean that, as Updike notes in another Tarbox story ("The Indian"), "You find you must drive down toward the beach once a week or it is like a week without love."

This proximity to the beach—(and perhaps the wild sensuous beauty of the ocean)—figures crucially in "A & P," for the girls who have entered the store are in bathing suits, and such casual wear is forbidden by the priggish store manager: "Girls, this isn't the beach." And, more priggishly, "We want you decently dressed when you come in here." Immediately we have a generational standoff: on one side, the girls in bathing suits and Sammy the admiring cashier, on the other the store manager Lengel, who happens to be an old friend of Sammy's parents ("Sammy, you don't want to do this to your mom and dad"—typically, a remark to make a rebellious adolescent feel guilty).

Sammy makes his gallant, if quixotic gesture—impulsively, he quits his job in protest of the store manager's behavior: "You didn't have to embarrass them." And when Sammy walks out of the store, the girls are gone. "My stomach kind of fell as I felt how hard the world was going to be to me from here on."

"A & P" is a wonderfully visual story. It is no surprise to learn that John Updike studied art, and that his fiction abounds with vividly realized and minutely delineated scenes. Though only a high school boy, Sammy has a sharp, droll eye: a middle-aged woman customer is seen as "a witch about fifty with rouge on her cheekbones and no eyebrows"—"if she'd been born at the right time they would have hung her over in Salem"; housewife-shoppers in the A & P he sneers at as "houseslaves in pin curlers." His intense interest is in the girls, or rather one of the girls, who is wearing a "kind of dirty-pink—beige maybe, I don't know—bathing suit with a little nubble all over it and, what got me, the straps were down. They were off her shoulders looped loose around the cool tops of her arms . . . all around the top of the cloth there was this shining rim . . . I mean, it was more than pretty."

We note that Sammy recounts the story as an anecdote that occurs both in the present tense ("In walks . . .") and the past tense ("The one that caught my eye first . . ."): why? Is this an error on the author's part or a shrewd decision? When we write/read/

think in the present tense, we are *not yet in possession of what comes next*; like a horse with blinders, yoked in place, unable to turn our heads and look back, we can only look forward, and we are helpless to "analyze" what is happening, since such a perspective can only come retrospectively. The present tense is the very tense of things unfolding—it's the present tense in which we actually live, though our wandering, questing, ruminating minds can take us very far even as we remain, in the eyes of an observer, in one place. Updike's narrator is retelling this story of how his life was changed when he was sixteen or seventeen, in the Tarbox A & P one momentous day—he's older now, and we might assume he is less impulsive. The reader is left to wonder: Did Sammy regret quitting his job at the A & P?

RALPH ELLISON'S "BATTLE ROYAL" is the most frequently anthologized stories by this distinguished Black American writer, most famous for his novel *Invisible Man* (1952); it is also recounted by a narrator looking back on his boyhood—"It goes a long way back, some twenty years." Both stories depict boys who make dramatic decisions that have affected their subsequent lives, and it's suggested in "A & P" that Sammy will always be an outsider in his smug, provincial society. But the (unnamed) narrator of the harrowing "Battle Royal" is truly an outsider in the white racist society in which he must live, and his horrific experience is virtually the antithesis of the quite mild, unthreatening experience of the (white) boy Sammy. (Indeed, we don't think of Sammy as "white" when we read "A & P"—we take for granted that he is of the majority race, which happens to be "white" in the United States. Only when we contrast Sammy with Ellison's teenaged boy do we realize the profound abyss between them.)

At the outset, Ellison's narrator is shocked by his seemingly meek grandfather's instructions to him on his death bed: "I never told you, our life is a war . . . Live with your head in the lion's mouth. I want you to overcome 'em with yeses, undermine 'em with grins, agree 'em to death and destruction, let 'em swoller you till they vomit or burst wide open." (By *'em* the grandfather means, of course, the enemy: white folks.)

Where "A & P" is a sweetly melancholy/comic story, "Battle Royal" is a horror story all the more horrible for being historically "real." (Though once, when I taught this famous story in a Princeton writing workshop, an undergraduate said, "This never happened. Nothing like this ever happened." The student was not of the white racial majority, and the rest of us simply sat stunned, in silence. How to reply? We said nothing—we did not defend Ralph Ellison's authority. My feeling was that Ellison's brave story was the only valid reply—the witnessing of truth by one who has experienced it, not one who is only summarizing it.)

Both "A & P" and "Battle Royal" are dramatic, and riveting. Both center on turning points in teenaged boys' lives. Both are beautifully written, though Ellison's is the richer in its background exposition, as it is the more profound in its indictment of the very complacency of the white society to which, we can assume, Updike's Lengel belongs. The experience of racist harassment and cruelty could not be more succinctly focused than in "Battle Royal," in which Black boys are forced to fight one another for the amusement of ignorant but powerful white men in a segregated city (very likely Oklahoma City, where Ellison grew up in the early years of the twentieth century), where a Negro high school valedictorian is instructed by a smug racist to "keep developing as you are and some day [this prize briefcase] will be filled with important papers that will help shape the destiny of your people."

It is a delicious irony. But it is a painful irony. For who among the simpering white racists could have foreseen that, indeed, the "important papers" of Ralph Ellison would one day be published as *Invisible Man*, among the greatest of American novels of the twentieth century?

BICH MINH NGUYEN

✦ ✦ ✦ ✦ ✦ ✦ ✦

CATHEDRAL
Raymond Carver

IN THE AMERICAN SOCIETY
Gish Jen

✦ ✦ ✦ ✦ ✦ ✦ ✦

IT USED TO BE that epiphany was all the rage. Short stories moved toward a moment of realization, a flash of understanding that a character reached near the end, signifying a change. I was first taught this in undergrad when we read James Joyce's *Dubliners*. Epiphany could be quiet, brief, futile, or a moment of grace, as people often said about the doomed grandmother in Flannery O'Connor's "A Good Man is Hard to Find." Epiphany happened for the clerk who quits his job in John Updike's "A & P," another often-assigned story. And it was the hallmark of Raymond Carver's "Cathedral," published in 1983 and widely anthologized after, in the scene where the unnamed narrator draws a picture. For many years, it seemed, creative writing students read, wrote, studied, and workshopped toward epiphany, asking: Is it earned? All of this might seem a little quaint now, or nostalgic, or old-fashioned. A "dubious phenomenon," as Charles Baxter called it in "Against Epiphanies," from *Burning Down the House: Essays on Fiction*. That phenomenon, now, is more in question than ever. Whether or not the role of epiphany merits endurance, it is a technique that many writers were (are) taught as a way to reveal a sense of discovery. A gesture toward profundity, guarded by restraint. A glint, and the rest is up to the reader.

When I started teaching creative writing and literature classes some twenty years ago, after my MFA, I taught some of the same stories I had been taught. "Cathedral" was one of them. It's straightforward, first person, voicey, often funny, with clear metaphors and enough backstory for teaching backstory. It follows Freytag's Pyramid. The basics of character, conflict, setting, and point of view are established within the first paragraph. The story deftly combines interiority with exteriority. The protagonist is misanthropic, insecure, and prejudiced, jealous that his wife's old friend Robert, "this blind man," is coming to visit. In classic Carver style, the characters talk and drink within a domestic environment. There's a vivid dinner scene that both entertains and implies a kind of communion. By the end, the protagonist achieves a reversal of feeling and a moment of spirituality with Robert when they watch a TV program about cathedrals and begin drawing one together: "His fingers rode my fingers as my hand went over the paper. It was like nothing else in my life up to now."

Sixteen years after "Cathedral," Gish Jen published "In the American Society," a story about Ralph Chang, a first-generation immigrant. Ralph owns a successful pancake restaurant in a suburb of New York but runs it like an overlord. His efforts to help undocumented Chinese workers go awry. Meanwhile, Ralph's wife and especially his two daughters seem to be having an easier time of it. As his wife says to the daughters: "Your father doesn't believe in joining the American society. . . . He wants his own society." The implications of this, and the binary it sets up, trouble the entire story. To what extent does Ralph Chang not believe in joining society and to what extent is he not permitted entrance? The story is a study in generational difference, most notably in how the narration belongs not to Ralph but to Callie, one of the daughters. Being second generation, she doesn't have the same difficulties in navigating cultures. The story's tension increases when the Changs' application to join a country club is denied. The family goes to a neighbor's party where a white man named Jeremy accosts Ralph. "Who are you?" Jeremy asks, the question of selfhood made plain. "This is my party and I've never seen you before in my life. Who are you?" In a burst of fury, Ralph throws his own jacket into the pool and the family heads home. Then he remembers that his keys are in the jacket; someone will have to dive for them. Ralph gives the great line of the story, a kind of epiphany: "'You girls are good swimmers,' he said finally. 'Not like me.'"

BOTH "CATHEDRAL" AND "IN the American Society" used to be staples of the creative writing classroom, offering later-twentieth-century American realism, issues of identity, and male protagonists who have to realize a core truth about who they are. In "Cathedral" epiphany is overt and in the moment, happening to the narrator who is telling the story. "It's really something," he says. He doesn't have the words for what he's feeling. His experience is entirely self-concerned; Robert is an ancillary character and the narrator's wife is on the sidelines. In "In the American Society," Ralph does have the words. His epiphany is shared, happening both to him and to his narrator daughter. She watches her father have this understanding, and it's this watching—the daughter's awareness of her father's awareness—that makes the epiphany complex.

A SEMESTER ISN'T THAT much time. There's only so much time to investigate a good range of stories, to encourage students to write toward risk and depth. As much as we talk about craft—

trying to understand, question, and complicate the meaning of the term—we also talk about subject and process and, yes, feeling—the sense that something, anything matters, that the work isn't an exercise or a game. As a student, I wanted to have realizations. I wanted to feel that fiction meant more than even writers could articulate. All these years later, I still do. I still hope that readers will recognize and understand characters who may be, seemingly, nothing like them. No doubt, overly obvious versions of epiphany abound (many people think "Cathedral" is one of them), but in many ways the technique is still the rage in short stories, poems, nonfiction, and endless memes. Perhaps its lasting allure is its forthrightness; it wants to get us to a state of meaningful awareness. Sometimes that feels like realization; sometimes it feels like heartbreak. The approaches may have changed, but the longing remains.

Writing is influenced by trends as much as any art form, and the way story structure has been taught to generations of creative writing students is rooted in white patriarchy. And so I do not read "Cathedral" or "In the American Society" the same way I did twenty years ago; it would be a lack of progress if I did. After all, we're supposed to change as writers and as readers. When I look back at these influential works, I think about how all writing is dated, and how that is not at all a criticism but rather an appreciation of context. I find it satisfying to reread, to reach back through time and text and remember who these characters were and what they did and what they realized, and to remember who I was, too, when I first met them. Who I was when I was first writing. And what it was like to walk through someone else's cathedral, someone else's darkness, heading home.

ANTONYA NELSON

✦ ✦ ✦ ✦ ✦ ✦ ✦

HEART OF DARKNESS
Joseph Conrad

THE GIRL WHO LEFT HER SOCK ON THE FLOOR
Deborah Eisenberg

✦ ✦ ✦ ✦ ✦ ✦ ✦

T HE THING THAT LINKS these two stories to one another is my love of them. Might as well confess that up front, and proceed from that conceit. They are more different than they are alike, and their appearing in an essay together has as its fundamental reason my affection and respect for them as stories.

That said, they begin to open for me a few similarities. The most central of these, I think, is their sense of humor and play in the midst of describing traumatic events. That is, their authors seem to believe, as I do, that human truth, no matter how grim, is also inevitably infused with the ridiculous and comic. This, too, has been my experience of life. The same material, in some more somber author's hands, might not ever allow for a laugh.

Joseph Conrad's *Heart of Darkness* provides the information that human character, despite era or continent, will, when handed absolute power, fall prey to absolute corruption. At heart, minus manners and other civilizing influences, man will be reduced to egomania and madness. When I teach the novella, I also show Francis Ford Coppola's iconic film version, *Apocalypse Now*, and then the documentary made by his wife, called

Hearts of Darkness, about the filming of *Apocalypse Now* in which Francis himself plays the nonfiction role of Kurtz gone berserk. This series of exposures to the same story reaffirms the original's technical impact: a narrator is recounting a story to a group of listeners, and the reader, reading the story, feels herself included in that ever-widening ripple effect caused by the essential anecdote, which is at the heart of the story, an event not unlike a stone thrown into a pond, the resulting rings of disruption extending in its wake.

But at various points in the story, the narrator pauses to expose the quite convincing levity—the gallows humor, the amusing vernacular, the absurdity—that punctuates all of human endeavor. Here is the narrator's description of the languishing cannibals who accompany him up the river: "I looked at them with a swift quickening of interest—not because it occurred to me I might be eaten by them before very long, though I own to you that just then I perceived—in a new light, as it were—how unwholesome the pilgrims looked, and I hoped, yes, I positively hoped, that my aspect was not so—what shall I say?—so—unappetizing. . . ." The niggling vanity of this description! The pure admission of it! The force of character that it animates! Ask anyone who's watched *Apocalypse Now* about a favorite scene and you're likely to get the surfing one as a response. Everywhere bombs and flames, but all Kilgore wants to look at is the way the waves break. Later, to punctuate his story concerning loving "the smell of napalm in the morning," he exclaims, like a punchline, "Smells like . . . victory."

"Mistah Kurtz—he dead."

These small gestures—inflected dialogue, the nonessential aside—do tremendous work in lengthening the spectrum along which the story's tonal range extends. For this reader, that expanse buys a lot of credibility and complicated pleasure.

DEBORAH EISENBERG'S NARRATOR—INTIMATE WITH the girl who leaves her sock on the floor—also convinces me of the verity of the situation by replicating that girl's thinking. Confronted with the death of her mother, Francine begins a long trek into the next stage of her life. All of the stops along the way provide opportunities for absolute pathos, yet Eisenberg never allows Francine to become that worst of all fictional characters: the victim.

The story is shaped by the suspended state of limbo Francine finds herself in, having lost her mother at story's beginning and found her father by the end. It is a structural wonder, yet what I admire most is being made to laugh on every page. At the hospital, Francine listens to Nurse Healy praise her mother, her politeness and stoicism. Yet what she deciphers for the reader is this: "Oh, great. Who but her mother could get someone to say that her pain was obvious but that she never complained? Who but her mother could get someone to say she was polite even though everyone could tell she didn't want their gifts? No doubt about it, the body they'd carted off almost a day and a half ago from Room 418 had been her mother's—Miss Healy had just laid waste, in her squelchy voice, to *that* last wisp of hope."

Francine continues to reveal to the reader the character of the woman who was her mother, proud, stubborn, defensive, and fundamentally dishonest. She would rather lie to Francine about her father—invent his violent death by hit and run—than reveal the fact that he is alive and well, and homosexual. The reader discovers his aliveness in the same way Francine does; her voice saturates the story, her teenage innocence and confusion and sarcasm and self-doubt provide a beautiful balance of unbearable sadness and redemptive hope. "Yargh." begins the narrative in one paragraph. Vulnerable, yes, but with a firm grasp on the range of emotional tonality that allows me to believe she will survive. Her story will never trade on bathos; it would be too unlike her.

THE BREAK IN DEADLY serious and mortal consequence convinces a reader like me of the truthfulness of what is being recalled. I don't as thoroughly trust a sensibility that won't acknowledge the human fallibility of finding something dire also awfully funny. Awfully.

RICK MOODY

✦ ✦ ✦ ✦ ✦ ✦ ✦

THE COMPANY OF WOLVES
Angela Carter

THE USE OF FORCE
William Carlos Williams

✦ ✦ ✦ ✦ ✦ ✦ ✦

THE LAST BOOK I read, on the beach, in August 1979, before heading off to Brown University for my freshman year, was *The World According to Garp* (1978), by John Irving, which I enjoyed thoroughly. Weeks later, I enrolled in a literature course required for freshmen interested in the English department, and in that class I read: *Murphy*, by Samuel Beckett; *Labyrinths*, by Jorge Luis Borges, *One Hundred Years of Solitude*, by Gabriel García Márquez, and *The Crying of Lot 49*, by Thomas Pynchon. After a semester in that classroom, the beach reading of my prior life seemed far away.

That literature class had occasion to employ *The Norton Anthology of Short Fiction*, edited by Brown University's own R.V. Cassill. He was near retirement at that point, I think, and was not much in evidence on campus. For me, *The Norton Anthology of Short Fiction* was a foundational document for American literature. I was just the right age for it. There were a dozen or more stories in it that became absolutely essential to me, and those stories which are so heavily outfitted with notes and marginalia at this point that my copy (second edition, I believe), with its compound-fractured binding, is more a historical document than a book you could actually read.

"The Use of Force," by William Carlos Williams, was one story I read in *The Norton Anthology of Short Fiction* in my first semester at school. Williams, better known for his spare, declarative poems and his epic *Paterson*, is not particularly celebrated for his short fiction. I'm sure there are those who would allege that "The Use of Force" is so blunt an object as to be more traumatic than effective as a short fiction. But for me, especially now having taught it many dozens of times, it is a hallowed thing, luminous, harrowing, provocative. The plot—because this story is nothing if not a study in brief of plot itself—is simple. A doctor (the W. C. Williams character, it must be said) goes on a house call (!), in which he intends to examine a young girl with a sore throat. When the girl, despite prodding by her mother and father, refuses to open her mouth for the exam, the action begins. The entire story, therefore, consists of the doctor's increasing vehemence. Onto this simplest of plots, every possible allegorical layer of philosophical conundrum is easily grafted. The story is frankly erotic, whether it wants to be or not. And it is about class (the girl, and her parents, are working class, while the doctor is middle class). And it is about medicine and medical intervention. It's also about war, and about force generally speaking. All this in the plainest language imaginable, and with deftly deployed characterizations that only begin to reveal how sophisticated they are upon repeated examination, as when the doctor says of the parents: "After all, I had already fallen in love with the savage brat, the parents were contemptible to me. In the ensuing struggle they grew more and more abject, crushed, exhausted while she surely rose to magnificent heights of insane fury of effort bred of her terror of me."

I'm not going to give away the ending, because it's so great. But what I will say is that everything you could ever want to know about "plot" versus "story" is contained in those mere fifteen hundred words. No mystery, no overplotted crime fiction, could ever exceed the perfection of Williams's brief investigation into force, though he was no specialized prose writer, or, at least, was never adjudged as such.

My second year at Brown, having drunk deep from the trough of international literature in the aforementioned freshman English class, I decided to try to study writing with a British writer who was visiting campus for one year. She was filling in for John Hawkes, who was on sabbatical. I didn't know anything about the British writer, and as I have mentioned elsewhere, during the first class someone had the temerity to ask this writer, Angela Carter, what her work was like, to which she replied, "My work cuts like a steel blade at the base of a man's penis." At which point, or soon thereafter, the class mostly emptied out.

I READ CARTER'S TRULY excellent collection of short fiction, *The Bloody Chamber and Other Stories* (1979), upon enrolling in her class. It's a book of rehabilitated and renovated fairy tales, mostly adapted from the Brothers Grimm and Perrault, retrofitted with feminist and Freudian and Marxian subtexts, though to say this does the work a profound disservice. *The Bloody Chamber* restores the awe to the fairy tales, the mystery and surprise, makes them less like teddy bears and more like grizzly bears, in which menace and subconscious crosscurrents are spelled out and made obvious. The Brothers Grimm stories, we forget, were full of murder and incest and all the things that children worry about and are encouraged to suppress. Carter teased out these substrata and made them manifest again.

"Little Red Riding Hood" comes in for several refurbishments in the Carter collection and chief among these is a short piece called "The Company of Wolves." As with "The Use of Force," for me "The Company of Wolves" was a primer on how to work with short fiction, but of a diametrically opposed sort. Where

"The Use of Force" is all about drama, and the cinematic urgency of conflict, "The Company of Wolves" meanders for pages before it arrives at its alleged story (a story we know so well as to forbid any uncertainty at all about its outcome). The narrator is completely intrusive, and, without a doubt, has opinions about everything, and she also doubles (like the voice at the opening of Joyce's "The Dead") as the voice of the townsfolk of the piece, in their communal whole. The story, once it arrives, turns everything we know about "Little Red Riding Hood" on its head, so that it's more about marriage rituals and defilement of girls than about wolves and forests. It's unrelentingly dark, this short story, but in a way that is highly pleasurable and often funny, because it tells you something true about the origin of folk literature: "You are always in danger in the forest, where no people are. Step between the portals of the great pines where the shaggy branches tangle about you, step between the gateposts of the forest with the greatest trepidation and infinite precautions, for if you stray from the path for one instant, the wolves will eat you. They are grey as famine, they are as unkind as plague."

Indeed, if "The Use of Force" serves as a template for how to make a modern realistic story, "The Company of Wolves" does just the opposite: it reminds us how storytelling immemorial, the thing that happened around campfires and in underheated drawing rooms of old, was full of fabulation, exaggeration, and all the insecurities of the human subconscious. "The Company of Wolves," therefore, also performs conceptual work. It makes a decisive turn away from the real, in the direction of the imaginary, the sublimated, the allegorical.

I needed both these things to develop as a writer. I needed both an American tradition that was about character and action, and I needed an international tradition, a counternarrative, that was about voice, philosophy, and a sometimes dark, unpredictable storytelling tradition that is thousands of years old. Never the one without the other, always the oscillation between the two.

What I'm also trying to suggest with these two very different stories is the idea of reading hungrily, of leaving no stone unturned in the quest to learn more and to feel more as a would-be writer. Read hungrily, like the famished wolf.

SUE MILLER

✦ ✦ ✦ ✦ ✦ ✦ ✦

SPANISH IN THE MORNING
Edward P. Jones

THE THINGS THEY CARRIED
Tim O'Brien

✦ ✦ ✦ ✦ ✦ ✦ ✦

T HERE IS SO MUCH that's dazzling about Tim O'Brien's "The Things They Carried," but what strikes me as a writer every time I read it is the improbable way it's made. These sections of an almost generic coming-of-age story of First Lieutenant Jimmy Cross, lost in dreams of a girl he barely knew before he came to war, alternating with a focus on the men in his platoon and the lists of objects they carry—solo, chorus, solo, chorus, solo— how does this almost musical structure achieve such power?

Partly, I think, because of the way the two elements in the story come together as O'Brien gradually reveals more and more about the central events—the death of Ted Lavender, and Jimmy Cross's sense of responsibility for that. Though even in the first iteration of the list, when O'Brien is working with what the men feel they need to carry, we hear three times, glancingly, in a phrase or a subordinate clause, of Lavender's death—a dark motif, a minor note struck in what seems otherwise an uncompli-cated, here and there even *humorous*, inventory. And in each sub-sequent turn back to this "chorus"—the list sometimes shaped by what rank the men hold, sometimes by what mission they're on—we get a darker and fuller account of Lavender's death, even as the nature of the items in the lists changes, deepens, begins to measure the weight of the psychic and emotional burdens the men carry along with what's in their packs or on their backs.

The story's power rises too from O'Brien's bitter rage at the war—rage mostly at the absurdity of the sheer abundance of things: the resupply choppers arriving with "more of the same . . . fresh watermelons and crates of ammunition and sunglasses and woolen sweaters . . . sparklers for the Fourth of July, colored eggs for Easter—it was the great American war chest—the fruits of science, the smokestacks, the canneries, the arsenals at Hartford, the Minnesota forests, the machine shops, the vast fields of corn and wheat . . . they would never be at a loss for things to carry."

And before we come for the final time to Jimmy Cross, alone, burning the letters from his girl, refined to maturity by war, by death, there is a last chorus, a near-rhapsodic crescendo rising away from the lists into the dream of escape the men share, a dream of being themselves carried. "They were naked, they were light and free . . . sailing that big silver freedom bird over the mountains and oceans, over America . . . they gave themselves over to lightness, they were carried, they were purely borne."

These two passages, one describing a man hardening himself to carry on, the other imagining the weightlessness of the war's end—these passages talk to each other in a heartbreaking way.

But do these two *stories* talk to each other at all? Is there any reason to write about them together?

It would seem not, at first. Edward P. Jones's "Spanish in the Morning" is a first-person narration by a preternaturally observant little girl about to enter kindergarten, a perhaps more "ordinary" story, told more conventionally than "The Things They Carried." But while the arc of the narrative seems to concern the issue of where the narrator will go to school, she tells us early on that this is not what the story is about—that it's about "my father's father. And me. And all of them."

And though it's certainly true that the question of school is the thing that pushes the narrative forward—her father has wanted her to go to the public school just across the street, her mother, as ambitious for her children as she is for herself (it's her habit of speaking Spanish to her family in the morning that gives the story its title) is insistent that she go to the more distant, more rigorous parochial school—the narrator does, in fact, give us a full account of the difficult, painful lives of her father and grandfather and a more abbreviated account of the other men she knows and cares for. All of these men are damaged in one way or another: half blinded by a policeman, crippled, ill, in jail, but all of them bring her gifts before she starts school, "as if, my mother was to say, I was going away and never coming back."

And, of course, that is precisely what the narrator will do— leave forever the world she shares with "all of them." For as the first weeks of school pass, she slowly takes in the way the little boys around her are disappearing, opting out or perhaps somehow being driven out of this new world that's so encouraging to her. And we readers begin simultaneously to realize that the sense in which this story is about "all of them" is that it's describing the way the white world works differentially on Black males and Black females, the way it pushes them apart.

A crisis arises for the narrator a few days after two of the children in her class are disciplined. Sensing something about the vulnerability of the Black children around her, she rises from her desk, faints, and hits her head. She wakes in her own bed. That night, she has a dream as wonderful in its way as the dream of escape O'Brien's men have. She imagines that all the men she knows—released from jail, their wounds healed, their lives restored—are gathered with her in her father's yard, feasting on the fruits he's grown. In the dream she knows she can't stay in this Eden, but she lingers.

The next day, her family, concerned about her happiness in school, gives her the option of transferring to the public school her father has wanted for her, where, as her grandfather says, she will "be safe and happy as you would be in that front yard." But—her mother's daughter after all—she decides to go back to the parochial school, where, as she says, "by late October, my wound was healing as best it could, and our class was down to nine boys."

Like Jimmy Cross, then, our narrator has somehow matured in the course of these events, but it's a growth achieved, like his, by a renunciation whose terrible cost is part of the story—here in Jones's version more subliminally revealed, with the little girl's almost unarticulated and yet sorrowful awareness of what the history of "the men in my life" is going to mean for her.

COLUM McCANN

✦ ✦ ✦ ✦ ✦ ✦ ✦

A BALL OF MALT AND MADAME BUTTERFLY
Benedict Kiely

THE LOVE OBJECT
Edna O'Brien

✦ ✦ ✦ ✦ ✦ ✦ ✦

G REAT FICTION BRINGS US elsewhere, then allows us—if we
so desire—to dwell there forever. Not only does good writing help us see, but it also allows us to feel, even in the most extraordinary circumstances, what it means to be somebody else, or
someplace else. It acknowledges the complexity of the world, and
it amplifies our experience of being alive. We are given access to
voices we have not necessarily heard before. We can step outside
of ourselves and into a new form. What is singular about this is
that we can experience, for example, the terror of another life
and yet emerge from it without scars. We can see the inside of
the battered world and be thankful, too, that we can walk away
from it. Literature is the ultimate Möbius strip—we go on a journey away from ourselves, only to come back around, entirely
changed by what we have seen.

That this can be done in the space of a few short pages is tan-
tamount to a miracle.

It has often been said that historically the best short story writers, alongside the Russians, are the Irish, though I have to admit
that the American short story is an incredibly healthy specimen

too, especially in the past few decades.

In terms of the Irish short story there are a litany of names to choose from—James Joyce, Mary Lavin, John McGahern, William Trevor, Maeve Brennan, Liam O'Flaherty and so many others that listing them becomes an exercise in abundance or perhaps even embarrassment that one might leave a great name out. Oh—Joe O'Connor. And Claire Keegan. And Colm Toibin. And Bernard MacLaverty. And Danielle McLoughlin. And. And. And.

But for me, on a strictly personal level, I don't think I would go anywhere without the work of two of my all-time favourites, Benedict Kiely and Edna O'Brien, both of whom have written stories that can be read in an hour and remembered for a lifetime.

"A BALL OF MALT and Madame Butterfly" is a story that knocked me off balance the first time I read it, at the tender age of sixteen. I simply didn't know that stories like that could be written. What was more remarkable was that the author Benedict Kiely was a friend of my father's and lived not too far from me, in Donnybrook. I went on a short pilgrimage to see him, which set me on the road to becoming a writer, but the real journey was contained within the story itself.

It is the tale of a half-Japanese Dubliner, Madame Butterfly, "a woman of questionable virginity," who plies her trade in the Dark Cow pub along the quays. The narrator, a newspaperman, tells the story of how a civil servant, Pike Hunter, falls in love with her, pursues her, loses her and, in the process, loses his mind. I didn't know it then, but there is a remarkable range of literary references and allusions in the story, including Synge, Joyce, Spenser, Maupassant, Gilbert and Sullivan, W.B. Yeats and Maud Gonne, (both of whom are characters in the story). Oblique literary references resound throughout, yet when Pike starts regaling Madame Butterfly with obscure Yeatsian love poems, she turns around to say that Pike would "puke you with poetry."

Kiely (who passed away in 2007) was—or rather, is—one of the most erudite and informed writers of recent times in Ireland, but the stories are never diseased with self-consciousness. He has absorbed the great works and is at ease in a variety of things (Balzac, Finnegan's Wake, theology, pop culture, you name it) and yet he is essentially rooted in the calm of his own voice. Language, of all the mediums we use, is the most volatile and unyielding, and therefore the most difficult to make memorable. Kiely, rather than stripping the language down, layers it, so that it becomes a resonant, hypnotic chant. The sense of movement upon movement, digression into digression, song piled onto song, is overwhelmingly in its intensity and warmth, creating a home for the reader, any reader, within the story. In the manner of Joyce, Kiely's stories are beautifully laced through with songs, ballads, myths, colloquialisms, all of which are often reappropriated and twisted, operating in a new sphere, bumping up against their old meanings and, like in all great work, this gives a number of levels to the stories. The layers and levels of narration in the story are stunning and yet the architecture is seemingly simple. This gift for apparent ease is actually the ultimate in craftwork.

Only someone who listened well could have produced the stories that Kiely told. He could sing and shout with the best of them. He could also haul a laugh out of the darkest corners. He spoke the truth in wild, gabby, discursive ways. He had a great affection for the anecdote, the song, the scrap of local verse that brought a wakeful grace to the language of ordinary people. And, most importantly, he understands the interior clockwork of the people he wrote about: farmers, journalists, tradesmen, barmaids, the firemen and countless others who have made up the bric'n'brac of Irish life.

In later years I shared many balls of malt—otherwise known as a glass of whiskey—with the great Ben Kiely. I told him that his story about Madame Butterfly was one of the finest and funniest and most profound pieces I had ever read. He lowered his head humbly and asked me if I would like another drink. I said I would.

A LITTLE OVER A decade after first reading Ben Kiely, I had my own first short collection, *Fishing the Sloe-Black River*, published. I had been living in Japan at the time and I went to London on publication day. The great shock to my soul was that nobody cared. Sure, my editor was nice to me, and I was introduced around to the folks in the public relations office and the design department, but essentially the book was a little whisper in a house of great noise. I was absolutely a first-time writer. I had no readings planned, no interviews, no festival invitations, no reviews that I knew of yet.

I wandered around the corridors and nourished my own sense of shock at the silence I was encountering. And then—at the far end of the corridor—I saw a striking silhouette, a very glamourous woman with a long pour of red hair. Could it be? Was it possible? Is that truly her? I rushed into my editor's office to ask me if she could introduce me to Edna O'Brien. Fifteen minutes later Edna—who had generously blurbed the book and was visiting her own editor—invited me to read with her at a bookshop in Camden Town. I had never read in public before and I think I took the podium for an embarrassingly long twenty minutes, reading from my story, *Cathal's Lake*, before she showed how it really should be done, with grace and style and wit and charm, when she read from *House of Splendid Isolation*.

I adored the work of Edna O'Brien before that, but her generosity helped ensure that would continue forever.

It is difficult to choose any one particular short story from Edna—it's akin to singling out a single speck in the vast sky-theatre, and so I will go for one of her early stories, "The Love Object," from 1967, which feels like a thrilling compendium of all her work—graceful, incisive, melodic and dramatic. Even the title itself is wonderfully ambiguous and suggestive. The story begins with the words "He simply said my name," and the affair—and the world of the narrator and "the man who dwells somewhere within me"—unfolds from there into a confessional. It feels stripped down and bare and yet it also searches for intimate human heights so that it is both tiny and epic at the same time.

In this story, as in all of her work, Edna pulls back the curtains and opens the windows of our rooms: sometimes with a blast of light that is uncomfortable enough for us to make us cover our eyes until we learn how to deal with the truth of it all. Part of her greatness is a lack of fear. She describes the finest nuances of human feeling and leaves it up to the reader as to whether "The Love Object" is autobiographical or not.

The measure of a work of art—or a number of works of art—is from how deep a life does it spring. Edna's is immeasurable: counter, original, new, spare, unafraid of the dark instincts of the human spirit. Her imagination is meteoric. Words crackle around her.

I FEEL HONORED TO have met both Edna O'Brien and Ben Kiely, and to have spent time with them both at various times over the years. They were good to me. They extended a hand of mentorship and friendship. They taught me how to navigate the world and to negotiate what was yet to come. I am lucky that I got to step into that territory with them. But I also find it thrilling to think that they extended the same sort of hand to readers everywhere. This, too, is the joy of literature. It extends the world. All the people we are not are available to us, often in the most profound and thrilling ways.

And so I envy those who are coming to these stories for the very first time. Step into their worlds—and your own will not likely be the same again. The great gift is that they connect us all with one another.

We become, then, what they have been: patriots of elsewhere.

LOIS LOWRY

+ + + + + + +

A SMALL, GOOD THING
Raymond Carver

THE MANAGEMENT OF GRIEF
Bharati Mukherjee

+ + + + + + +

PHONE. THE INSISTENT RING. And it is not yet light. Four a.m. maybe, four thirty? So you know. Still, during the groggy fumble and grope for the lamp, the receiver, you tell yourself: wrong number. Butt-dial from a drunk. Or: prank. *Is your refrigerator running?* No, not at four a.m. So you know, really. And now you're awake, and you hear the words, and it's not a dream, not a nightmare, it's real, and your son is dead; he will always be dead, even though yesterday he was alive, and last week he was alive, and—listen, if I just tell you how alive he was! How smart, how good-looking, how—well, then you'll see that he can't be dead, can't possibly be dead.

Shaila Bhave, in Bharati Mukherjee's "The Management of Grief," points out that her boy was a good swimmer. Mrs. Bhave is a competent, intelligent woman. Still, one manages grief by grasping. Her son was a good swimmer. Last year he took diving as well! And where the plane went down in the Atlantic—well, in that area there are small islands, aren't there? There is still the possibility that her boy swam to an island! And towed his little brother, too! Yes! That could happen. One must hope. *It is one's duty to hope.*

And so Ann Weiss, in Raymond Carver's "A Small, Good Thing," comforts herself as well. "At least he doesn't have a fever," she says reassuringly, touching her dying son's cold forehead.

It is one's duty to hope.

Enter the secondary characters who always hover on the periphery of tragedy. Judith Templeton, the government functionary, with her cordovan briefcase and pearl drop earrings, mouths her platitudes at Mrs. Bhave; and at Scotty's bedside, Dr. Francis, wearing his striped tie and ivory cufflinks, actually says to Ann Weiss, "You try not to worry, little mother." And both women take it, nod their heads, reply politely. *Until.* (I knew, reading, that there would be an *until*, because there had been, for me.)

Shaila Bhave loses it in an airport and screams "You bastard!" at a customs official. Ann Weiss, so contained, falls apart in a bakery: "It isn't fair," she says, sobbing, leaning over the flour-covered table. "It isn't, isn't fair." (The victim of my own loss of composure—my personal *until*—was the security officer in the Frankfurt Airport who reached for and wanted to open and examine the wooden box I was holding; it contained the folded flag that had covered my son's casket.)

And what is the point, really, of writing about—Bharati Mukherjee, or Raymond Carver, writing about—the management of grief? Do the stories convey a larger truth, a new way of seeing? Not for me, they don't.

But they make me remember a note I received, following my son's death, from a friend who was a Shakespearean actor. I had seen him play Malvolio once, on the stage. I opened his letter and instead of the cloying condolences that I had read in so many others, he had simply written out a line from *Macbeth*:

> Give sorrow words; the grief that does not speak / Whispers the o'er-fraught heart and bids it break.

And that is what these stories contain: the words that keep the fraught heart from breaking. In the Mukherjee story, the populous community that surrounds Shaila Bhave distracts and irritates her with mindless, wailing advice as she tries to grasp the enormity of loss. But the widowed doctor scattering stolen roses on the sea that has claimed his wife says to her, "Mrs. Bhave, you are wanting to throw in some roses for your loved ones? I have two big ones left." Strangers approach her in the street and offer halting sympathy. A policeman cries and says, "I am sorry. I am so sorry, ma'am." There is odd comfort in the awkward encounters.

And the moment when the numb, wordless silence that has enveloped Ann and Howard Weiss is pierced, in one heartbreaking moment, by the baker they encounter at midnight in his closed bakery, and who holds out to them, as an offering, the small, good thing—a warm roll still steaming with cinnamon—and who begins to talk to them.

"'Smell this,' the baker said, breaking open a dark loaf. 'It's a heavy bread, but rich.'" They smelled it, then he had them taste it. It had the taste of molasses and coarse grains. They listened to him. They ate what they could. They swallowed the dark bread. It was like daylight under the fluorescent trays of light. They talked on into the early morning, the high, pale cast of light in the windows, and they did not think of leaving.

They did not think of leaving. In contrast, Shaila Bhave stands in a path looking north to Queen's Park and west to the university and hears her family's voices one last time. Go, they tell her. Be brave. She begins to walk.

The management of grief does, indeed, consist of small, good things. Both of these stories remind me of that and that once, I, too, did not think of leaving, but that eventually, propelled by words from others and from my own inner self—and because we do; we have no choice—I, too, began to walk.

DENNIS LEHANE

✦ ✦ ✦ ✦ ✦ ✦ ✦

WHY DON'T YOU DANCE
Raymond Carver

THE SECOND TREE FROM THE CORNER
E. B. White

✦ ✦ ✦ ✦ ✦ ✦ ✦

I FIRST READ "WHY Don't You Dance?" when I was nineteen
and working in a bookstore, where I spent my days opening
boxes, removing the books inside, and placing them on wheeled
carts to be shelved. One of those books—I can still see it nest-
ing between Styrofoam packing popcorn and other books—was
What We Talk About When We Talk About Love, by Raymond Carver, a slim white paperback with stark, Hopperesque cover art of
a nightstand, a lamp, a window, and a small bed with no pillow.
"Why Don't You Dance?" is the first story in the collection and
short enough, at seven pages, to read three times on a lunch
break, which is how I communed with it one day.

I had no idea what to make of it. As I understood story at
that point, it didn't seem to be one. A man whose wife has left
him puts all their furniture on the front lawn of his house. It's a
tragically exhibitionist act—*Here is all the failure and inadequacy of
my love*. A young couple happens by and believes it's a yard sale.
They proceed to bid on things. The man goes along and sells off
his life (and its curses, one could argue) to the young couple. He
drunkenly dances with the girl. The young couple goes home and

a few weeks later the girl tries to tell friends about the experience—she can feel its tragedy; her boyfriend can't—and ends up incapable of articulating it. The End.

I read the story three times because I didn't understand how something so slight in event could have had such an unsettling effect on me. (I had zero idea what minimalism was at this point.) I bought the book and read the other stories in the collection, some quite powerful, a few unforgettable. But it was "Why Don't You Dance?" that continued to haunt me. A year later the book was in my bag when I went off to college to study creative writing. By that point, I'd lost track of how many times I'd read the story, but it had unlocked itself to me a fair amount.

The story's title stems from a line the Sad Older Man asks the Young Vibrant Girl and the Young Dumb Boy: "Why don't you dance?" They do so in his driveway. The boy drunkenly sits down and the man steps in. The girl, perceptive beyond her years though wholly unable to articulate it, feels the man's loss, his permanent sadness, and mumbles, "You must be desperate or something." What the girl feels is her own possible future in the dance of love and relationships. Depending on which character's perspective we consider and at which time in their lives we find them the question can be posed with varied emphasis—*Why* don't you dance? becomes Why *don't* you dance? or Why don't *you* dance? or Why don't you *dance?* These are all questions or possibly accusations that cut to the core of how one approaches both love and life. The story ends on ". . . she was trying to get it talked out. After a time, she quit trying." And in seven pages, Carver carried a single unnamed character from innocence to experience and maybe even beyond into the first stages of willful disconnection from the emotional carnage that might await her in adulthood.

In one of my classes that year, we read E. B. White's "Second Tree from the Corner." It was another deceptively simple story in which very little seems to happen. Trexler, a nervous man given to "bizarre thoughts," visits his psychiatrist. Trexler is filled with indefinable dreads common to the period in which the story was written (shortly after the end of World War II). "Forty years," he thinks at one point, "and I still can't stay on life's bucky horse." His psychiatrist dominates the anxious little man. He wants to know about those "bizarre thoughts," wants Trexler to own up to being a misfit, an unhealthy outlier. "What do you want?" the good doctor asks in their final session. Trexler turns the question on the psychiatrist and the psychiatrist's answer—"I want a wing on the small house I own . . . I want more money and more leisure—" is so base and shallow that it forces Trexler to see the man upon who he's been conferring so much power in a new light. He sees *him* as small and afraid. "Poor scared overworked bastard," he thinks as he leaves his office.

It could be transference, yes, but it could also be something more—by empathizing with the universal insecurity of all human beings, Trexler frees himself, however temporarily, from the shackles of his own existential dread. And as the story closes, it moves from being quite clean and simple in its prose to something more symphonic when Trexler, walking toward Central Park with the "the last daylight applying a high lacquer to the brick and brownstone walls," knows "what he wanted, and what, in general all men wanted; and he was glad, in a way, that it was both inexpressible and unattainable, and that it wasn't a wing . . . [It] was at once great and microscopic, and although it borrowed from the nature of large deeds and of youthful love and old songs and early intimations, it was not any of those things, and it had not been isolated or pinned down, and a man who attempted to define it in the privacy of a doctor's office would fall flat on his face."

Trexler, "content to be sick, unembarrassed at being afraid," strikes a blow for anyone who mistrusts the easy certainties and facile rewards to be found in acquisition and consumption, the twin engines of twentieth-century capitalism. In the same way that the girl in "Why Don't You Dance?" understands for the first time that the human condition is far more complex than she'd ever imagined, so does Trexler, but whereas the girl is already beginning to distance herself from that knowledge, Trexler heartily embraces it.

In the two stories, stylistically disparate and philosophically divergent though they may be, my twenty-year-old self found kinship. Often to be human is to be lost and afraid and only as happy as your last good moment. Carver found a chilly despair in that knowledge. White found hope and liberation. Neither was wrong.

PHIL KLAY

✦ ✦ ✦ ✦ ✦ ✦ ✦

THE GRAND INQUISITOR
Fyodor Dostoyevsky

THE HARVEST
Amy Hempel

✦ ✦ ✦ ✦ ✦ ✦ ✦

I SUPPOSE, ALL THINGS considered, that my first reading of Dostoyevsky's "The Grand Inquisitor" was substantially improved by first almost accidentally killing myself. I'd been hiking in Montana, alone. I was sixteen, with a day pack, a copy of *The Brothers Karamazov*, and a plan to find the ideal spot to read it. Just a hundred meters or so off the trail was a group of beautiful cliffs, at the top of which, undoubtedly, there'd be just the perfect place. I had nothing in the way of climbing gear or climbing experience.

Midway up a foothold broke. I instinctively shifted all my weight to another foothold, causing that to break as well. I dropped a few inches, clutching two good handholds, and then dangled, flat against the cliff. After the first burst of panic and adrenaline I closed my eyes, controlled my breathing, and brought my heart rate back to normal. Then I opened my eyes and assessed my options. There were no obvious ways to get up or down. I dangled some more. The thought occurred to me, looking at the rocky ground below me, that it was possible I'd just hang there until my arms tired and I'd fall and die. That thought sat in my brain for a good five to ten seconds, much longer than it sounds, while I scanned the cliff for something of use. Far off to the right the rock curved out a bit. I realized I might be able to get some leverage by stretching my legs wide apart and pushing against the wall to create a little more friction—what climbers call stemming. This helped me push myself up, grab another hold, and continue climbing. When I got to the top I stood at the edge, looking out on the mountain valley below me, and I roared. Then I took a sip of water, sat down, and opened my book to where I'd left off, with Ivan saying something about the suffering of children.

As FIRST EXPOSURES TO "The Grand Inquisitor" go, I couldn't have asked for a better one. Not because a brief, if ridiculous, brush with my own mortality put me in the right frame of mind to contemplate the stakes of Dostoyevsky's universe, but because it gave me something tremendously valuable for any writer—the humbling knowledge that I am often an idiot, often make terrible judgment calls, and should thus employ a good deal more self-doubt.

In his writing, Dostoyevsky exercised a very specific form of self-doubt. The literary critic Mikhail Bakhtin claimed that Dostoyevsky's characters are not "voiceless slaves, but free people, capable of standing next to their creator, capable of not agreeing with him and even of rebelling against him," and "The Grand Inquisitor" is the clearest articulation of Ivan Karamazov's rebellion against Christianity, the religion of his creator. Dostoyevsky once responded to critics: "The dolts have ridiculed my obscurantism and the reactionary character of my faith. These fools could not even conceive so strong a denial of God as the one to which I gave expression." And that's why his work has power—he strove to articulate everything he didn't want to believe, everything he'd have liked to banish from his field of view. Instead of arrogantly dismissing his ideological opponents, he employs the full force of his genius to give them voice.

The writer is the God of their fictional world. If they want their characters to confirm to them that God is good, or that religion is evil, or that the antebellum South was a place full of charm and grace, or that Republicans have only the stupidest views of everything, or that the world is nothing but moochers and supermen . . . well . . . they can construct their world such that they get the answer they want. This doesn't always produce bad fiction, but when you see characters pinned to their author's intentions like insects displayed on a board, it's hard not to wonder what it'd be like to see them alive, at flight.

AMY HEMPEL EMPLOYS A somewhat different form of doubt—one that puts far more than simply religious beliefs at risk. Though, sadly, I didn't read "The Harvest" after a near death experience (I read it in a plywood hut on a very secure base in Iraq), I'd like to believe it was an equally exhilarating first read.

Hempel opens her story: "The year I began to say *vahz* instead of *vase*, a man I barely knew nearly accidentally killed me," and the sentences keep getting better from there, one after another: "In the hospital, after injections, I knew there was pain in the room—I just didn't know whose pain it was." "What happened to one of my legs required four hundred stitches, which, when I told it, became five hundred stitches, because nothing is ever quite as bad as it 'be.'" "As soon as I knew that I would be all right, I was sure that I was dead and didn't know it."

And then, midway through the story, comes the kicker. "I leave a lot out when I tell the truth. The same when I write a story. I'm going to start now to tell you what I have left out of 'The Harvest,' and maybe begin to wonder why I had to leave it out." And she proceeds to hunt down not only why she might evade or exaggerate, but also why we, the reader, might want her to: "The man of a week, whose motorcycle it was, was not a married man. But when you thought he had a wife, wasn't I liable to do anything? And didn't I have it coming?"

Up until reading Hempel, I'd felt a vague distaste for what I considered "metafiction." The notion of storytelling about storytelling seemed self-indulgent, a game of interest only to writers. But Hempel wasn't playing games. She was pulling up our motivations behind the ways we choose to remember, looking at the way the memory of an experience is bound together with the telling, the way the telling is shaped by the listener, and the way both of those become a part of the experience itself. The worlds we walk around in are constructed by the myths we tell ourselves and others, so when Hempel starts pulling on that thread, a whole lot begins to unravel.

I know I tell myself stories that probably don't match up to reality so well. There are big ones, about what kind of person I am, and little ones, like my little cliffhanger story. I bet if I went back to Montana I'd have to confront something far less impressive—stubby little cliffs, crumbling and sad, too small to really put a climber's life at risk, though still something only a fool would attempt.

CHARLES JOHNSON

+ + + + + + +

AN OCCURRENCE AT OWL CREEK BRIDGE
Ambrose Bierce

TRUMPETER
John Gardner

+ + + + + + +

IN ONE OF MY essays on aesthetics, "Storytelling and the Alpha Narrative" (*Southern Review*, winter 2005), I invite readers
to meditate with me on the perennial question of why certain
stories endure and others do not. Looking at literature, it seems
to me that a writer may have to work a lifetime before he or she
stumbles upon *that* story that embodies an archetype for our
thoughts, feelings, and experiences. If a writer during a long career hits that kind of story *once*, then he has been treated well
by the gods. If she delivers this kind of baby *twice*, we are looking at a true major talent. And when the rare writer creates such
a story *three* times or more (as Shakespeare, Mark Twain, and
Charles Dickens did)—a story that three generations or more of
readers embrace as an interpretative tool for their experience and
ideals—then he or she may be considered one of the towering
literary giants of all time. Some writers are blessed with such an
enduring performance only once, but that once can be enough if
one's goal is to enrich literary culture.

Alpha Narratives, as I call such stories, share a number of
traits. First, these works achieve that deceptively simple yet most

difficult of achievements: delivering a whopping good, imaginative, and original story. A story so good, as Aristotle says in his *Poetics*, that its reader should be able to just turn to the person next to him and summarize its plot, and his listener, on the basis of that précis, will be moved to pity and fear. Second, after fifty years or more, stories and novels of this kind cease to be just stories and become cultural artifacts—that is, they help us "read" a moment in a culture's history, or the human condition generally. Alpha Narratives are elegant, compact, and crystalline. They satisfy our definition of a classic work because they express something so perfectly that they do not need to be rewritten. And, to paraphrase something once said by the writer/cartoonist Tim Kreider, over time we find ourselves describing certain experiences or people by just alluding to such a literary work, for example, when we call someone a Don Quixote or say something was a *Rashomon* situation.

Ambrose Bierce's masterpiece, "An Occurrence at Owl Creek Bridge," is that kind of Alpha Narrative. Examining this story, we notice immediately that its plot is economical and efficient. You can summarize it in just three sentences. Peyton Farquhar, an Alabama planter during the Civil War, supports the Confederacy and longs for "the larger life of the soldier, the opportunity for distinction." That opportunity arises when a "gray-clad soldier," who unbeknownst to Farquhar is a "Federal scout," informs him that the Yanks have restored Owl Creek Bridge, built a stockade nearby, and that the bridge can be destroyed if someone sets fire to it. Farquhar attempts to destroy the bridge, is captured, and is executed by hanging.

As a plot, this is simple enough. But it is upon this simplicity that Bierce builds an unforgettable literary experience. One of the many pleasures of "Occurrence," published in 1890 in the *San Francisco Examiner*, is the granularity of the details Bierce brings to the smallest actions of the soldiers who will execute Farquhar. They window onto a world long ago. And at the story's center is the ambiguity of time, how it speeds up and slows down, depending on our state of consciousness. "What, then, is time?" St. Augustine asks in his *Confessions*. "If no one ask of me, I know; if I wish to explain to him who asks, I know not . . ." Bierce plunges us so powerfully into this universal mystery that "Occurrence" has inspired other artists to return to it, allude to it, engage in dialogue with it, and reimagine it in their own styles for 125 years. That transformation of a story into cultural shareware is one hallmark of enduring literary art. No writer could hope for more than having his or her creation received this way as a gift so valued by others.

JOHN GARDNER'S STORY "TRUMPETER" also speaks to art's endurance by representing the impact a creator's vision can have on other writers. Gardner was arguably one of the greatest, most innovative, and most hardworking creative writing teachers in our time. I was one of the thousands of students privileged to work with him. In his oeuvre of some thirty books and in his works on literary craft such as *The Art of Fiction*, *On Becoming a Novelist*, and *On Moral Fiction*, Gardner was distinguished among contemporary authors by his understanding of the inexhaustible possibilities for literary form, especially the ancestral forms of storytelling that predate and provide a foundation for fiction today.

"Trumpeter" is indebted to one of those ancestral forms, the animal fable common in Western cultures (Aesop's stories), Africa (Anansi the Spider stories), and the East (the Buddhist *Jātaka* tales). Gardner understood that the reality of the world governing the fable and all other tales is that of a *moral* universe. In *The Forms of Fiction*, he wrote that its laws "may not be those of cause-and-effect, but even when they are not, they seem natural because they are psychologically and poetically true." Thus, in "Trumpeter," mad Queen Louisa can "transform herself suddenly into a large green toad." The story overflows with enchantments of style—a beautifully orchestrated opening sentence that is a page long; lambent wit; an authoritative narrative voice; and, most delightful of all, a viewpoint limited to the queen's vigilant watchdog, Trumpeter. Through his nonhuman eyes we experience the follies of our own species. It was "Trumpeter" that got me thinking of how wonderful it would be if every writer's body of work offered at least one thought-provoking animal fable and led to two of my own stories in that genre, Menagerie, A Child's Fable, and the sci-fi fable/fabliau, Guinea Pig. For that artistic awakening, I will always be grateful to John Gardner.

PAM HOUSTON

✦ ✦ ✦ ✦ ✦ ✦ ✦

SARA COLE: A TYPE OF LOVE STORY
Russell Banks

A NOTE ON THE TYPE
Ron Carlson

✦ ✦ ✦ ✦ ✦ ✦ ✦

"SARAH COLE: A TYPE of Love Story" has the most audacious opening paragraph I know of. Reading it for the first time, in graduate school, made me understand that short stories are like car bombs: they can detonate at any moment with the slightest reaction from the reader. My job as a writer, I understood Banks to be telling me, was to do whatever it took to elicit the reaction that blows up the car. "Sarah Cole" is a veritable funhouse of literary disorientations, so many feints and dodges, so many half-truths and withholdings and one gorgeously unabashed lie, all designed to make the reader startle and wince and gasp.

Kaboom.

"Sarah Cole" is also an advanced course in point of view. Our narrator starts off in the first person, "To begin then, here is a scene in which I am the man and my friend Sarah Cole is the woman." But even the wording of that sentence is a clue to the narrative doubling that will follow. Soon, that *I*, becoming increasingly uncomfortable with his confession, will resort to the third person: "Around six o'clock on a Wednesday evening in late May, a man enters a bar . . . our man, call him Ronald, Ron

141

. . ." and it isn't long before Sarah Cole bellies up to the bar with him. Only a few scenes later the *I* steps back in, in his newly complicated persona: "I am still the man in this story, and Sarah Cole is still the women, but I am telling it this way because what I have to tell you now confuses me, embarrasses me, and makes me sad, and consequently, I'm likely to tell it falsely."

In this part of the story, Banks makes so many smart decisions that it causes the fillings in my teeth to hum every time I read it. This narrator, who is simultaneously Ron and someone even *less* trustworthy, is so ingeniously manipulative, so practiced at emotional sleight of hand that the reader has to tie herself in knots to feel she is capable of any judgment whatsoever.

When you're training championship show jumpers, high-strung Thoroughbreds, mostly you teach them to do something called a flying lead change, where they switch the foot they land on in midair, at a full canter, making it possible for them to change direction quickly, to stay on course, to face the next fence in the complicated pattern. "Sarah Cole" is a story of perfectly executed flying lead changes and perfectly executed jumps over a series of fences that it keeps throwing up in front if itself.

After schooling us thoroughly in the way exponentially accelerating unreliability can lead, as we suspected it would, to an even more painful übertruth, Banks pulls off a move so unexpected that I can't talk about it here without compromising *your* reading experience. So I won't, except to say that he makes the story tilt ninety degrees up on itself, or perhaps it is the reader's world that is forced to tilt, to try to keep up with the story. It is one of life's small cruelties that no one can read "Sarah Cole: A Type of Love Story" for the first time twice.

THE NARRATOR OF RON Carlson's "A Note on the Type"—a habitual criminal and practitioner of letter craft named Ray—tells us, "I became a car thief because it seemed a quick and efficient way to get away from my father's fists and I became a font maker because I was caught." In prison, Ray invents a font called Ray Bold, and after stealing a lab coat and making a clipboard in shop ("the single most powerful accessory," he believes, "to any costume"), he walks straight out of the Windchime, Nevada, State Prison unquestioned. On the run between towns with names like Triplet and Marvin and Old Delphi, he stops only long enough to carve his name into every silo, stock tank, dumpster, and boxcar in the Rocky Mountain region. It doesn't seem to occur to Ray that the authorities would have a harder time keeping up with him if he would only stop signing his name.

One day, Ray steals a car with a woman inside it, and because "when you find a woman in the car you are stealing, there is a good chance the law will view that as kidnapping," he decides to give her a ride home, where she makes him a "good feather bed" in the tack room and bakes him an apple pie to thank him for replacing the culvert at the end of her driveway. The next thing you know Ray is "affected," the urge to run temporarily put on hold.

Like "Sarah Cole," "A Note on the Type" is driven by voice and stance, the opportunities and complexities of a charismatic first-person narrator. But unlike our man Ron, who seduces the reader with deception, Ray is all good humor and good nature, nothing but earnestness in his desire to set the record straight. Whereas "Sarah Cole" explores every nook and cranny of unreliability, Ray's narration plumbs the depths of the reliable, all its subtle reveals, its nuanced suggestions of the magical contained within the mundane. He dares us to believe in characters named Bobby Lee Swinghammer and Little Ricky Grudnaut, in a place called Fort Nippers Juvenile Facility, in a world in which the sight of a woman leaning against a doorway with a pie in her hands could make you never need to carve your name into anything again.

"To run is to write," says Ray, somewhere in a canal duct between Marvin and Shutout. "Character is fate," says Ron, just before he climbs the stairs to Sarah's dark and cluttered apartment and they finally kiss for the first time. Like all of my other favorite stories, these two are about the acts of writing and rewriting. When we read them we understand, on a cellular level, the way stories have a life of their own, separate from the lives they arise from: how they can shape-shift along the fault lines of our shame and our desires, according to what we need to be forgiven for, and by whom. They remind us that often the metaphor knows more than we do, and if the subconscious hasn't been invited to the party, there is no reason to show up at all.

Finally, they both contain the obvious if untenable suggestion (ultimately rejected) that writers are people whose lives might be a little easier if we would only stop carving our names into culverts and silos, if we would keep a little of our shame, sometimes, to ourselves.

"Why do it?" reporters ask Ray. "You want to be famous?"

"It is a question," he tells them, "so wrongheaded it kind of hurts."

"You shouldn't believe anything I tell you," the narrator of "Sarah Cole" reminds us repeatedly, yet we lean in closer to hear every word.

ANN HOOD

+ + + + + + +

GIRL
Jamaica Kincaid

HOME
Jayne Anne Phillips

+ + + + + + +

O N THE SURFACE, "GIRL," by Jamaica Kincaid, and "Home," by Jayne Anne Phillips, have little in common. Kincaid's story takes place in Antigua and is rich with details from the island: pumpkin fritters, okra trees, pepper pot, dasheen. The setting of "Home" is typical Middle America with its Veteran of Foreign Wars rummage sales, *Reader's Digest*, Walter Cronkite, and *The Sound of Music* soundtrack. The stories are stylistically very different too. "Girl" reads like a prose poem, and is sometimes labeled as such rather than as a short story. "Home," which was contained in *Black Tickets*, Phillips's 1979 collection, is realistic fiction typical of stories written then.

Yet it is the similarities between the two stories that strike me.

"Girl" was first published in the *New Yorker* in 1978. Its unusual tone and voice emerge from its unconventional form. At approximately five hundred words ("Girl" is often characterized as flash fiction or a short-short), the story uses semicolons and repetition to create its breathlessness. The voice is a mother giving advice and directions to her daughter to help her become a woman in this traditional society. She tells her how to walk, whom to talk to, how to cook and shop and dress, all in the hope that her daughter will be a lady and not "a slut." The daughter interjects only twice, and in brief italicized phrases. "*I don't sing benna on Sundays and never in Sunday school,*" she says. "*But what if the baker won't let me feel the bread?*" she asks near the end of the story.

"Home" is a more traditional story in which a twenty-three-year-old woman returns home to live with her mother because "I ran out of money and I wasn't in love." The mother struggles to maintain rules too, but they no longer apply in the modern world. She too gives advice: "Don't be silly." "Don't use profanity." "Save your money." "If you are guilty, you should feel guilty." "Sex is for those who are married." But ultimately she admits, "I don't know what to do about anything."

Both mothers want their daughters to become respectable women. Yet both worry that their daughters, who live in a different, changing world, will not be able to achieve that despite their advice and opinions. The mothers are represented as traditional women. In "Girl," the rules reflect the mother's own domestic and societal accomplishments. She can tell her daughter how to live well because she herself follows these rules, which cover every aspect of life, from cooking, to gardening, to how to act in different situations. And the advice moves quickly and easily across these topics. "This is how you set a table for breakfast; this is how to behave in the presence of men who don't know you very well . . ."

Throughout the story, the mother in "Home" performs traditional domestic tasks. Every night after work she watches television and knits afghans. The daughter says: "She stops and counts, so many stitches across, so many down. Yes, she is on the right track." This observation is both literal and metaphorical—her knitting count is accurate and by doing this domestic work night after night, she is on the right track as a woman and as a mother. She took care of her dying mother, got married with a white gardenia in her hair, goes to church.

However, the advice of these mothers—one through the relentless listing of rules of behavior, the other coming from frustration at the way her daughter lives—becomes almost oppressive. In "Girl," the mother does not pause long enough for any real communication; in "Home," the mother's and daughter's lives are so different, their attitudes so opposite, that attempts at communication always deteriorate. "I want to make her back down," the daughter says.

In a way, in both of these stories the mothers are trying to make their daughters back down, especially in regard to their sexuality. "[O]n Sundays try to walk like a lady and not like the slut you are so bent on becoming," the mother in "Girl" warns. And later: "This is how to hem a dress when you see the hem coming down and so to prevent yourself from looking like the slut I know you are so bent on becoming." When at the end of the story the daughter asks her mother what if the baker won't let her feel the bread, her mother replies, "You mean to say that after all you are really going to be the kind of woman who the baker won't let near the bread?" Yet the mother also tells her how to make a medicine to get rid of a child "before it becomes a child."

The mother and daughter in "Home" engage in a debate about sexuality. The daughter, a twenty-three-year-old, believes in premarital sex whereas her mother, the symbol of tradition and rules, believes sex is for those who are married. This disagreement takes a sharp turn when the daughter's ex-lover, Daniel, shows up for a visit. At first, the mother acts like a perfect hostess, making whiskey sours and popcorn. But when Daniel goes to bed for the night, the mother and daughter continue their argument. When the mother comments on how nice he is, the daughter points out that Daniel respects her even though they've been lovers.

She pushes her point after her mother goes to bed. The daughter goes into Daniel's room and engages in sexual activity with him, even though she knows her mother can hear them. This aggressive act ties together a recurring theme of a cancer that has hit this house, something that was stealthy and destructive. After reading the story of a grizzly bear attacking a girl in *Reader's Digest*, the daughter has a sexual dream about her father. The many ways in which guilt, secrets, and scars are explored in the story lead the reader to believe that there has been sexual abuse between the father and daughter, and that the mother hides behind her traditional female role to ignore it.

The morning after she and Daniel have sex, the daughter she finds her mother standing at the sink washing dishes, another traditional domestic task. Her mother refuses to speak to her. Instead, she performs the simple act of cleaning—running hot water, adding soap, and then pushing the dishes down into the water, which is exactly what she has done with the secrets in the house: she has buried them. When her mother begins to sob, the daughter hugs her. "I heard you," the mother says. "I heard it." At last she has confessed that she heard the earlier abuse. "Here, in my own house," she continues, but now taking her now wobbly stance as a pillar of womanhood. It is at this point that she says, "I don't know what to do about anything." This admission is the denouement, the realization that despite all of her rules, despite doing everything right, she is lost.

Although there is no such backing down in "Girl," this mother too holds on to rules and traditions that no longer make a girl into a proper woman. It is not coincidence that these two stories, published in 1978 and 1979, were written after the sexual revolution, at a time when traditions and roles were questioned. Both stories contrast these worlds, the old one and the modern one, and force everyone—the mothers and their daughters and the readers—to review and reassess what home is and what makes a girl a woman.

PAUL HARDING

✦ ✦ ✦ ✦ ✦ ✦ ✦

THE SWIMMER
John Cheever

THE JEWELS OF THE CABOTS
John Cheever

✦ ✦ ✦ ✦ ✦ ✦ ✦

W HEN YOU READ "THE Swimmer" and "The Jewels of the
    Cabots," keep in mind that both stories are powered by
posing the same rhetorical questions almost verbatim about
their protagonists. The narrator in "The Swimmer" asks of
Neddy Merrill, a ruined and oblivious king of suburban Connecticut who decides to swim the eight miles back to his house
by using his acquaintances' swimming pools, "Was he losing his
memory, had his gift for concealing painful facts let him forget
that he had sold his house, that his children were in trouble,
and that his friend had been ill?" and "Was his memory failing
or had he so disciplined it in the repression of unpleasant facts
that he had damaged his sense of the truth?" The narrator of
"The Jewels of the Cabots," a fictional alter ego of Cheever, asks
of himself and his generation: were they "so drilled in evasiveness that they would be denied forever the splendors of passionate confrontation?"

Whereas these questions about evasiveness are the same in
both stories and they share aesthetic DNA, they produce fasci-
natingly different results by virtue of being posed in the case of

"The Swimmer" from the outside, so to speak, in third person and in "The Jewels of the Cabots" from the inside, in the first person. "The Swimmer" is sharp, emblematic, chilly—ruthless, even. It smacks of satire. "The Jewels of the Cabots" is intimate, tortured, and inconclusive. It reads like a kind of modern attempt at Augustinian confession.

"The Swimmer" has the concentrated effect of a grim fable. Neddy Merrill is not so much an individual person as a caricature of a particular sort of privileged, unreflective vigor. His enthusiasms and appetites are heroic in proportion. But he is heedless, and as he imagines swimming in sequence a string of suburban Connecticut pools back to his own, in exuberant but also cartoonish terms of exploration and pilgrimage, reality—"the facts" of his life from which he has until now managed to divorce himself—finally outstrips him and is waiting to meet him on the doorstep when he arrives home. The brilliant, concentrated eeriness at the end of the story is achieved by the stark counterpoint of the grim facts set against Neddy's perfect suppression of them.

Like Neddy, the protagonist of "The Jewels" sits atop the social ladder. Like Neddy, too, he avails himself of his social privilege. But because the essential question about repression has been internalized and he brings it to bear upon *himself*, he is, in perfect contrast to Neddy, nearly paralyzed by self-consciousness. Unlike Neddy, he is painfully aware of his privilege and of its consequences, even as he constantly takes advantage of it. He understands that he has been "drilled in evasiveness." He is not contemplating repression and concealment from above the rift but instead from within it. In a juxtaposition as elegant as that in "The Swimmer," Cheever gives his main character two powerful, equal, and opposite impulses, that of evasiveness and that of confession. The narrator means to confess and repent of his evasiveness, in moral terms, but being so successfully trained in it, he continually resorts to it when the facts become too painful to face, which is always and more or less immediately.

The narrator's cognitive dissonance is what gives the story its associative shape, its apparent feeling of random drift on first reading, its complexity and ambivalence. The telling is as intricate as the struggling consciousness it portrays. Although Neddy has succeeded in repressing fact from his awareness altogether, the narrator of "The Jewels," a journalist professionally and here ironically trained in writing about the facts, attempts to grapple with them, even as he tries to quarantine them in an abstract realm, separate from his participation in them.

The story is one of advances and retreats, of displacements, misdirection, and backhanded revelation. Such emotional tactics pervade every page, from the level of the sentences, where true subjects are often hidden in plain sight by being grammatically positioned as predicates (or within parentheses, as on the first page) to the nominal subject of the whole story, those jewels toward which the narrator almost immediately heads after opening the story with news of the murder of one of his neighbors. The murder is not returned to until the very last lines, when the narrator reveals that he knows who the murderer is but has again unconsciously taken advantage of his social position in order not to bring the murderer to justice. The very title of the story is an act of misdirection, a "crabwise" way of sidling up to the truth without looking directly at it.

Repression and concealment are arguably Cheever's artistic preoccupations. They are not to be engaged in popular clinical or, as he once said, "symptomatic" terms, or as generalized themes. They are not diagnoses. They are meant to be experienced aesthetically, in a realm of profound moral struggle. They are the sources of his stories' sublime beauty and their swan dives into misery and squalor, hope and despair, and often a wise, melancholy humor, and are arrayed across an opus that ranges from brilliant parody to sheer tragedy. "The Swimmer" is satirical;

"The Jewels of the Cabots" is tragic. The one story simplifies; the other complicates. Neddy Merrill is the fool; the narrator of "The Jewels" is more like Hamlet. Both are extraordinary facets of Cheever's body of work.

RON HANSEN

✦ ✦ ✦ ✦ ✦ ✦ ✦

TO BUILD A FIRE
Jack London

MASTER AND MAN
Leo Tolstoy

✦ ✦ ✦ ✦ ✦ ✦ ✦

I N JANUARY 1985 I accepted a one-semester teaching position
at the Iowa Writers' Workshop. Just a day earlier I'd been snor-
keling in Key West, Florida, but on the morning I arrived in Iowa
City it was twenty-five below zero. Within a few hours the battery
of my Mazda died, so I bought another at an auto parts store
and in exchanging new for old I took off my ski glove to make
a critical adjustment, and within a half-minute the fingers of my
right hand felt like a terrier was cruelly gnawing at them. With
that first hint of frostbite, I hurriedly put on my ski glove again,
thinking, *What did you almost do?*

Jack London had firsthand experience of even scarier tem-
peratures, having joined at age twenty-one the Klondike gold
rush in Alaska, where the cold can reach eighty below. In fact,
Jack London's face did get scarred by so much sub-zero weather
and he got scurvy from the malnourishment of a winter up there
and lost four front teeth.

Remembering his time in the Yukon in 1902, he published
a children's story with a happy ending in *The Youth's Companion*, but six years later he returned to the same material and

revised "To Build a Fire" into the grimmer, unforgettable work you have here.

The plot is wonderfully simple. An unnamed man who's fairly new to Alaska is walking at the rate of four miles per hour on the frozen Yukon River with the intent of getting to "the old claim on Henderson's Creek" by six that evening. His friends will have a hot supper waiting. Hanging with him is a husky whose skepticism about the journey and worries about the man's intentions reflect a sane reader's own attitudes. The temperature is given as seventy-five below zero. The hiker has been warned not to travel alone in such an extreme, but he ignores that advice, and he's wearing just thick stockings under moccasins, wool trousers, I guess, mittens, a jacket and shirt but no long johns, and not even a scarf over his nose and cheeks.

We're told he's without thoughts or imagination, but he *is* enterprising and has had the foresight to pack with him a sandwich, a packet of matches, and some tree bark to use as kindling for a fire. And he'll need that fire to dry his things after he breaks through a skin of ice to freshwater below, recognizing that his feet will freeze without heat. Each move he makes after that just rachets up the suspense.

I first read "To Build a Fire" as a freshman in high school and I can still recall the thrill and anxiety I felt as the protagonist fell into ever deeper peril in his efforts, hindered by cold, just to survive. In my freshman class we discussed the Darwinian, the "naturalist" view of human life and actions, and the ways in which "To Build a Fire" variously represented Jack London's atheism and socialism; but he was a frankly commercial writer, so I'm pretty sure he wanted first and foremost to write a spellbinding adventure, and that he did.

When Leo Tolstoy was first famous, at twenty-nine, Ivan Turgenev characterized him as a "poet, Calvinist, fanatic, aristocrat." At age sixty-six, when he wrote "Master and Man," Count Tolstoy was changed only in having given up Calvinism for a fanatical Christian religion wholly his own and having forfeited a great deal of his wealth and prestige in order to live, to his mind, the holy life of a *muzhiki*, or peasant.

Writing of the conflicting urges in his psychology at the time of his religious conversion, he described the feeling as like being lost in a snowstorm, and "Master and Man" can be read as a fictional elaboration of that metaphor, positing, in Brekhunoff, Tolstoy's self-portrait of pride, independence, waywardness, and death; and in Nikíta his hoped-for future self of simplicity, participation, certitude, and the firm road to life everlasting. Brekhunoff fancies himself formidable and self-sufficient, but in crisis he's hapless, selfish, and lost, a church elder whose religious feelings have been a sham, a scheming businessman whose intrigues are useless in the wilds. Nikíta has no illusions about himself. Wholly lacking in possessions, importance, or aspirations, scorned as an "old fool," a drunkard, and cuckold, Nikíta is free to be affectionate, genuine, humble, in harmony with nature, faithful to God, and unafraid of death. Tolstoy's own fierce struggle for integrity and religious consolation is given form in these hugely different men who ultimately find and heed the same life force.

Tolstoy annihilated a great deal of fiction for me with "Master and Man." Everything I'd been reading up till then seemed meretricious and unimportant. Like Brekhunoff I could not understand how I could bear to interest myself in such things as I did. It was in the seventies, in winter; I was a first-year graduate student in the Iowa Writers' Workshop, where I would later teach, and fat flakes of snow were softly falling as I hiked the two miles to Vance Bourjaily's afternoon class on Tolstoy's masterpieces. And as I hunched forward in a Russian cold with Tolstoy's story in my head, I felt challenged to be the kind of writer he was, but I was also haunted by the fear that he'd raised the standard of good fiction far too high.

And so it was for Tolstoy, too. Except for a handful of fables and the flawed novel *Resurrection*, "Master and Man" was the last fictional work Leo Tolstoy would publish. In October 1910, he took flight from his estate hoping to find refuge in an Eastern monastery, and he was on his way there when he died in a railroad station at the age of eighty-two.

His dying must have seemed to him a good deal like Nikíta's— not at home, but with *ikons* and candles, his wife left behind but forgiven, his focus wholly on "that other life which had been growing more and more familiar and alluring."

JANE HAMILTON

✦ ✦ ✦ ✦ ✦ ✦ ✦

GOODBYE, MY BROTHER
John Cheever

WHITE ANGEL
Michael Cunningham

✦ ✦ ✦ ✦ ✦ ✦ ✦

WHEN THE YOUNG BUCK, the talented punk, speaks explicitly in his work to the Old Master, comparison is not only
inevitable; it's an invitation. My guess is that Michael Cunningham, coming through the grades, read "Goodbye, My Brother"
as one does chapter and verse, returning to it periodically to re-
new his faith. The day would come when he felt ready, felt called,
maybe, to speak to the story, and through the work to the master himself. Did Cheever read a draft of "White Angel" before
he died? Did he and Cunningham know each other? Their stories exist together in the etheric realm, no need in that place for
strict chronology. "White Angel" is Cunningham's love song to
Cheever: it is an act of courage and an act of faith.

The first paragraphs of each story lay out the essentials of
place, time, family members, and class, the student not mimicking but echoing the structure of the master.

"White Angel"
*We lived then in Cleveland, in the middle of everything . . . It
was before the city of Cleveland went broke, before its river*

157

caught fire. We were four. My mother and father, Carleton and me . . . Between us were several brothers and sisters, weak flames quenched in our mother's womb. We are not a fruitful or many-branched line. Our family name is Morrow.

"Goodbye, My Brother"
We are a family that has always been very close in spirit . . . I don't think about the family much, but when I remember its members and the coast where they lived and the sea salt that I think is in our blood, I am happy to recall that I am a Pom-meroy—that I have the nose, the coloring, and the promise of longevity . . . We are four children . . .

Cheever's story, the avowed masterpiece. Kid Cunningham's is, if not a story for the ages, most certainly a perfect story. Cheever's narrator has to speak in his elaborate Cheever-ese because it is his birthright and because he's snowing us. Who wouldn't be happy to be charmed to death by the bitterly funny melancholic, keen to win our sympathy, who reveals more than he means to? Whereas Bobby, oh God, Bobby in "White Angel" will never have another story to tell. He's condemned to live in this one forever, and therefore he must tell it in the present tense, and he's got to tell it straight. Even if Bobby wanted to write with the mythy depth and texture of Cheever's character he cannot, he must not; his purpose would be thwarted. (Still, Cunningham allows Bobby occasional echoes of the master's cadences and grandiosity: "weak flames quenched in our mother's womb" and sentences such as "Farther away, in a richer section, miniature mosques and Parthenons spoke silently to Cleveland of man's accomplishments." Bobby's family, not from the East, but from homely, industrial Cleveland, where a river will burn, no harsh and venerable Puritan past dogging the members, Cotton Mather on no one's tongue, and yet even in Cleveland there are spooks, past and present.

The student naturally has to stake his own claim, and Cunningham does so by writing a story that must remain incomplete. Each character but one has many names, each character in every scene shifts roles and often is rechristened in that role. The character who willfully cannot be named is the heroine, the girl who in her way is a missing piece, the girl who keeps the story firmly in limbo.

Cheever's story ends with the fulfillment that is perhaps particularly WASPish, a story made for New Criticism with that old urge toward redemption, communion in a single image, the moment of beauty. The story works at the poetic level with every reading, the reader catching glimmers of meaning, the images hovering deep in the brainpan as well as the solar plexus. The mystery of the Pommeroys continues to open and haunt, the reader's pleasure is ever keen, the wonder fresh.

We return to "White Angel" to marvel at the perfect story, each detail precisely rendered and in harmony, one to the next. (The drug the boys are taking on the first page is Window Pane, the story blithely prefigured in the fourth paragraph.) We return to it for the terrible pleasure of having our hearts broken, for the piercing ache that is a comfort, the shipwreck and loneliness gorgeously wrought. Not least, the story is sharply funny. Fourth-grader Bobby, having witnessed his brother's deflowering, says, "I am about to ask, as casually as I can, about the relationship between love and bodily pain, when our mother cuts into the room."

Both stories are about family alliances, the delicate and blunt shifts in allegiances, and at the center of each is Mother. Oh, they are bitter, those mothers, they are full of rage, women to cross at your own peril. Each mother could very nimbly walk out of her story and into the other's. Imagine Isabel Morrow and Mrs. Pommeroy on the porch on Lake Erie, Mrs. P. tending toward the Midwest—why not?—cocktail in hand. It's dark. They've been drinking for several hours now. One of them says, "I don't know . . . I don't know if it's better if the kids are alive or dead." There is a moment of shock. And then they both laugh. They mean what they've said, their despair like rot. They know, they knew full well that all mothers are powerless, all mothers suffer at the hands of their children, alive or dead. They are the kind of women who don't avoid each other the next morning but instead look straight into the other's eyes: *Yes, we said that.*

I like to think that if Cheever read Cunningham's story he was pleased by the student's labor, impressed, glad that the beat goes on, gratified by the echoes of his own story in "White Angel." Not so long ago I ran into Cunningham, the only time we've met, and I mentioned the connection between the two stories. I'd only noticed the similarities because I'd happened to read them back to back. That "White Angel" was an homage seemed obvious. He looked startled, as if he'd been busted. "It's true!" he said. I didn't think to ask if he'd studied with Cheever, or any other questions that would speak to this essay. But no matter. The master is secure in his firmament, and the brilliant student is, too, the conversation between the old man and young man alive for as long as print goes on.

JENNIFER HAIGH

✦ ✦ ✦ ✦ ✦ ✦ ✦

THE ICE WAGON GOING DOWN THE STREET
Mavis Gallant

FAMILY FURNISHINGS
Alice Munro

✦ ✦ ✦ ✦ ✦ ✦ ✦

I WAS RAISED WITH what now strikes me as comically naive ideas about class. I blame my early education at the hands of earnest, folk-singing Catholic nuns and also my parents—first-generation Americans who believed the New World fairy tale that social mobility is possible for all. Geography preserved my innocence in these matters. We lived in a dying coal town where many people had nothing and nobody had much, so I grew up largely blind to signifiers of class. It was in reading Alice Munro and Mavis Gallant, two Canadian masters of the short story, that I learned to see.

Munro's "Family Furnishings" looks at a rural family's secrets through the lens of class. The narrator is an Ontario teenager with a sociologist's eye. Her family, she notes, "did not have a regular social life"—in contrast to the one she later marries into, who "invited people who were not related to them to dinner. . . . It was a life such as I had read of in magazine stories, and it seemed to place my in-laws in a world of storybook privilege." Her own relatives are laconic farmers and farm wives—practical souls, resolutely anti-intellectual. Her father, a closet reader, uses bad grammar in a show of solidarity when his kin come to visit. At family dinners, "there was a feeling that conversation that passed beyond certain understood limits might be a disruption, a show-ing-off. . . . Mention of intimate bodily matters seemed never to be so out of place, or suspect, as the mention of something read in a magazine, or an item in the news—it was improper somehow to pay attention to anything that was not close at hand." These rules are breached only by her father's cousin Alfrida, an unmar-ried "career girl" who writes a ladies column for a city newspa-per. Fond of jokes and ribald gossip, Alfrida "talked to my father about things that were happening in the world . . . My father read the paper, he listened to the radio, he had opinions about these things but rarely had a chance to talk about them."

The young narrator considers Alfrida clever and sophisticat-ed. Only later does she understand that for all her verve, Alfrida is not so different from the other women in the family. Invited to dinner at Alfrida's apartment in the city, she is surprised to find it chock-full of the eponymous family furnishings: "It was all more like the aunts' houses than I would have thought possible." Even more striking are Alfrida's attempts to draw her diffident male companion into the dinner conversation: "She seemed almost to hold her breath, as if he was her child taking unsupported steps, or a first lone wobble on a bicycle." At the time the narrator finds this mystifying. True understanding will come later: "All of my experience of a woman with men, a woman listening to her man, hoping and hoping that he will establish himself as someone she can reasonably be proud of, was in the future."

In "The Ice Wagon Going Down the Street," Mavis Gallant follows one Peter Frazier, a hapless son determined to restore to social prominence his once-wealthy Toronto family. Gallant traces, in a few deft strokes, the Fraziers' class trajectory: "One generation made it, the granite Presbyterian immigrants from

Scotland. Their children, a generation of daunted women and maiden men, held still. Peter's father's crowd spent [and] Peter and his sister and his cousins lived on the remains." Led by an almost mystical sense of destiny, Peter moves his family to Europe with a vague idea of pursuing a diplomatic career, cheered on by his English wife, Sheilah, a ruthless social climber whose ambitions—like those of the women in "Family Furnishings"—are refracted, always, through her man. There, Peter is stymied by a social order he finds impossible to penetrate. It is, Gallant suggests, a uniquely New World problem, as it stems from the belief that social mobility is possible: "If he had been European, he would have ridden to work on a bicycle, in the uniform of his class and condition."

In Geneva, Peter lands a clerical job alongside a fellow Canadian, the plain and dutiful Agnes Brusen. When she hangs her framed college diploma on the office wall, he thinks "she must be one of a family of immigrants for whom education is everything . . . They are white-hot Protestants, and they live with a load of work and debt and obligation." For all his self-deception, Peter is a social taxonomist of consummate precision; his judgments about Agnes are spot on. And yet his foreign colleagues seem to discern no difference between the two Canadians, to Peter's consternation: "his social compass was out of order . . . There was a world of difference between them, yet it was she who had been brought in to sit at the larger of the two desks."

Invited to a costume party at the home of the chic and wealthy Burleighs, Peter and Sheilah are dazzled by possibility. Agnes attends the same party and is appalled by the drunkenness of the guests: "All my life I heard, educated people don't do this, educated people don't do that. And now I'm here, and you're all educated people, and you're nothing but pigs." The party is a turning point for Peter, who realizes, in a rare and painful moment of lucidity, that he and Agnes have a commonality that runs deeper than class. Agnes's pride in accomplishment, her anxious sense of duty and doughty work ethic, are symptoms of an intrinsic Canadianness he finds repulsive in her and in himself, an identity he doesn't share with his wife and doesn't want to. ("I'd be like Agnes if I didn't have Sheilah," he thinks with some relief.)

Quietly revolutionary, these stories of Alice Munro and Mavis Gallant take aim at the New World myth of a classless society. For their characters, the unspoken rules and invisible limitations of class are innate and determinative. "I know I've got far too much stuff in here," Alfrida tells her young relative. "It's family furnishings, and I couldn't let it go."

LAUREN GROFF

✦ ✦ ✦ ✦ ✦ ✦ ✦

THE OVERCOAT
Nikolai Gogol

THE SHAWL
Cynthia Ozick

✦ ✦ ✦ ✦ ✦ ✦ ✦

E VERY TIME A WRITER sits down to work, the stories she loves most curl up on her desk beside her. I first read Nikolai Gogol's "The Overcoat" and Cynthia Ozick's "The Shawl" in college; since then, every story I've written has the purr of one or the other in it.

On their surfaces, the stories couldn't be more different: Gogol's is told in a loopy voice with confiding warmth and humor; Ozick's is a quick blaze that strikes the reader like a lightning bolt. Fyodor Dostoyevsky said, "We all come out from Gogol's 'Overcoat'"; this is also true of Cynthia Ozick's 'Shawl.'"

"The Overcoat" is the deceptively simple tale of the clerk Akaky Akakyevitch, a name that in its evocation of *caca* is deliberately scatological in sound. Akakyevitch is a timid creature with little internal life: when asked to modify a text instead of copying it, he cannot, and after going home to his sparse supper, he fills his evening hours with more copying for his own pleasure. He is paid poorly and bullied at work. He is intensely distressed when his old overcoat is found to be so thin and rotten that it cannot be saved and he must find the rubles for a new one. After he deprives himself for months, his tailor brings the clerk an overcoat that is so splendid and warm that the other clerks invite him to a party. Something cracks open in Akakyevitch, then; he takes pleasure in the cold night air, in the party with its champagne and tarts and the others' admiration of his coat, and on the way home he almost runs to follow a woman who passes by "like lightning with every part of her frame in violent motion."

In the clerk's dawning joy, in this new stirring of virility, we see his soul coming to life. But that very night, a terrible thing happens: Akakyevitch is mugged, the overcoat stolen. He complains ineptly to higher-ups, who refuse to help and who even abuse him. The brokenhearted clerk takes cold, then dies. But Akakyevitch enacts his magnificent revenge, because his corpse comes back to mug other men of their overcoats, finally terrifying and robbing the very Person of Consequence who was indirectly responsible for his death.

Gogol slides fantasy into the comedic realism of "The Overcoat"; the clerk's corpse returning to wreak vengeance is the most obvious, but the overcoat itself is a supernatural item, its bestowal upon Akaky Akakyevitch quickening the dormant internal life of the poor meek clerk. Fantastical elements often deepen and highlight emotion in fiction, the way shadowing in painting can make the painted object clear against its background. The clerk's circumscribed life and his painful acquisition of the overcoat inspire pity in the reader, but he becomes a real, round character only when he has a powerful thing to lose.

IN OZICK'S SWIFT AND devastating story, an article of clothing, the eponymous shawl, is also fantastical. A mother marches to a concentration camp with her two daughters; when the mother, Rosa, has no more milk, the shawl gives warmth and shelter and even nourishment to Magda, the baby, who milks the corner of the shawl instead. "It was a magic shawl," Ozick writes, "it could nourish an infant for three days and three nights." The shawl hides Magda at the camp and keeps her silent during the long hours during roll call when Rosa and Stella, the sister, have to be away from the baby. But Stella is jealous, starving, cold to the bone. She steals Magda's shawl. The baby toddles out into the dangerous daylight to find it, where everyone can see her. Rosa instantly knows her baby is going to die.

But here's the swerve in the story, the bolt of greatness in Ozick: even as Rosa sees her daughter's fate, "a fearful joy" runs in her because the baby is howling. Ever since the child's last scream on the road, Rosa had believed that her daughter was a mute, that something had gone wrong with her, that "Magda was defective, without a voice; perhaps she was deaf; there might be something amiss with her intelligence; Magda was dumb." Even in Rosa's deepest despair, there is relief, a blistering recognition of Magda's buried humanity. Just as with Gogol, one very important article of clothing is an agent of interiority, of awakened humanity. But in Gogol, the overcoat with all its material warmth and symbolism is the item that awakens humanity; in Ozick, it's the removal of the shawl that awakens the humanity in Magda.

The death of Magda comes with terrible swiftness. There are voices in the electrified fence; Magda floats toward it "like a butterfly touching a silver vine." Ozick's voice in this story is both precise and dreamy, the suffering in the story sketched so lightly that the moments when we touch it full on are accompanied with great pain. Cynthia Ozick says her story illustrates that "in the madness of despair lies the sanity of hope."

Both writers have an ability to look at humanity with clear eyes, showing the reader its cruelty and horror, and yet are able to acknowledge a simultaneous depth of human warmth and love. "The Overcoat" is saved from being an outright farce by the stirrings of the characters' souls: the Person of Consequence repents bitterly of his treatment of Akakyevitch even before he is mugged by the corpse, and one of the clerks who torments Akakyevitch later understands his own cruelty and it makes him hide his face in shame. There is a similar, subtler recognition in Ozick when her prose alights briefly on beauty in the midst of all the soul-breaking horror. It is liberating as a writer to recognize that although Gogol and Ozick use methods so divergent as to be almost in opposition, colloquial satire versus incantatory fable, the writers' essential humanity can gleam with such similar light out of such terrifying darkness.

ROBERT BOSWELL

✦ ✦ ✦ ✦ ✦ ✦ ✦

MADAGASCAR
Steven Schwartz

THE DEATH OF IVAN ILYCH
Leo Tolstoy

✦ ✦ ✦ ✦ ✦ ✦ ✦

A
S A WRITING AND literature teacher, I long ago discovered that if you introduce undergraduate students to remarkable work, they give you part of the credit. Most graduate students, however, are well read and not easily impressed. Yet when I assign Steven Schwartz's "Madagascar," I know my reputation will be on the rise. No one in the class will have heard of it, and all will genuinely admire it.

I first read "Madagascar" in the *Chicago Tribune* when it won the Nelson Algren Prize, in the late 1980s. I'd met Steven Schwartz, but I didn't know his fiction. The story knocked me out. It was the first work by a writer of my generation that seemed destined to become a classic. This not only impressed me; it also gave me hope for the rest of us—and this is no small matter.

Writing literary fiction is a peculiarly hopeful endeavor. (Ask a writer to name her best story, and she will answer, "The one I'm working on now.") But it is also a lonely and frequently humiliating task, and the likelihood of creating something that will endure beyond the year of its publication is remote. One must occasionally find evidence that one's hope has merit; otherwise, the work becomes intolerable. "Madagascar," then, was doubly significant for me: as a reader I was deeply affected and as a writer I was renewed.

Obviously, if the story had achieved the iconic status that I imagined for it, my students would be less impressed with me. I might find this circumstance discouraging but I prefer to believe that the story's brilliance will yet be recognized.

"The baker tells my father to climb into an oven no longer in use."

"Madagascar" is hugely ambitious and utterly fearless. The narrative covers fifty years and embraces large world events, yet it feels intensely personal and the final movements are emotionally powerful. The story is not propelled by cause and effect; rather, its scenes rhyme in a delicate pattern, much like a poem or perhaps a waltz. If I were to approximate the central question that "Madagascar" raises, it might be the following: How does one endure the impossible? The story does not presume to answer the question, but I believe its beautiful sorrow instills in the reader a new resiliency.

"Ivan Ilych's life was most simple and most ordinary and therefore most terrible."

I first read "The Death of Ivan Ilych" in graduate school. The course was taught by Francine Prose—a teacher I revered—and her zeal for the story impressed me, but I was in my twenties, cocky, confident, and none too bright. Moreover, at some precognitive level, I felt quite sure that I would never die.

So I thought it was a good story but I wasn't all that impressed.

A few years passed before I read it again. By this time, I was an assistant professor of English at Northwestern University. "The Death of Ivan Ilych" appeared in the anthology I was using, and my admiration for Francine Prose led me to assign it. The circumstances of my life were radically different: I was in my thirties, married, and my wife was pregnant. We owned a condo in Evanston, and we were having our floors sanded.

This time when I read the story I trembled. I had to place the book on the kitchen table and lean over the pages to continue. Upon finishing it, I immediately read it again. The story terrified me—not with the fear of death but with the fear of living foolishly—yet I could not quit reading it. I began the story a third time, but my wife in her nightgown, round with the future, appeared in the kitchen doorway.

"Why aren't you coming to bed?" she asked.

It was almost four in the morning.

"I was just about to," I said, a white lie to avoid sounding crazy: *I don't want to waste my life.*

That was close to thirty years ago, and I cannot estimate how many times I've read the story since. I refer to it in many of my craft lectures, and the topics range widely. In my initial lecture I note that the early drafts of the story are in the first person. I argue that Tolstoy's move to omniscience represents a shift in the magnitude of his intention. He is not content to show a character whose life changes; rather, he wants to compel the reader to remake her own life. In a later lecture, I analyze stories in which a character trades places in a social paradigm, and "The Death of Ivan Ilych" provides the perfect example. As a judge, Ilych prides himself on eliminating the personal factors of each case to deal only with the facts. Later, as a patient, he is devastated by the doctor's insistence on talking about his symptoms rather than his person. The world has turned upside down, and he longs for someone to recognize his humanity. I also refer to the story in a class I teach about the use of objects in narrative: to examine the emptiness of materialism, Tolstoy grants objects volition. Objects quite literally kill Ivan Ilych.

And I bring up the story whenever I talk about actions that embody meaning (Ivan's hand lands on the answer to his ultimate question), degrees of omniscience (no story makes greater claim to full omniscience), release of information (even the title announces that the main character is dead), narrative shape (a classic figure eight), and authorial custody (Tolstoy is a high-custody author and nowhere is it more evident than in "The Death of Ivan Ilych").

I will likely study this story for the remainder of my life, but it was not admiration for Tolstoy's craft that made me tremble at the kitchen table. *What if my whole life has been wrong?* Ivan Ilych is forced to ask this question by the proximity of death, and the reader is forced to ask the same question by the genius of Tolstoy's narrative. Very few stories are its equal.

RUSSELL BANKS

✦ ✦ ✦ ✦ ✦ ✦ ✦

THE ARTIFICIAL NIGGER
Flannery O'Connor

NO PLACE FOR YOU MY LOVE
Eudora Welty

✦ ✦ ✦ ✦ ✦ ✦ ✦

ODDLY, THESE ARE AMONG the least read stories by two of the greatest short story writers in the American canon. Rarely anthologized, Eudora Welty's "No Place for You, My Love" has been overlooked possibly because the two central characters in her story are not characteristically Southern; they're from Syracuse, New York, and Toledo, Ohio, and we don't like our Southern writers to write about Northerners. I suspect the usual absence of Flannery O'Connor's story can be attributed to its title, which pointedly, with unmistakable irony, alludes to O'Connor's paired protagonists' shared name for those onetime ubiquitous lawn statues of a Black jockey, the luminous—one might say *numinous*—central image of the story. Whatever the reasons, both stories are great works of fiction, as profound and moving as anything either writer has given us and as capable of cracking open our minds and hearts as any story in the English language.

Welty's "No Place for You, My Love" was published in 1955 in the collection *The Bride of the Innisfallen*, the same year that O'Connor's "The Artificial Nigger" appeared in the *Kenyon Review*, collected later in *A Good Man is Hard to Find*. I read them

173

separately long ago and many years apart and at first saw nothing that they bore in common, other than having been written around mid-century by Southern white women, one from Mississippi, the other from Georgia.

In "No Place for You, My Love" two unnamed strangers, a married man and "a woman who was having an affair" (or so the man intuits), meet at a tedious luncheon in New Orleans and impulsively drive in the man's rented car south on diminishing roads across the levees and bayous to the Gulf, where at an end-of-the-road waterside café they slow-dance to a juke box tune, after which they return to New Orleans and separate. Not much else happens, so that the few small, precisely described things that do happen and the threatening images that appear as they travel "south of south" and the few ambiguous words exchanged between the man and woman all take on great significance. It can easily be read as a Southern noir version of Orpheus's and Eurydice's fateful visit to the Underworld and return.

Welty told *The Paris Review* in 1972, "I saw that setting only one time—the Delta of the Mississippi River itself, down below New Orleans where it winds toward the Gulf—one time only. Which smote me." What "smote" her, what she and her unnamed man and woman saw south of south that "one time only," was the Underworld, its tempting beauty and terrifying implacability, giving her and her characters (and us) a glimpse of the overpowering, dangerous mystery of love.

"The Artificial Nigger" also has two characters in transit—and here we begin to see similarities between the stories. A poor white farmer, Mr. Head, and his grandson, Nelson, travel by train from their isolated Georgia cabin to Atlanta, where the old man and the boy bump up against the bewildering social and racial and economic realities of a fallen urban world. Given the imagery, it's a more Christian vision of Hades than Welty's. Not much happens in this story, either. The two wander the mean streets of the city, lose their way and one another in a Black neighborhood, find each other again, and manage finally to get aboard the last train departing the city for the safety of home.

From the start their actions and decisions are driven by prideful competition. The boy has been raised from infancy by his grandfather, and though born in the city, has no memory of the place. Nonetheless, as a result, he feels socially smarter and more worldly than the old man, who intends to show him up by taking him to the city and exposing his ignorance of it. Both characters are egoistic and proud and meanly competitive with one another, but also woefully insecure and frightened. The cathartic moment in the story, where both are transformed and redeemed, is their sudden encounter with "the artificial nigger." Yes, it's a story about race and grace, but like "No Place for You, My Love," it's also a story about the profound mystery of love.

But for me, the most striking and intriguing aspect shared by the two stories is their unusual structure. (I have actually tried over the years to borrow it for several of my own stories, for instance "Sarah Cole: A Type of Love Story" and "Snowbirds.") There is no central character in either story. Rather, there are two, paired like the strands of a double helix. The close third-person point of view switches regularly every few paragraphs or pages from one character to the other, so that you can't say which character the story is *about*. Welty's unnamed married man, or the woman "having an affair"? O'Connor's grandfather, Mr. Head, or his grandson, Nelson? They are in fact about *both* characters, each of whom, throughout, is driven by an unspoken attempt to capture and dominate the other (and in the process take over the story). First one character is the predator, the other the prey, until, after a few paragraphs or pages, there occurs a reversal of roles, a shift in point of view, and predator becomes prey, prey becomes predator, all the way to the end, where, like exhausted lovers, they finally merge and become one.

For Welty it's a transformative erotic experience; for O'Connor it's a moment of spiritual (and saving) grace.

The structure is dialectical, in as much as the paired characters, alternately functioning in opposition as thesis and antithesis, are led through a series of complications along a circuitous, not-quite-Kantian path to a synthesis that transfigures both. It begins with two conflicted points of view evenly balanced, quickly tipped out of balance by an unforeseen event or by mere happenstance: a lonely married man offers a woman he thinks is having an affair to leave the boring lunch party for a joyride; on the train to Atlanta the first Black man the boy has ever seen enters the car, the grandfather says, "What's that?" the boy answers, "A man," and the grandfather mocks him for not knowing: "That was a nigger." The losing, dominated party attempts to reset the balance between them, which can only be done by upping the ante, taking both characters further and further from their initial, perfectly balanced state of conflict. Conflict as such is inert, static, non-dramatic; you can't make a story from it alone. You have to destroy it over and over. Hemingway's "Hills Like White Elephants" and Cheever's "Goodbye, My Brother" are similarly designed, but it's a difficult structure to deploy and rarely employed. It puts a lot of pressure on the imagery and language and requires constant reversal and counter-reversal without depending on plot for suspense. I can think of no better examples than these two masterpieces, one by Eudora Welty and the other by Flannery O'Connor.

JULIA GLASS

✦ ✦ ✦ ✦ ✦ ✦ ✦

A FATHER'S STORY
Andre Dubus

YOUNG GOODMAN BROWN
Nathaniel Hawthorne

✦ ✦ ✦ ✦ ✦ ✦ ✦

*He had taken a dreary road, darkened by all the gloomiest
trees of the forest, which barely stood aside to let the narrow
path creep through, and closed immediately behind. It was all
as lonely as could be; and there is this peculiarity in such a
solitude, that the traveller knows not who may be concealed
by the innumerable trunks and the thick boughs overhead . . .*
—From "Young Goodman Brown"

H E WAS CLEVER, MY ninth-grade English teacher. Among other wise moves, he did not offer the conventional entrée to
Nathaniel Hawthorne. I suspect he knew that if he did, we would
forever picture that literary dreamboat sporting a scarlet B (for
Bore; for Blowhard; for Bummer). He knew that Hawthorne was
a better short story writer than he was a novelist. And so we began with "Young Goodman Brown," an allegory about the bestial
urges lurking beneath the mannerly veneer of civilization, the triumph of sin over virtue. Its melodrama and even its misanthropy
had a timely appeal to me and my fellow adolescents; this was the
year of the Kent State shootings, the escalation of a misbegotten

war. Hawthorne's portrait of society's elders as two-faced corrupt-
ers only confirmed the generalized view of our parents as peers,
even enablers, of leaders like Nixon and McNamara.

That English class took place in Concord, Massachusetts, less
than a mile from the Old Manse, which lent its name to *Mosses
from an Old Manse*, the second collection of Hawthorne's stories
to include "Young Goodman Brown." The dense woods into
which the protagonist ventures are ostensibly in Salem, back at
the time of the witchcraft hysteria, yet they are as much an "ev-
erywoods" as Brown is Everyman. Even now, Hawthorne's description of the landscape evokes the prized conservation tracts
that make Concord and its neighboring towns so costly. That is
what you pay for: pockets of wilderness shielded by wealth. It is a
privilege, not a hazard, to step out your back door onto miles of
narrow trails unspooling with deliberate indirection among maples, oaks, and evergreens, passing through stonewalled meadows, alongside hidden ponds. Here you will encounter songbirds
and foxes, dog walkers and skiers, not devils bearing serpentine
staffs or savages dancing around a fire. The woods do not threat-
en with temptation or satanic rites; they offer release from urban
cares, protect your home from prying eyes. They are, in fact, no
tamer than they were in Hawthorne's time. (*Walden* was published just twenty years after "Young Goodman Brown.")

Out the back door of my childhood home stretched hundreds
of acres preserved for the purpose of "escape." Those woods, especially in my teens, were the first place I went to seek liberating
solitude, where I practiced, beyond the reach of parental scolding,
the art of the daydream, often with a book in hand.

The woods in "Young Goodman Brown" were the counter-
culture of mine; Hawthorne's Calvinist view of humanity as
irredeemably sinful had no place in the Dickinson and Barrett
Browning poems I read aloud to the squirrels and jays when I fled
"out back." But I loved Hawthorne, too, and I think of him now
as the first writer I admired purely for his short stories. I plunged

ardently, on my own, into "Rappaccini's Daughter," "The Minister's Black Veil," "The Birth-Mark." They were Poe without the grisly occult, Camus without the bleakness. They were Jonathan Edwards unplugged.

It's interesting that the only substantial conversations in Hawthorne's story are between the hapless hero and a corporeal devil; God is present only in glimpses of the distant starry sky. Curiously, there is no bargain, no Faustian offer of immortality or riches. The more the trees creak, the more the wind blows, the more the stars are blighted by clouds, the closer Brown's off-road folly brings him to his ultimate undoing—even as, ironically, he flees. Hawthorne spares no mercy for a single, solitary soul; evil is the consequence not of particular choices made but of human nature itself. We are all, once we enter the woods, fallen. If God is all-seeing, Satan is all-possessing. Notions of conscience, atonement, and salvation are moot.

The story has three distinct sections: a succinct prelude; the lush, extravagantly descriptive drama in the woods; and a brief, chilling epilogue. After witnessing the most esteemed of his townsfolk cavorting with savages—among them his wife, Faith— Brown tries to refuse the Devil's offer of this perverse "communion." The next morning, he returns to the village "bewildered": did his horrific memories constitute only a "wild dream"? Yet thereafter, on the village street, at Sabbath services, inside his home, though nothing looks any different on its face, Goodman Brown has glimpsed the wickedness within. He lives out a long life in gloomy distrust, robbed of joy and piety—all, perhaps, because of a hallucination. Yet he was *summoned* into that forest— and who can stick to the well-traveled road? By what false certainties do all of us live, trivial or grand, God-fearing or profane?

I sit in the kitchen near the rear of the house and drink coffee and smoke and watch the sky growing light before sunrise, the trees of the woods near the barn taking shape, becoming sin-

gle pines and elms and oaks and maples. Sometimes a rabbit
comes out of the treeline, or is already sitting there, invisible till
the light finds him. —From "A Father's Story"

For the decade after high school, my central passion was painting—but my appetite for fiction remained insatiable. Through
my twenties, I lived alone. I divided my job-free time between
making pictures and reading books. I devoured, in particular, collections of stories, and I suspect that affinity is what turned me
back toward writing fiction for the first time since high school.

Among other collections, I bought those annual "best of" anthologies. I consumed them like platters of dim sum. I can remember lying on my bed one Saturday afternoon in the mid-1980s and,
in one such anthology, coming across the first story I would ever
read by Andre Dubus. (Eventually, in wonder and—once I started writing my own—in grateful envy, I would read them all.) "A
Father's Story" is long, exquisitely written, cinematically detailed,
and rife with idiosyncratic wisdoms. At its heart—toward which
one spirals slowly, as if through a narrowing nautilus—is a devil
of a moral choice, every bit as specific and personal as the choice
made by Hawthorne's hero is broad, even public. Like "Young
Goodman Brown," it is also a tripartite story—but this time, the
long, elaborate prelude bears the greatest narrative weight.

"A Father's Story" begins like an accounting, an unburdening:
"My name is Luke Ripley, and here is what I call my life." *Here is*
the face I present to you and to the world, he says, and the more he
lays out of his day-to-day habits and rituals—deliberate and con-
templative yet tinted with rue—the more acutely we anticipate,
with prurience and dread, the revelation of what lies beneath.

Like Goodman Brown, Luke Ripley lives in "northeastern
Massachusetts," on a country road dividing the "dark woods."
He owns and rides horses (short of elephants, perhaps, the apo-
gee of bestiality tamed). Unlike Brown, he is a man of late middle
age—long divorced, willfully celibate, living alone. He is a devout

if routinely sinful Catholic, a smoker, an opera lover, an early riser. Not the least bit allegorical in texture, he is a sweating, regretting, whiskey-drinking, churchgoing, conscientious Good Man; if introspection counts as a virtue (and in our times it does), then a Very Good Man.

For Andre Dubus's characters, religious faith is often a kind of true north: an invisible point toward which the needle on the compass quivers with longing but from which it must also stray. Its gravity pulls at but cannot dictate their motives, failures, and justifications. Broken contracts with loved ones are, often equally, broken contracts with God. Sin to the soul is like rain to a roof: despite the most attentive care, over time it will find a way in.

What makes "A Father's Story" so indelible, however, is that the contract broken is, simultaneously, a contract kept. Ripley must choose between his spiritual allegiance to the Holy Father—and, by extension, to his social responsibilities—and his earthly allegiance to his own fatherhood, more specifically to the primitive (and masculine) sense of himself as his daughter's protector from all harm. The daughter, Jennifer, is a barely grown girl as allegorical as the errant wife of Goodman Brown: not just Daughter but Woman. Ripley thinks of her as entering the "deep forest" of womanhood, a place where "men find their way . . . only on clearly marked trails, while women move about in it like birds."

It is while driving through the literal forest, however—late at night, alone, tipsy from a night out with friends, "on country roads where pines curved in the wind and big deciduous trees swayed and shook as if they might leap from the earth"—that Jennifer unwittingly strikes a pedestrian. She does not stop but instead goes straight to her father's house and wakes him.

Luke Ripley's choice becomes clear to him before it does to the reader. The choice is not whether to go straight to the scene of the crime but what to do when he gets there, once he goes into the woods by the side of the road, in the dark, to find—if there is one to find—the body.

And this is when the other characters of the story fall away as insignificant. Just as the crucial relationship in "Young Goodman Brown" is not between Brown and his wife but between the mortal hero and the Devil, so the relationship at stake in "A Father's Story" is not Ripley's complex, fragile bond with his daughter but his complex, fragile filial tie to God. Whose will, whose commandments, matter more: those of a father or those of the Father?

I'm not a Catholic. Though raised Episcopalian, I left church behind decades ago. I call myself a mournful atheist. But inside the Catholic cosmos of a story by Andre Dubus, I gladly enter the state of faith I often wish were mine—or perhaps it's simpler to say that I welcome his vision of a world where folly is balanced by redemption, guilt by forgiveness, and where grace (whether religious or secular) is achievable for most of us. That cosmos is, of course, the obverse of Hawthorne's. The human struggle in one is against the tyranny of sin; in the other, it is against the dictates of humility. Both struggles are lost—at least in part—yet the stories end on profoundly different notes. For Goodman Brown, there is no God with whom to plead his innocence or argue his doubts. For Luke Ripley, that conversation never ends.

When I think about what makes both of these stories compelling to me, I realize that they converge at a common point, in a very specific and privately significant place: in the deep New England woods of my inner self, the "out back" where I went to dream, to indulge, to imagine (by Puritan standards, to tarry with the devil). I believe that each of us has a primal landscape within us, that we are emotionally imprinted with early places: inner city, suburban cul-de-sac, bayou, desert, rocky shore. Our places form us, challenge us, test us, comfort us, and sometimes call us back. Only recently did I realize that many of my favorite authors are those in whose stories the landscape exerts an almost moral force on the characters, where not just geography but sometimes even topography is destiny. Hardy, Munro, García Márquez, Baldwin, Harrison, Faulkner . . . certainly Hawthorne and Dubus.

The wind is a vital descriptive element in both "Young Goodman Brown" and "A Father's Story." In both, it gusts ominously, insistent and loud, as the stakes rise—and dies down with the return of day and the restoration of appearances. But there is something benevolent about the way Dubus describes its waning: "I looked at the still maple near the window, and thought of the wind leaving farms and towns and the coast, going out over the sea to die on the waves." Pantheism, Dubus tells us earlier in the story, is a part of Catholicism; in nature, there is mercy.

To read Hawthorne is to be reminded that Eden is firmly and forever behind us, moral failure our universal fate. To read Dubus is to begin by accepting all that—and then to be forgiven: to emerge from the woods, into the light, with a clear eye if not a clear conscience.

DAGOBERTO GILB

✦ ✦ ✦ ✦ ✦ ✦ ✦

LA NOCHE BUENA
Tomás Rivera

THE BURNING PLAIN
Juan Rulfo

✦ ✦ ✦ ✦ ✦ ✦ ✦

B ACK IN THE OLD, old days of American literature—call that
pre-1975—not every writer was expected to live and study in
the same way. If being smart enough was a baseline, being educated was essential, but that didn't mean a writer was a perfect
student, with perfect grades, who went to the perfect schools
and got perfect jobs. The writers I loved lived in an outside land
that expected engagement—generally that was with the wealthy
(even the poor like to read about the much better off), a real
adventure with risk, but it could be inside a poor or weekly pay-
check community, all of which probably reflected the writer's
actual personal life, region, and occupation. Ideas came from
inside a day-to-day world, were learned. So different for the
American writer of now, who formulates ideas and research-
es material from a library or its equivalent, the stories shaped
from inside the head, not by experience and surprise. I've even
noted that a writer now is "from" a grad school she attended,
"from" a program he teaches creative writing in . . . and that's
when I hear Pete Seeger:

There's a green one and a pink one
And a blue one and a yellow one
And they're all made out of ticky-tacky,
And they all look just the same.

And the people in the houses . . .

. . . they all get put in boxes
And they all come out the same.

I didn't grow up wanting to become a writer, an aspiration as never heard of as someone wanting to be a governor. In my home and neighborhood there weren't many books or readers of them around—any, as far as I knew. But there were a lot of storytellers. Lots of them were liars or scam artists or bullshitters, players and hustlers both male and female, and saps, suckers, and losers, each with stories charged by the unreal in the real, which had consequences that seemed unreal but were too real. I was so thrilled when—in my twenties—I found out about literature. It became the religion I believed in. The writers I loved were saviors howling in joy or lamentation at inappropriate times, seekers of mysteries and truths whispered privately between the lines. Their characters had lives I recognized, ones who took me home even when it wasn't really very close to where I ever lived. They wrote stories that were more myth tales: they gave me ideas that seemed fresh and new but were, at the same time, ones I already carried deep inside me.

They, characters and writers, were not raised only in family happiness and comfort, and they sometimes chose wrong and worked bad jobs; they met the best people who were in fact sleazes, or the least interesting who were invisible saints. And they came back to tell, to reassure me, their reader, that I too was living a life fully, not like an oh-so-cool celebrity in the successful birth spotlight, but like the simple, admirable ones who few paid any attention to, who lived commonly and died commonly—remembered only by the myths of the small stories left behind.

Excuse this aside: Lots treat the story as "short," as in junior, and mean it's not as ambitious or important as a novel at the adult table (evidence, that it isn't called a "long" story). There are those who'd go after poetry for even being shorter still. A story has a closer kinship to poetry than to novels. A great story, like a great poem, is made huge by its myopic obsession on the small, saying more in the fewest lines, in carefully executed language and scene.

And so many writers and stories I loved, and from so many countries and regions not mine—and probably because they were, it wasn't until I read those from my own mental and visual landscape that I realized what writing might be for me: people I knew, culture I lived in, places I'd been but that the American literature I read didn't acknowledge as existing.

Tomás Rivera's "La Noche Buena," on the surface, would seem to be simply about a very poor provincial mother so trapped by her own agoraphobia that she's unable to go only a few blocks in a small Texas city to buy Christmas Eve presents for her young sons, who want the American holiday. Easy analysis is of the difficult generational transition from Mexican to American, the poverty of these people on the border. But that misses so much. Setting aside the colloquial Tejano Spanish used, the literary shock of that itself (in a collection first published bilingually), here was a world unseen in print by the many of us who know the exact house she lives in, who know those tracks she crosses unto such confusion, have even been in that Kress drugstore—and not from the point of view of an Anglo, Larry McMurtry Texas, but as it is to the other half of the residents of the state. What takes a little more to realize is that doña Maria's love of her children is so great that she is willing to overcome her most humiliating fears to please them. In a sense to lose them, to let them grow up away from what she can—and can't—give them, which is only, ironically, her stability—a home where she stays and takes care of them. That simple woman with an apron, a mother, soon enough a grandmother. And you leave the story, this unsophisticated woman you knew well and left behind, and ask, How right was she? What would history say?

It was Juan Rulfo, the finest Mexican master, who made me read fiction as I would poetry—more slowly, like walking a distance on a scorching day. In Rulfo's stories, life, reality, is a hallucination. Where most writers are consumed by characters, here the land is God, poverty, the human condition. Every conversation, every activity, every emotion was affected by and reflected in the chapped, pitiless landscape that is northern Mexico. I have never been able to resist what for me is one of the greatest stories I've ever read, "Paso del Norte." It is primarily but a conversation between a grown son and his aging father. Broke, the son has nothing left to do but go north to the United States, cross into El Paso, and find any paying work. He is asking his father to care for his small children and his wife until he can take them back. It is a conversation that cannot be good under any circumstance, anywhere, but here it is drawn as brutally unsentimental as is possible while still being real. And when the son returns, failed, there is the stunning end, with the saddest, fullest, most layered last line ever written.

STUART DYBEK

✦ ✦ ✦ ✦ ✦ ✦ ✦

THE GRASSHOPPER AND BELL CRICKET
Yasunari Kawabata

BIRDS
John O'Brien

✦ ✦ ✦ ✦ ✦ ✦ ✦

"The Grasshopper and the Bell Cricket" is dated 1924. It is four pages long, which is one way to measure the length of a story. There are, of course, other measures—the number of times one has felt compelled to reread it, or the length of the shadow it throws, or the depth it reaches in the heart. Yasunari Kawabata isn't a writer who has crossed over into the American canon in the way that say, Haruki Murakami has, and I often use "The Grasshopper and the Bell Cricket" to introduce his work to my classes. The story's compression is such that it manages to encapsulate almost every feature of the writer's signature voice—Kawabata's clarity of language, his layered imagery and sensual detail, his obsession with age and beauty, and a sensibility that, as the citation for his Nobel Prize reads, "expresses the essence of the Japanese mind." Were such a story to be lost, Kawabata's oeuvre would be the poorer for it, as Kafka's would be without "A Country Doctor" or Hemingway's without "Hills Like White Elephants."

Today, "The Grasshopper and the Bell Cricket" might be labeled flash fiction. In 1924, Kawabata called such pieces palm-of-the-hand stories. A note at the beginning of Lane Dunlop's and J. Martin Holman's masterful translation of Kawabata's *Palm-of-the-Hand Stories* quotes Kawabata: "Many writers in their youth write poetry; I, instead of poetry, wrote the palm-of-the-hand stories."

The title, "The Grasshopper and Bell Cricket," calls to mind Aesop's fables. Perhaps that was Kawabata's intention, for the story's ending mimics the classic closure for a fable: a moral. A moral in Aesop is a lesson drawn from experience or observation, a down-to-earth wisdom that the story imparts to the reader, and Kawabata's take on the moral is at once wise and beautiful. As if the story were a sonnet, there's a turn in which dispassionate observation becomes sudden, arresting emotion.

Besides its ending, what has always impressed me about the story is its compression. Compression begins with the conception: a simple scene, shot, so to speak, in a single take. There are no jump cuts until the flash-forward of closure; otherwise, the pace seems unhurried, allowing the imagery of the children's lanterns to bloom into an interplay of light and its reflections. Reflections are a motif in Kawabata's work, moments of heightened perception for the characters that notice them. (I'm reminded especially of a scene in his novel *Snow Country* in which the reflection of a woman's face appears to a man on the steamy cold window of a train.) The seventy stories in *Palm-of-the-Hand* assume a variety of shapes—narrative, dramatic, slice of life, anecdotal. "The Grasshopper and Bell Cricket" leans toward the lyrical. A simple anecdote of children at play becomes an increasingly complex flow of images whose deeper meaning becomes clear only at the intersection of maturity and innocence.

"Birds" was published in the summer 1972 issue of the *Iowa Review*. I've been careful to keep my original copy of the magazine. According to the bio note, it's John O'Brien's first published

story. O'Brien, the note continues, "is living with the Athabas-
ca Indians, 200 miles into the Alaskan bush, 30 below, dogsled,
etc." That's a long way from Philly, where John grew up. The
story makes the same point. A year before its publication, I'd
read "Birds" in a mimeographed version John brought to a class
we shared at the Iowa Writers' Workshop, and was blown away
by it. I remember asking him how he'd come up with the story's
form. John told me he admired the way Jerzy Kosinski arranged
the chapters of his novel *Steps*, so that it read as if the writer were
relying on instinct rather than on a linear narrative pattern. The
loosely chronological arrangement that John settled on for the
published the story funnels the earlier scenes into a sequence
of scenes set in Alaska. Although the story's form trades linear
narration for a more musical theme and variation, there's still a
sense of forward movement.

There is also, from the opening sentence to the last, a beautiful modulation of prose rhythm, and of the intimate voice of
the narrator. The accumulation of anecdotes puts the reader in
the grip of a natural raconteur, a storyteller with more stories
than he knows what to do with. Whatever "Birds" gives up in
plot, it repays with invention: memorable anecdotes, the fresh-
ness of its lyricism, and its conflation of human emotion with
the natural world.

Once I began using the story in my writing classes, I never
stopped. Over the years I've found that many writers have at
least one such story to tell. "Birds" demonstrates that the sense of
cause and effect inherent in linear, chronological narration is not
the only way to lay out a life. One might organize a life around
an object—some recurrent, resonant image—cars, shoes, knives,
kisses. In such a story, cause and effect is not a given. In fact,
that's the very point made by "Bird's" lyrical closure.

Actually, there's an ingenious kind of double closure in "Birds."
In the next-to-last vignette, the narrator recounts how once while
hunting in Alaska he "shot a kittiwake out of boredom and spite."

Another kittiwake circles, calling to the downed bird, and then lands beside it and stays with the body. The section ends, "I haven't shot anything since then." It's a statement that could certainly serve as closure. The narrator has had a realization, learned greater empathy, matured. Instead, Obrien ends with a section of three sentences: "We left the island by mail plane. Flying over the water, we saw gulls like white puffs on the water and crossed over an eagle too. The shadow of the eagle swam on the water." Without cause and effect, a story risks ending on confusion. It isn't confusion O'Brien arrives at but rather the mystery that is a life. The final image is for me one of the most gorgeous in contemporary literature: the shadow of an eagle flying over water. It is there so vividly, so real, and yet it can never be grasped.

EMMA DONOGHUE

✦ ✦ ✦ ✦ ✦ ✦ ✦

AN ATTACH OF HUNGER
Maeve Brennan

THE YELLOW WALLPAPER
Charlotte Perkins Gilman

✦ ✦ ✦ ✦ ✦ ✦ ✦

I READ "THE YELLOW Wallpaper" at nineteen, and took it personally. I don't think I reread it, over the next two decades;
I didn't need to, because it was lodged like a painful splinter in
the back of my mind. At forty, writing about a young woman
raising her child in a locked shed in my novel *Room*, without
even realizing it I drew on the suffocating atmosphere of Perkins Gilman's story.

"The Yellow Wallpaper" is famous for everything outside its
text, such as the circumstances of its composition, the stir it
caused, and the preeminent role its author would go on to have
as a feminist polemicist. But let's forget all that for a moment and
look at the style. First-person narration that anticipates modern-
ism in its following of the wandering stream of consciousness;
paragraphs so short and staccato that at certain points the story
reads like a prose poem about psychosis.

Far from being a straightforward fictionalization of the author's own breakdowns (postpartum and marital), the story flirts
with several literary traditions. Starting with a reference to moving into a possibly "haunted house," it resembles other ghost

stories (a thriving Victorian genre) in which women narrators
are sensitive to supernatural presences in a way that their ratio-
nal, sensible peers are not. It also invokes the gothic novel, and
before that dark legends such as Bluebeard. Edgar Allan Poe's
psychological horror stories are not far away, especially "The
Tell-Tale Heart," with its murderer narrator driven insane by the
lingering pulse of his victim from under the floorboards.

All these literary allegiances help to camouflage the story's
feminism—its narrator's fairly explicit declarations that she is
sick of being told what to do. Something else that saves "The
Yellow Wallpaper" from settling into the stiff modes of lecture
and cautionary tale is its undecidedness. Details contradict each
other in a way that wouldn't happen in a more generic piece of
fiction. For example, the couple's bedroom has the most hideous
reeking, staining wallpaper, as well as other sinister fittings left
over from its nursery days (barred windows, rings in the walls)
. . . but it is also sunny and airy, with splendid and varied views
of a "*delicious* garden," and the narrator claims to be fond of the
room in spite of the terrible wallpaper, or maybe even because
of it. The "creeping woman" (or perhaps women) she glimpses
in the wallpaper—if the narrator identifies with her and longs
to free her, then why get hold of a rope to tie her up? Also, the
narrator constantly tells us how frail and tired she feels, but the
prose is driven along by what her husband calls her "imaginative
power and habit of story-making." As she falls into confusion
and paranoia, she admits with a dark flash of humor that "life is
very much more exciting now."

So, like the wallpaper itself, "The Yellow Wallpaper" is always
in motion, evading a simple or fixed interpretation. It works because it turns a culturally specific protest (against the infamous
"rest cure" of Dr S. Weir Mitchell) into a, dare I say it, universal cry: "Get me out of here!" Like Samuel Richardson's *Clarissa*,
like Charlotte Brontë's *Jane Eyre*, like Shirley Jackson's *We Have
Always Lived in the Castle*, or like V. C. Andrews's *Flowers in the*

Attic, it is a study of confinement, and the uncanny powers of the powerless.

MAEVE BRENNAN, THE SUBJECT of my 2012 play, *The Talk of the Town*, wrote repeatedly about the kind of marriage—Irish Catholic, traditionally patriarchal, with children—that she made sure to avoid entering into herself. (The five years she spent hitched to a colleague at the *New Yorker* were an entirely different modern, cocktail-fueled venture.)

"An Attack of Hunger" is one of a series of stories about the Derdons, and finds Mrs. Derdon suffering from what we would now call empty-nest syndrome. Like the narrator of "The Yellow Wallpaper," Mrs. Derdon is worn out, "dwindling" fast, depressed to the point of wanting to lie down all the time. Her visceral longing for John, the son who has become a priest, works here like a classic *Madame Bovary* adultery plot, exposing the hollowness of both the marriage and the self-deluding passion that disrupts it.

Like Perkins Gilman's narrator, Mrs. Derdon is a bored fantasist with a dreamy mind that "might even break free and sail off up like a child's balloon." She uses her imagination destructively to conjure up the deaths of her son, herself, above all her husband, whose bland features she convinces herself hide "the face of a *villain* . . . capable of saying and doing the most passionate and awful things."

And what wife wouldn't prefer outright villainy to the subtle passive-aggression with which Mr. Derdon doles out the housekeeping money? "There was no hope for her inside the house," Brennan's narrator warns. Like "The Yellow Wallpaper," this story is a howl of protest against domesticity, with hints of the gothic: stained cushions, cups that crack themselves, a rosebush "crippled" by the kick of a child's ball. There is a thrilling moment when Mrs. Derdon finally walks out, and we think this may be a *Hedda Gabler* story of wifely liberation:

She felt an indulgent astonishment at her former anguish and helplessness and at the importance she had attached to the house and all its little furnishings, when all the time all she had ever really wanted was to run away as far as she could go.

Instead she is dragged back, not just by practicalities (having no income) but by the limits of her own courage.

Brennan is a mistress of the petty detail: consider Mrs. Derdon's nostalgia for the "rusty little wad of newspaper" with which John used to wedge shut the door of his wardrobe. Perhaps the reason this story moves me so much is that it is not just about marriage but also mortality itself. Everything rots or erodes: a house is only a "remnant," a marker for "the shabbiness of time."

JUNOT DÍAZ

✦ ✦ ✦ ✦ ✦ ✦ ✦

BLOODCHILD
Octavia Butler

NIGHT WOMEN
Edwidge Danticat

✦ ✦ ✦ ✦ ✦ ✦ ✦

T HE UNNAMED NIGHT WOMAN of Edwidge Danticat's story lives in a world of unrelenting adversity, "a place where
nothing lasts." To survive, this single mother engages in sex work
under the cover of night, separated from her sleeping son by only
the thinnest of sheets. As a precaution in case he ever awakens,
she regales the young boy with fantastic stories of visitations and
angels, but the son is growing fast and soon neither the "fabrica-
tions" she prepares nor the radio he sleeps with will be able to
obscure the bitter reality of what goes on beyond the sheet.

That's the heartbreaking predicament at the center of this tale
that I consider among the finest in our canon.

On almost every level "Night Women" is extraordinary. It's
certainly a masterclass in the extraordinary capabilities of the
form. Only six pages long and yet Danticat taps into the short
story's suggestive powers, its Tardis-like ability to be both expan-
sive and concise, to offer her readers a life, a world, and ultimately
an invaluable corrective to how we've been taught to *see the world*.

Danticat does so much so well here. Consider the Night Woman herself: she is a singular narrative presence, her voice among

Danticat's finest achievements. Aching and poetic and impossibly *real*. Her lyricism and folkloric knowledge are not writerly affectations but instead characterological information, helping to illuminate both her sense of the world and her longings for liberation and transformation. (After all, if a mosquito can learn "the gift of lightning itself" cannot we as well?) The intimacy that voice invites (and the effortless manner in which Danticat produces it) is worth noting and for those of us interested in writing something to aspire to. As a reader, one feels as though the barrier separating us from that suffocating one-room house is even thinner than the sheet dividing the mother and the son.

Night Woman is nothing if not unblinkingly honest about her situation, about the world around her—the holes in the roof of her house, the mosquitoes that leave her son's face freckled in blood, the men with their breadfruit heads who visit her in the dark and who do not offer to fix her roof because they enjoy "the view"—and yet for all her "real-ness" Night Woman is also profoundly imaginative, a storyteller of no mean talent who limns her bleak world with metaphor, poetry, dream, myth, hope. "There is a place in Ville Rose where ghost women ride the crests of waves while brushing the stars out of their hair" and "My fingers coil into visions of birds on his nose" are typical of her. What's truly marvelous here is the pas de deux that Danticat performs in these six pages, allowing neither Night Woman's mythopeic lyricism nor her "traumatic realism" to get the upper hand or to negate the other.

By giving us a Night Woman who can see the hole in the roof *and* the stars beyond, Danticat's story honors both the endemic difficulties that many Haitians must confront and the superhuman resilience and powerful creative labors that Haitian women mobilize in their struggles for self-possession. This is a story that dramatizes (and is itself a wondrous example of) the true work of the Night Women of Haiti and all the Night Women on our neoliberal planet.

And then we have the alarming tour de force that is Octavia Butler's Bloodchild. Whereas Danticat focuses on the calamitous present of Caribbean Blackness, Octavia Butler turns to an interstellar future so that she might access the dark origin story of our civilization (and of Danticat's Night Woman): the nightmare of New World slavery. Condensing the wrenching complexity of that experience down to a singular chilling story speaks to Butler's craft and to her all the more colossal imaginative powers.

Equal parts body horror, neo-slave narrative, and dystopian nightmare, "Bloodchild" revolves around a human colony stranded on an alien planet. Cut off from rescue and unable to return to Earth, the surviving colonists have been forced into a gruesome symbiotic relationship with superior Tlic natives. The Tlic impregnate humans regardless of their gender with their grublike issue (turns out eggs hosted in human bodies produce stronger, healthier young). As long as the grubs are removed before they grow too big, the human hosts can survive the implantation— otherwise the grubs will start to eat the flesh of their hosts. Contact with Tlic eggs extends human life and by extension increases their worth as breeding stock. Though the Tlic argue otherwise, humans in this tale have no control over their bodies. The Tlic violate human flesh and gender norms and humans are regularly doled out to Tlic clans for breeding, valuable commodities. Humans are segregated onto a reservation-like Preserve and wear bands with their owners' names on them; they cannot drive or bear arms; their sole purpose is to host Tlic grubs and to multiply in order to better serve the Tlic. It's as hellish a scenario as it sounds and for those of us descended from enslaved Africans all too believable.

At the core of our story is Gan, a young human who has reached the age of implantation, and his growing awareness of the system of control and oppression that govern the lives of all humans on the Preserve. A pregnant "runaway" intrudes on the "domestic" idyll Gan is enjoying with the Tlic he has been promised to and suddenly the full weight of what he is being prepared for is laid bare before Gan in the eviscerated body of the runaway.

Butler does not flinch from portraying the complex physical, emotional, and psychic consequences of the Tlic captivity and offers no happy emancipation at the end. What Gan's final stand does seem to indicate is that even if, in the face of such an overwhelming system, our positive options are few, they must still be pursued bravely if one is to hope for a future when any real sense of a self will be possible. Butler seems to be arguing that surviving sometimes is the only victory possible, which might seem like cold comfort indeed and yet when looked at from the great distance of centuries (or through the lens of the African diasporic experience) surviving might in fact be an even greater heroic deed than any Achilles or Beowulf might have dreamed of.

Like Danticat, Butler does so much here. She is flying to the future to touch the past without which we cannot understand our present. She presents in "Bloodchild" what Glissant has called a "prophetic vision of history." And by alloying the slave narrative to some of the oldest tropes of science fiction, she helps reveal the colonial root of all our speculative genres. Science fiction might claim to be about technology and alterity and visions of the future, but Butler seems to be indicating that it is equally about the unspoken history of coloniality that gave birth to our modernities. Butler's extraordinary story helps us re-member this apocalyptic origin, re-member it in our minds, our hearts, and yes, our bodies.

MICHAEL CUNNINGHAM

+ + + + + + +

WORK
Denis Johnson

THE DEAD
James Joyce

+ + + + + + +

W RITING STUDENTS ASK ALL kinds of questions about how
to write. As they should. Some of their questions have answers and some do not. On the occasions when I have no answer
to give, I tell them so.

I remind them that the writing of fiction is on the one hand a
craft that can be learned but on the other is, obdurately, a mysterious act. Mixed in with a story's or novel's identifiable qualities are
gestures, moments, twists of phrase and event, revelations of character, that are stunningly effective and yet seem to defy analysis.

This can, of course, be a frustrating experience for young people who've signed up for a course that offers to teach them how
to write.

By way of compensation, meager though it may be, I sometimes tell my students that I aspire, one day, to teach a series of
seminars called, "Hell If I Know," during which we will, week by
week, confront various questions about writing that defeat any
attempt to arrive at an answer.

The sessions would be brief. They'd possess a certain Zen
quality, in that both teacher and students would acknowledge

that some miracle has been wrought by means of paper and ink alone, and that any ambition to explain the miracle is not only doomed but also discouraging. Who, after all, would want an explicable miracle?

After a brief silence, I imagine us all filing, quietly and reverently, back out of the room.

I tell my students that the first session in the "Hell If I Know" series would be called, "How to End a Story."

I'd choose that as the opening subject because students so often come to me in a state of confusion about how to bring their stories (which had seemed to be moving along fairly well, through their beginnings and middles) to a close.

I can, in fact, sometimes help them, but I'll save whatever advice I may harbor about the ways writers might discover a story's proper ending for another essay. We're here to consider a larger question, one that is by no means confined to student writers.

How the Hell Do I Know . . .

. . . how to produce, in those final lines, a sense of distinct and even profound closure without being tidy or smug . . . how to end a story in a way that simultaneously solves and deepens its central mystery . . . how to land a story at a point that's both surprising (a story must be surprising, in one way or another) and inevitable.

In this regard, a story, any story, should resemble a standard-issue, old-fashioned mystery. Here, reader, is the outcome, and it's been right in front of you all along. I, the writer, have so cleverly diverted your attention that you failed to realize where the story was headed until its actual destination was revealed. If, in a mystery, the killer turns out to be a random psychopath—a stranger who hasn't appeared at all until the final lines—the mystery's no good.

The same applies to fiction of all kinds. A story's ending should elicit, from its reader, some reaction along the lines of, *Right, of course, how could I have missed that?*

This comparison to the traditional mystery story, however, takes us only so far. In a mystery, the climactic revelation is, in part, a demonstration of the writer's ingenuity; it's the exposure of the machinery that's been driving the plot.

In fiction of another kind the revelation functions, if anything, to deny the fact that machinery, or machinations, have been at work at all. It may pay tribute to the writer's skills, but a great ending to a great story should feel like an enormous truth conjured up by the writer, a truth as surprising to them as it is to the reader.

It is, in short, both a trick and an anti-trick. The conjurer may have started with a few simple, familiar props—the hat, the wand, the cabinet—but by the time the act is over, something deeper and more consequential, perhaps something of terrifying power, has to have been summoned, and it must far surpass the plucked-from-nowhere bouquet or the vanished assistant.

I'd like to talk about two stories that come to miraculous, mysterious ends: James Joyce's "The Dead" and Denis Johnson's "Work."

Before going into the specifics of those two stories, however, there's this to consider about stories in general and endings in particular.

Every story, whatever its nature, is by definition a single writer's attempt to tell some section of a story too vast to be told: a story that begins with the first fish that wriggled out of the ocean and onto land and ends when the sun supernovas and incinerates the solar system.

Anyone who writes fiction is telling their segment of that story, which is not only too large for any individual, but also too large for all the writers who've ever lived, or ever will. What we're offering, as writers, is fragments. The more resonantly and truly the fragment speaks to the imponderably bigger picture, the more integral it feels, the more ground it covers, the greater the story.

Beginnings aren't easy. Nothing about writing fiction is easy. But writers can, in fact, enter the continuum at just about any point, from those ambitious fish whose fins were slowly developing into feet to the ten seconds before the sun explodes. It's all part of the same untellable tale, whether it starts during the Crimean War or at a garden party held the day before yesterday.

The thornier question is, having entered, where and when does one step away? How and where and when to end one's story, with the implication that the writer is leaving these people and these situations for now, while imparting to the reader the clear understanding that there's more, a great deal more, still to come: that there's always more to come, but whatever it may be, it lies beyond the confines of this particular account.

In short, we don't exactly *end* a story. We leave a story, at what seems like the right—the precisely, painfully, revealingly right—departure point.

I suspect most of us are familiar with Joyce's "The Dead," which has been canonized for many, extremely good, reasons, particular among them its dazzling finale:

> A few light taps upon the pane made [Gabriel] turn to the window. It had begun to snow again. He watched sleepily the flakes, silver and dark, falling obliquely against the lamplight. The time had come for him to set out on his journey westward. Yes, the newspapers were right: snow was general all over Ireland. It was falling on every part of the dark central plain, on the treeless hills, falling softly upon the Bog of Allen and, farther westward, softly falling into the dark mutinous Shannon waves. It was falling, too, upon every part of the lonely churchyard on the hill where Michael Furey lay buried. It lay thickly drifted on the crooked crosses and headstones, on the spears of the little gate, on the barren thorns. His soul swooned slowly as he heard the snow falling faintly through the universe and faintly falling, like the descent of their last end, upon all the living and the dead.

What's preceded this final paragraph is a story that, although not conventional—Joyce never wrote anything that could rightly be called "conventional"—is rather unexceptional in its characters and events.

The bulk of the story takes place during an annual party given, on the Feast of the Epiphany, by two Irish spinsters and attended, most prominently, by one Gabriel Conroy and his wife, Gretta.

It is not an especially fabulous or memorable party. It's a good-enough party. During the course of the celebration, not much occurs. Gabriel unintentionally insults Lily, the maid, and will be, later in the evening, insulted in turn by another guest, who resents his conservative political views. A young woman plays the piano. People dance. People sing. A man who's had too much to drink proves to be disruptive. That's about it.

We do understand, however, as the party progresses, that Gabriel is rather self-satisfied, a little pompous, and very much a regular guy. He's fond of his little comforts. He doesn't aspire to much more than little comforts.

Here is the story's opening paragraph:

> Lily, the caretaker's daughter, was literally run off her feet. Hardly had she brought one gentleman into the little pantry behind the office on the ground floor and helped him off with his overcoat than the wheezy hall-door bell clanged again and she had to scamper along the bare hallway to let in another guest. It was well for her she had not to attend to the ladies also. But Miss Kate and Miss Julia had thought of that and had converted the bathroom upstairs into a ladies' dressing-room. Miss Kate and Miss Julia were there, gossiping and laughing and fussing, walking after each other to the head of the stairs, peering down over the banisters and calling down to Lily to ask her who had come.

Consider that paragraph, from its depiction of simple domesticity to the relative plainness of its language, in light of the closing paragraph. Clearly, from opening to end, a great deal has, in fact, occurred.

The ending starts to rev up when Gabriel and Gretta arrive at the hotel room they've reserved for the night, their house being rather far off and the evening being beset by Irish sleet and snow. At the hotel, Gabriel anticipates, happily, a night of familiar marital love-making.

Gretta, however, is distracted. When Gabriel asks her why, she breaks down weeping. She tells him that one of the songs sung at the party reminded her of a boy she knew, when she was much younger.

Gabriel is, naturally enough, disconcerted, and jealous. Why, he demands to know, is his wife so undone by the memory of a boy she knew years ago? Does she imagine she might see him again?

> He is dead, she said at length. He died when he was only seventeen. Isn't it a terrible thing, to die so young as that?

Gabriel interrogates her further. How did the boy die? Was it consumption?

Greta answers: "I think he died for me."

She continues:

> Poor fellow. He was very fond of me and he was such a gentle boy. We used to go out together, walking, you know, Gabriel, like the way they do in the country. He was going to study singing, but for his health. He had a very good voice, poor Michael Furey.
>
> Well; and then? asked Gabriel.
>
> And then when it came to the time for me to leave

Galway and come up to the convent he was much worse and I wouldn't be let see him so I wrote him a letter saying I was going up to Dublin and would be back in the summer and hoping he would be better then.

She paused for a moment to get her voice under control and then went on:

Then the night before I left I was in my Grandmother's house in Nun's Island, packing up, and I heard gravel thrown up against the window. The window was so wet I couldn't see so I ran downstairs as I was and slipped out the back into the garden and there was the poor fellow at the end of the garden, shivering.

And did you not tell him to go back, asked Gabriel.

I implored him to go back at once and told him he would get his death in the rain. But he said he did not want to live. I can see his eyes as well as well! He was standing at the end of the wall where there was a tree.

And did he go home? asked Gabriel.

Yes he went home. And when I was only a week in the convent he died and was buried in Oughterard where his people came from. O the day I heard that, that he was dead!

She stopped, choking with sobs, and, overcome with emotion, flung herself face downward on the bed, sobbing in the quilt. Gabriel held her hand for a moment longer, irresolutely, and then, shy of intruding on her grief, let it fall gently and walked quietly to the window.

Soon thereafter, we arrive at that closing paragraph, which is one of the greatest paragraphs produced by human hand. We've gone to the most ordinary imaginable holiday party, carved the traditional goose, sung the traditional songs and, by evening's end, found ourselves face to face with loss and aging and mortality itself.

Denis Johnson's short story, "Work," like "The Dead," involves a series of commonplace events, although the nature of the "commonplace" among Johnson's characters is quite different from that of Joyce's well-fed Irish Catholics.

This is the opening paragraph of "Work":

> I'd been staying at the Holiday Inn with my girlfriend, honestly the most beautiful woman I'd ever known, for three days under a phony name, shooting heroin. We made love in the bed, ate steaks in the restaurant, shot up in the john, puked, cried, accused one another, begged of one another, forgave, promised, and carried one another to heaven.

Unlike the orderly progression of events that compose "The Dead," "Work" jerks shaggily forward. The narrator abandons his girlfriend and eventually wanders into a bar, where he encounters an old friend named Wayne, who is every bit as aimless and drug-addled as the narrator. The two agree to pick up a few dollars by stealing the copper wiring out of an abandoned house on the outskirts of town which, after the wire has been taken, is revealed to have been Wayne's own house, once, before the bank foreclosed on it.

As the two men make their way back to town, they share a vision of a beautiful red-haired woman, parasailing over a river, naked. It's the story's only surreal moment.

They stop by the home of Wayne's ex-wife. The narrator believes the ex-wife to have been the naked woman he saw, aloft. They sell the wire and drink up the profits. The narrator observes, of the woman behind the bar:

> Who should be pouring drinks there but a young woman whose name I can't remember. But I remember the way she poured. It was like doubling your money. She

wasn't going to make her employers rich. Needless to say, she was revered among us.

Drink in hand, the narrator experiences a reverie:

> I was eighteen and in bed with my first wife, before we were married. Our naked bodies started glowing, and the air turned such a strange color I thought my life must be leaving me, and with every young fiber and cell I wanted to hold on to it for another breath. A clattering sound was tearing up my head as I staggered upright and opened the door on a vision I will never see again: Where are my women now, with their sweet wet words and ways, and the miraculous balls of hail popping in a green translucence in the yards?
>
> We put on our clothes, she and I, and walked out into a town flooded ankle-deep with white, buoyant stones. Birth should have been like that.

Shortly after, we arrive at the story's closing paragraph:

> The Vine had no jukebox but a real stereo, continually playing tunes of alcoholic self-pity and sentimental divorce. "Nurse," I sobbed. She poured doubles like an angel, right up to the lip of a cocktail glass, no measuring. "You have a lovely pitching arm." You had to go down to them like a hummingbird to a blossom. I saw her much later, not too many years ago, and when I smiled she seemed to believe I was making advances. But it was only that I remembered. I'll never forget you. Your husband will beat you with an extension cord and the bus will pull away leaving you standing there in tears, but you were my mother.

Which is my own, personal nomination for second-best clos-ing paragraph ever produced by human hand.

If the closing paragraph of "The Dead" is unexpected but per-fectly logical, the closing paragraph of "Work" is unexpected and, on first reading, somewhat baffling.

No one's mother has appeared in the story. There have, in fact, been no consistent characters at all, except the narrator and Wayne.

There have, however, been five women (albeit one of them a hallucination), all on the one hand tangential but, on the oth-er, all vital—all objects of love bordering on veneration for the narrator, all incarnations of the narrator's fundamental idea of womanliness: nurturing, beautiful, generous, kind; as much man-ifestations of the divine as they are human beings; members of a superior race who conduct their business on a plane higher than that of Wayne and the narrator and the other men who appear peripherally in the story. In "Work," most members of the race known as *men* are dishonest, lazy, cruel, and petty.

The men in the story are children, the women are mothers. Idealized mothers, absolutely. But mothers are, for the most part, meant to be idealized, especially as we grow older. Not every mother. But for many of us, the woman who raised us, who when we were children denied us the things we most ardently want-ed, punished us for misbehaving, embarrassed us at certain times with their cosseting and ignored us at other times when we need-ed them most. That woman, in memory, beyond childhood's end, tends to be glorified. For many of us—certainly for the narrator in "Work"—that complicated figure, that goddess who usurped and forbade as well as loved and provided, is sanctified, her laps-es forgiven if not forgotten. We can see, as adults, the titanic effort required merely to keep us alive all those years, from the age at which we were determined to put our mouths to electrical outlets to the age at which we were determined to drive when we were too drunk to walk.

That's the brilliance of "Work's" closing paragraph. That's the surprise that isn't really a surprise, after all. Without consciously realizing it, we've been reading a story about bad boys and the mothers who look after them, the women who ascend, after they've been forsaken, to a pantheon of feminine virtue and sacrifice.

With "The Dead," we have the unanticipated resurrection of a boy who was willing to die for love, as Gabriel surely would not. In "Work" we have the sudden invocation of a put-upon mother-goddess who, like Michael Furey in "The Dead," lives as a memory, an ideal, the embodiment of an Eden from which we, the living, have been banished.

And yet.

The fact that a certain logic can be extracted from the bodies of both stories does not, in the final analysis, fully elucidate their mysteries.

As in a whodunit, the final revelation does not, cannot, come from nowhere. The murderer, the lost love, the ghostly mother, have been there all along, right in front of us. If that weren't the case, the endings wouldn't be satisfying. They would not, in fact, be endings at all.

There remains, however, the mystery inside the mystery. Joyce knew to leave Gabriel looking out the window into a world filling up with snow, which falls at first specifically—on the Bog of Allen, on the River Shannon, on the churchyard in which Michael Furey is buried. Joyce knew then to enlarge upon those specifics, to take the big risk, to assert that the snow is "falling faintly through the universe and faintly falling, like the descent of their last end, upon all the living and the dead."

A line like that could so easily have felt pretentious and obvious. It somehow, however, does not.

Johnson, on the other hand, knew to stay with specifics, to allow the last reveal to reside not in an assertion of mortal vastness like the one conjured up by Joyce but rather in a concrete yet utterly unexpected association. "Your husband will beat you with an extension cord and the bus will pull away leaving you standing there in tears, but you were my mother."

If we can follow Joyce's and Johnson's concealed logic, if we can to a certain extent decipher their routes, we can't account for the rightness of their execution. How did Joyce come up with the reverse repetition—snow that is "falling faintly" and "faintly falling" in the same line—or Johnson with the fact that the invoked mother was beaten with an extension cord, and that a bus pulled away, leaving her in tears? We know only that, in both cases, those final lines wouldn't quite work, not without the poetic repetition, not without the bus and the extension cord.

It's magic. It's genius.

Hell if I know how they did it.

LAN SAMANTHA CHANG

+ + + + + + +

FRENCH LESSON I: LE MEURTRE
Lydia Davis

THE CASK OF AMONTILLADO
Edgar Allen Poe

+ + + + + + +

Ι FIRST ENCOUNTERED EDGAR Allan Poe's masterpiece "The Cask of Amontillado" under the fluorescent lights of a public school classroom. A misfit in eighth grade, shunned by my classmates and perpetually bored, I turned the pages of my literature anthology in search of a spell to take me away from the claustrophobic misery of winter in northeastern Wisconsin. It was the perfect setting in which to read Poe's unforgettable first line: "The thousand injuries of Fortunato I had borne as I best could; but when he ventured upon insult, I vowed revenge." Thus, I was lifted happily away, delighted by the strangeness and flamboyance of the narrator, Montresor.

Decades later, I came to understand my eighth-grade teacher's claim that Poe was an inventor of the short story. A brilliant short story is a work of breathtaking impact and efficiency. Poe makes a startling move in that first sentence, beginning when the trouble between Fortunato and the narrator, Montresor, is well under way. What, we readers wonder, were the "thousand injuries"? And how will the narrator fulfill his vow? Poe eschews any explanation of *what* Fortunato's injuries and insult to the narrator have been. He

212

begins in the middle, *in medias res*, setting up the destination of the story: revenge. In a few more sentences, Montresor tells his unknown listener of the specific *requirements* for his revenge: that he *get away with it*—that he exact revenge with impunity—and, above all, that Fortunato *know* of Montresor's intentions.

Having established this ruthless premise, Poe carries it through, with admirable thoroughness, to its very end. Montresor gets his revenge. *How* does he get it? As an eighth-grade reader, I was so taken with the tale's exotic setting that I barely noticed the relentless momentum of its plot. Years later I especially admire this relentlessness. Step by step, using the promise of a rare Italian vintage, Montresor entices the inebriated Fortunato into his ancient family palazzo and through the archway that leads into the vaults, down innumerable stairs, through the dark catacombs enclosed by chill, wet walls laced with the mysterious and seemingly deadly *nitre*, into the deep and stifling recess of the innermost chambers, past forbidding piles of human remains, and finally into the small, still crypt in which the unfortunate Fortunato is to be chained to a granite wall and sealed into the crypt, literally *buried alive*. Layer by layer, *stone by stone*, Fortunato is stripped of his blithe ignorance of what is being done to him. His final cry, "For the love of God, Montresor," goes unheeded.

To compose a work like this, even to imagine it, takes craziness, ruthlessness, and guts. Poe struggled with gambling, debts, alcoholism, and health problems. He was kicked out of military academy, married his thirteen-year-old cousin, and died when he was only forty. To make such a mess of his life and yet to produce such extraordinary work is a feat that strains credulity. But Poe's brilliance shines with undeniable authority—it shines centuries ahead, through the iciest of northern winters.

Lydia Davis, writing close to one hundred fifty years after Poe, takes many of his pioneered elements of short fiction as convention; her work, rather than imitating them, revitalizes and transforms them. With the title of her short story, "French Lesson i: Le Meurtre," Davis announces two intentions: We will receive a French lesson and the lesson will include a murder. Then Davis begins, patiently and with the clarity of a linguistic master, to teach the reader a new language. "See the *vaches* ambling up the hill, head to rump, head to rump. Learn what a *vache* is. A *vache* is milked in the morning, and milked again in the evening, twitching her dung-soaked tail, her head in a stanchion. Always start learning your foreign language with the name of farm animals."

The murder, it seems, is put to the side. "We can now introduce the definite articles, *le, la,* and *les,* which we know already from certain phrases we see in our own country, such as *le car, le sandwich, le café, les girls.*" Yet, step by step, a setting is created. The weather-beaten *ferme,* with its mysteriously new tractor. The farmer's wife, with her red-knuckled hands. The vivid presence of the animals: the dogs that cringe in the presence of their master; the cats that slink by, mewing; the chickens, which are first loved as pets, then slaughtered, plucked, and consumed by the farmer's family.

At this point the story opens unexpectedly into philosophy. The narrator announces, "We will now introduce a piece of language history, and then, following it, a language concept." In precise, beautifully developed paragraphs, Davis responds to Wittengenstein's argument that language is defined by community, comparing how an American might imagine a tree to how a French person might see one. Thus the French word *arbre* "is not the elm or maple shading the main street of our New England town in the infinitely long, hot and listless, vacant summer of our childhoods." An *arbre,* she explains, "is a plane tree in an ancient town square with lopped, stubby branches and patchy, leprous bark in a row of similar plane trees across from the town hall, in front of which a bicycle ridden by a man with thick, reddish skin and an old cap wavers past and turns into a narrow lane." She acknowledges that these differences can make language lessons inadequate. "We have just said that we have our own words in English for the same things. This is not strictly true. We can't really say there are several words for the same thing. It is in fact just the opposite—there is only one word for many things, and usually even that word, when it is a noun, is too general." Thus each italicized French word—*la ferme, la femme*—gains a sense of deep particularity.

Davis's voice is lucid, witty, philosophically bent, psychologically astute, and knowing, yet curiously humble. After these paragraphs, I am willing to follow her story anywhere, even if it does not go where I have come to expect a story to lead me. I am given only a setting: It is five o'clock on a winter evening. The *vaches* are lowing because their udders are full. The farmer is missing. The farm wife, waiting in the kitchen, looks anxiously out across the yard. The next morning, when the farm wife goes to collect the eggs, she will discover something in the poultry yard that does not belong there.

Davis acknowledges the elements of short narrative made so vivid by Poe. Beginning *in medias res*. Suspense from a declarative opening—a time, a setting, *la ferme*, a cast of characters, a mystery. The murder, while definitively presented, is presented not as the center of the piece, but as a counterpart to the breathtaking, incisive philosophy on language. The most vivid paragraphs describe the specificity and mystery of language and memory. They breathe life into the setting of the barn, the kitchen. In "French Lesson 1: Le Meurtre," there is virtually no action, but the setting contains the elements of a human drama suspended in time. With this still portrait, Davis delves into the essential mystery of human behavior, expanding our understanding of what a story is.

RON CARLSON

✦ ✦ ✦ ✦ ✦ ✦ ✦

BABYLON REVISITED
F. Scott Fitzgerald

THE TELL-TALE HEART
Edgar Allen Poe

✦ ✦ ✦ ✦ ✦ ✦ ✦

W HEN I WAS TWENTY, I took a single-author course taught by
the eminent scholar Dr. Kenneth Eble at the University of
Utah. It was "F. Scott Fitzgerald," and the course—along with all
of the things that happen when a person is twenty—changed my
life, turned it toward literature, and showed me I was drawn to
and claimed by characters larger than life, characters who moved
beautifully toward things that would harm them, even aware of
the harm, and who turned to the next mistake with what I took
for ardor.

I'd always been a reader and a lover of stories, but I'd never
read anything like the stories of Fitzgerald. The timing was right.
I read *This Side of Paradise* and walked the beautiful campus at
Utah in the middle of the night, Emily Dickinson's poems in one
pocket and Fitzgerald's stories in the other. I could show you the
books. I could show you my route: up the old horseshoe under
the Park Building and beside it through the tall birch trees and
up onto the Union quad by the library and Orson Spencer Hall.
I walked with my hands clasped behind my back and I talked
to myself, saying the two or three poems I had memorized, and

starting stories too beautiful to finish. I moved my bed underneath the window of my dorm room and began writing lists of the qualities of light. I actually did these things! I was under a spell and I wanted to be under a spell. My god, I wasn't going to be an engineer after all. I didn't know what I was going to be. I said that grand sentence aloud some nights walking through that charmed garden.

Although I was a reader, I wasn't a perspicacious reader. I couldn't tell Hemingway from Katherine Ann Porter. I knew the stories these authors wrote and I knew if they were slow or fast, and then I crashed into this course with Dr. Eble and I read "Absolution" and "The Sensible Thing" and "The Diamond as Big as the Ritz" and "May Day" and "The Rich Boy" and I reread *This Side of Paradise*, which when you're twenty reads like a letter you might find on your bed returning from a late-night walk, and I reread *The Great Gatsby* and I was hooked. The best of his work hurt me like a bruise. I wanted to be up in the beauty, to be at the party, to be part of it; I ached to. But I also wanted, with a longing that I've found can be a real part of literary work, all these dear people to make better decisions. I read about him and I read his stories until it all seemed one story and there is part of me today that feels it might be.

Fitzgerald, they say, spent his genius boiling the pot, writing stories for the *Saturday Evening Post* at four thousand dollars each—and this in the Roaring Twenties. He feared that he was writing stories about boys and girls nobody cared about, and when the party ended with the financial crash of 1929, he was already asea, working on a book about the rich in Europe, which starts with a page of his beautiful poetry about a hotel beach and ends with a page that is more stylistically like Hemingway than anyone will say. *Tender Is the Night* was published in 1934 to great silence. The country had other concerns.

That book is filled with the maturity that is reflected in his little masterpiece "Babylon Revisited," in which the damaged protagonist, Charlie Wales, returns to the scene of his lavish and destructive dissipation, a word the story holds up like a candle, to see if he might reclaim his daughter. Fitzgerald himself was a pernicious alcoholic in an era before that was even a word. He did dissipate his talents and the bright edge of his life, and in this sobering story he reckons with the deep real rue that comes with a hangover. In the early 1930s, Charlie Wales returns to his Babylon—Paris—and finds it empty of the meretricious delights of the orgy of three years before. It is hollow and harrowing for him and the story would make a good walking tour of that great city. "The Place de Concorde moved by in pink majesty; they crossed the logical Seine, and Charlie felt the sudden provincial quality of the Left Bank." Charlie visits his old haunts and finds them properly and deeply haunting.

The excess of yesteryear is signaled right away in the opening with a reference to Paul, a barman who could afford a custom built-car in the day. Money was nothing. Charlie himself tipped an orchestra a thousand francs to play one song. Now he's on the narrow and the straight, taking one drink a day, his new regimen, something that Alcoholics Anonymous would have disallowed, but they were five or six years in the future. At one point in his tour, he picks up a *cocotte*, in a variation on a scene from Hemingway's first novel *The Sun Also Rises*, and buys her dinner. Polished with his resolve and shame, Charlie presents himself to his sister-in-law and her husband with hopes of winning back his aptly named daughter, Honoria. Fitzgerald's story sense was firmly intact as he wrote the assembly of Charlie's hopes, bit by bit, and two-thirds of the way through his Paris visit, it looks like he may win the day with his in-laws. But we can sense that the past, his mistakes and the residue he left behind, will undermine all of his efforts. Honor has been dissipated as well. These are characters we care about, and the stakes here are as high as any Fitzgerald laid out.

Charlie Wales is no longer young, but he has a resolve at the end of this story, an optimism which is not shiny nor insouciant or brimming with youthful ardor. This is a mature writer drawing from his most substantial moments to make moving fiction.

WHENEVER I'VE TAUGHT "The Tell-Tale Heart," and our guy has foamed and raved and finally advised the authorities to tear up the planks and reveal his deed, I ask the readers, "What was the murder weapon?"

This famous story got on everyone. There are hundreds of narrators who followed Edgar Allan Poe protesting—too much— their sanity, which we all know from childhood is the first signal for trouble ahead. You can't say, "I'm not mad!" without us leaning forward to see how mad you are, and a "Ha!" is such a signal we should bring it back. "The Tell-Tale Heart" offers up one of our first psychopaths, who is sometimes called the arch-unreliable narrator. As teachers we make a bit of a lesson out of that, though we needn't bother as any fourteen-year-old knows that the guy is lying from the get go. He's, in fact, the reliable narrator laying out his own craziness in breathless urgency. I've always loved the opening: "True!—nervous—very very nervous I had been and am; but why will you say that I am mad?" Just the grammar makes me mad. He's nuts from the start and thereby stone-solid reliable.

I read the story as a sophomore with Miss Porter fifty years ago in the gothic old long-gone Union Building at West High in Salt Lake City which had been, before that, one of the first red stone structures of the University of Utah. She was young and enthusiastic in the way of young teachers that even *Silas Marner* and "The Tell-Tale Heart" couldn't dampen. It was a hard story on us because though we loved the madman and his cautious, cautious, cautious, steady, steady, stealthy, stealthy emphatic preparations and his burning antipathy for the old man, my scrupulous teacher used the text as a host for her punishing vocabulary tests which were always a surprise: *dissimulation, sagaci-*

ty, *scantlings, tattoo, deputed, audacity, suavity, gesticulation, derision.* Poe was supplying inventory for the vocabulary cabinet for eons beyond his short, tortured life; he'd like that.

The story is a fierce lesson in the economy of scene, using the two rooms and arguably one. There is no larger world and little daylight to dissipate the pressure, the certain claustrophobia, and an abiding rule of the mystery or detective story is the circle; the criminal should be someone the detective knows well, perhaps the closest person to him or her; the scene of the crime should not be some other even exotic spot, but charged and close to home. Our dear madman in his glory puts the chairs on the floor above the body and sits with the law like a pot on a hot stove, and we watch him come to a boil, sound by sound, gradually increasing like every process in the tale.

I've taught it from time to time as I said and it goes well. When we're done I always ask my question. It is met with a hesitation, as the answer is the bed, so uniquely like Poe. The prepared madman had—eight days later, after all his homicidal care and forethought—entered the old man's chamber without a weapon. It would be enough to blunt an intentional murder charge in court. But then I answer the question by saying, *the mattress,* waiting a beat and saying, "It was a *mattress-cide.*" When no one laughs— because I've been all my days blessed with bright students—I tell them they should have because it will be the only joke of the term. And usually, for all the right reasons, it is.

CHARLES BAXTER

✦ ✦ ✦ ✦ ✦ ✦ ✦

THE CORN PLANTING
Sherwood Anderson

A CONVERSATION WITH MY FATHER
Grace Paley

✦ ✦ ✦ ✦ ✦ ✦ ✦

G REAT FICTION OFTEN TELLS us how we live, and, perhaps
more important, how we may respond to the deaths of others, especially those whom we love. These two stories, Sherwood
Anderson's "The Corn Planting" and Grace Paley's "A Conversation with My Father," treat the fact of a loved one's death in
two ways. The first story, though told in words, is nonverbal. The
second is full of talk, animated conversation. But both are very
moving, even when, as in Paley's wonderful story, the response
to death creates the kind of comedy that lies close to tragedy.

I had never read Anderson's "The Corn Planting" until I came
upon it among his uncollected stories. Anderson was a kind of
literary father to an entire generation of writers who followed
him, including Faulkner and Hemingway. But until 2012 this story was never reprinted after it appeared in *American Magazine*, in
1934, so it is not one of Anderson's better-known tales. Reading
it, you will be making a great discovery.

The story is short and relatively simple. Hatch Hutchenson
and his wife in middle age have raised a son, an only child, Will.
This son, talented at art, grows up, leaves his family's farm, and

moves to Chicago. Like most art students, he goes to parties and drinks. He is killed—the story does not say how—in an auto accident. Having received a telegram about the death, the narrator's friend and the narrator himself walk out to the Hutchenson farm to tell Will's father and mother about their son's death. They knock at the door; old Hatch answers, and after hearing about Will's death, he doesn't say a word. He slams the door. The narrator and his friend, however, do not leave, and then they witness the story's great, astounding, hair-raisingly beautiful scene, of what Hatch and his wife do out in the fields, by moonlight, to grieve their son.

These people have worked all their lives. Work is what they really know. Unlike many or most of us, they are uncomfortable with leisure. They are not talkative, either, so they don't spread their grief around by talking on the phone (they don't have one, wrong era) or anywhere else. Think of how everyone now is capable of spreading grief by phone, text, Facebook, blogs, and tweets. By contrast to our own generation's way of grieving, their mourning goes on in silence, "uncanny, sublime, and extraordinary," as the writer Ben Marcus says about Anderson's other stories, and the effect is heightened by our sense of the intensity of what the narrator is feeling as he watches Hatch and his wife. The story is not just about what *happens*; it's also about how it makes you *feel*.

In Grace Paley's "A Conversation with My Father" the narrative rhythms are completely different: urban, urbane, Jewish, comic. We have two people, the narrator and her elderly father (in bed, taking oxygen), talking. He's a retired doctor. What are they talking about? How to tell a story. What's the story? A woman, a single mother who lives down the block from the narrator, has become a junkie in solidarity with her son, also a junkie. The son gives up his habit, but the mother does not. What happens to her then? Her life is up for grabs. Does a woman with an addiction become a slave to her addiction?

That's the problem, but it's not the only problem. As a diagnostician, the old man thinks you always need a lot of backstory to make sense of anything: you need to know where people are from, what their families are like, how they look. His daughter, who's telling the story, wants to jettison all that information because she thinks it's determinative and therefore grim. Instead, she wants to give everyone in her stories, and in her life, an "open destiny," that is, freedom, or what she calls in another story "enormous changes at the last minute."

But if we're paying attention, we notice that there's another story in "A Conversation with My Father"—the story of the old man, who is dying before his daughter's eyes. His death is not going to go away, and you can't exactly laugh it off. And, as is proper, the old man has the last word. "Tragedy! You too. When will you look it in the face?" And whose face is she looking into at that very moment? Her father's, a man who is dying.

I find both of these stories terribly moving and terribly wise. Sherwood Anderson knows that in the depths of our greatest emotions, we cannot always speak. Instead, we will simply do what we are used to doing. When the news of 9/11 came, for example, I was at home, and I went out to mow the lawn, which did not need mowing. I had mowed the lawn the day before. Mowing the lawn was a habit with me, and by doing a customary action, something I was used to and could do without thinking, I was hoping to restore the world to the way it was before the catastrophe.

The wisdom of Grace Paley's story is that she knows, all the way into her bones, that some of us will talk until doomsday, and maybe past it. We will keep our spirits up with jokes, and why not? But the great wonder of her story, its brilliance, is in the silence with which it ends, when the story itself ends, and the joking stops, as it must.

RICHARD BAUSCH

✦ ✦ ✦ ✦ ✦ ✦ ✦

HILLS LIKE WHITE ELEPHANTS
Ernest Hemingway

THE REAL THING
Henry James

✦ ✦ ✦ ✦ ✦ ✦ ✦

I READ "HILLS LIKE White Elephants" when I was at Chanute
Air Force Base, in 1966. I was twenty-one. I had borrowed *The
Stories of Ernest Hemingway* from the base library. Chanute is long
gone now, thirty years gone, and of course the story is still with us.
When I first read it, I thought it was surely a conversation the author must've overheard. It seemed so simple, and such a naturally
flowing event from life. I would gaze at the picture that adorned
the back of the book, that famous image of the rough-hewn man
at his typewriter, and think of everything he wrote as a form of re-
porting on and recording his experience. I had learned the myths
of the adventurer, the hunter, the man of action, with his rifles
and his trophies, and at my green age I made the easy assumption
that to write fiction was to give forth one's own lived life on the
page: *write what you know* was the operative phrase.

Later that summer I came upon "The Real Thing." Since
James's protagonist was a painter, I assumed from my experience
of reading Hemingway and Thomas Wolfe that James had simply
turned himself into a painter for the benefit of the story. I was
reading him, back then, for two reasons: I thought I could gain

something in my hope to write longer stories by reading this writer of longish stories and I wanted to be able to say I'd read him (remember, I was twenty-one). But I liked the governed, discursive fullness, the multilayered richness of the prose.

The two stories seemed antithetical, and I came to think of them as exemplifying two strains of expression in prose fiction; that is, I had unwittingly formed something like the distinction Philip Rahv had made six years before I was born in his famous essay "Paleface and Redskin." That essay grouped writers into two categories: the "palefaces," writers like Henry James, and Hawthorne, whose concerns were intellectual or philosophical, and the "redskins"—with the chief redskin being Walt Whitman: wild, emotional, instinctive red-blooded types.

I offer again my youth and inexperience as an explanation, if not an excuse. Anyway, for years I carried the sense of the two stories as being very much of that dichotomy: "The Real Thing" was about the ways in which art surpasses the daily reality out of which it springs; the painter has before him the middle-aged, unfortunate couple who are the thing itself, people of their class who have come upon hard times. And as subjects for his painting of people of that very station in life, they're completely inappropriate; he can't use them. I thought "Hills Like White Elephants" was the powerful effusion of a writer less sophisticated than James—a more emotional, instinctive writer of feeling rather than intellect.

It wasn't until I got into my thirties and began trying to write short stories myself that I came to understand how much I had missed about the two stories, how wrong I had been about them. Both stories are about love. Both, in their way, deal with the risks of love, the fragility of it, and the strength of it, too. And the subtleties in both stories are perfectly, artfully realized.

When I was nearly forty, I saw a typescript page from Hemingway's work on "Hills Like White Elephants." There is a passage near the end of this very difficult conversation between a man and a woman, lovers, who are with child. He wants her to abort it ("It's really an awfully simple operation, Jig . . . It's not really an operation at all . . . It's really not anything. It's just to let the air in"), and she wants very badly and clearly to keep it ("Doesn't it mean anything to you? We could get along"). After this exchange, the man goes into the station bar, having carried their bags around to the other side of the station. "He drank an Anis at the bar and looked at the people. They were all waiting reasonably for the train."

The typescript page was a series of paragraphs that showed clearly the writer's work on that moment in the story. As I remember it, there was a series of paragraphs that ran something like this: *There was a place where people told you what they meant and you could trust it. There was a place where things were simple and clear, and the trains ran on time . . .*

Hemingway was working out the scene with the man sitting in the station bar looking at the people. The last two sentences on the page were the ones I quoted above. And in the margin to the right, in pencil, was written "heh, heh." So, there was young Hemingway, cocky and sure of himself and celebrating a brilliancy, which must have struck him exactly as it struck us, reading it. "They were all waiting reasonably for the train." And of course the loudest sound in those two sentences is the word *reasonably.* The use of that word, in its place, helps illuminate the matters showing forth in all the subtle reaches of the story, and one begins to realize the artistry involved.

You are aware of James's artistry from the very outset, and the baroque construction of the sentences enhances your sense of being carried along by the sheer storm of language. But the actual language requires our fullest attention. And curiously enough, the subject matter in both stories is love; in "Hills" we see the kind of malice callously reserved for the opportune moment, and of course that moment has already passed; in "The Real Thing," through the consideration and the quiet dignity of the Monarchs, you see the very thing itself in action: love. It is so powerfully present in those last lines of the story that the artist himself seems to slip out of character just enough to say that he would gladly trade the strut and pride of his own work for what the two out-of-luck Monarchs have shown him by example: The real thing. Love.

I have always admired these two great and very differently constructed stories, which show opposite sides of the same coin.

WRITING PROMPTS
FROM THE CONTRIBUTORS

✦ ✦ ✦ ✦ ✦ ✦ ✦

CHARLES BAXTER

How do people you know honor—or maybe dishonor—the memory of someone they knew who has passed on?

RUSSELL BANKS

Write a scene with two characters in conflict, then a second scene from the point of view of one of the two, and a third from the point of view of the second character. And so on, alternating the point of view, until one of the two characters is able to dominate the other (i.e., resolving the initiating conflict). Do not decide who the story is about until the very end.

RICHARD BAUSCH

Follow out this opening line: "I'd have crawled across a roomful of broken glass to answer that door if I'd known it was (she or he) making that little tapping on the other side."

ANN BEATTIE

It matters what a story sounds like. There's a majestic matter-of-factness to the tone of Craig Nova's "The Prince." We also recognize the tone of a fairy tale. (There are also the tinkling bells of literary allusion: *The Great Gatsby*; *Le Petit Prince*, etc.). Write a story that begins by being merely straightforward and factual and see what other tones can be brought in, like your own orchestra.

228

There has to be a reason for doing it, of course, so your reason will be to create "music" with a distinct and unusual sound—one that only exists to define a character in a particular story that is uniquely yours.

MADISON SMARTT BELL

Be the person you can't stand. Be inside that person. Imagine, understand, and write from the place where that person—whom you hate and despise, maybe for cause, maybe for injuries done by that person to you or yours, or injuries intended. Live, in your imagination, as the person you most can't bear, and write what that experience is. Not to you, but to the person whose whole being, for the purpose of this exercise, you wear.

ROBERT BOSWELL

One way of thinking about "The Death of Ivan Ilych" is that Tolstoy shows his main character in a position of power in one paradigm and then in a position of weakness in a second paradigm. This combination reveals his character and, too, something about the nature of power. And that experience leads to a change in the way the character behaves.

Imagine a character with power in a particular social paradigm who finds himself involved in another social paradigm, as well, but in a position of little power. You may use the term *paradigm* loosely.

For example, you might have a social worker as your main character, and her manner of dealing with clients has become rote, even cynical. She *processes* people. But she has begun a romantic relationship with a man or woman that leads to a holiday weekend with the beloved's family—and they are elite intellectuals and artists. She feels at first intimidated and then the object of condescension. When she returns to her work, she finds herself behaving differently.

Obviously, this isn't meant to be a formula for the invention story but a way to begin an investigation of character.

T. C. BOYLE

Read the newspaper for a couple of days. Find the odd story and dramatize it. The newspaper account lays out the facts, but only the fiction writer can give us the story buried beneath them.

RON CARLSON

Write a first-person excuse for burning down the house. Or sinking the boat. Or both. Let it unspool so that one thing leads to another. Try to include a recipe for lasagna or tuna casserole. Not both.

MICHAEL CUNNINGHAM

Observe a stranger, at random. It can be anyone, as long as you're able to unobtrusively watch that person for long enough to go home and write a list of physical—only physical—details about that person.

It's essentially a laundry list of outward attributes, but it should be as exhaustive as it can be. Race, gender (or outwardly apparent gender) (or gender impossible to determine), height, etc., of course, and dress, and physical features, but also stance, quality of movement, tone of voice (if you're able to hear the person speak), everything you can obtain, without getting arrested. How the person smells, if you can get that close. Everything.

Be prepared to make a list of at least 20 physical observations. This is not literature. It's a very straightforward list. No similes or any other literary devices, please.

And please, no speculation. If the person's hands are rough and calloused, that's it, don't add "like a handyman's hands," or any such. It's only what you're able to observe (and hear, smell, etc.).

Dyed hair only if the dye job is obvious. Occupation probably unknowable unless the person wears a jacket that says "Joe's Plumbing Supplies," but even then, that doesn't necessarily mean the person is a plumber.

I think you'll be surprised by the detailed character who emerges from an exhaustive list of physical qualities. Many of us tend to imagine a person as a sort of emotional and spiritual entity, and then come up with outward traits, which is not a *wrong* way to work. But it can be illuminating to see how much we derive about said emotional and spiritual qualities if we simply start from the outside and move inward.

Then look over your list, and choose three or four—no more than four—of the qualities you'll use to introduce the character. Look for qualities that are simultaneously consistent and, to some degree, contradictory. As in, a woman who's clearly in her late seventies, walking slowly and with difficulty, wearing a Pink Floyd sweatshirt.

It's exactly that combination of the consistent and the inconsistent from which believable characters come fully—and yet economically—to life.

JUNOT DÍAZ

Your narrator has kept a secret for a long time. Have your narrator write a letter to the person who had obliged her to keep the secret, explaining why she won't be silent anymore.

ANTHONY DOERR

While I understand that the strategy of creating visual correlatives for the structures of stories, or trying to, can be reductive, see if you can draw the shape of something you've written.

Is it a spiral, a muddle, a labyrinth, a Freytag-ian pyramid? Does it have three parts, or five, or sixty-two? Where is the slack and where is the tension? Does it explode conventional notions of rising action, or does it execute them perfectly? Sometimes making the effort to illustrate the whole shape of a narrative can help you better understand where it's lumpy, where it's tight, and where it might need a bit more attention.

EMMA DONOGHUE
Write about a room you remember from your childhood, using all your senses.

STUART DYBEK
This story is a wonderful example of how image can be used as the engine to generate and organize a story. Rather than organizing a life along a linear narrative, a life can be composed around a presiding image and told in anecdotes. Choose an image (an object works—shoes, cars, songs . . . and let it guide you through a story that, were it a musical composition, would be called theme and variations.

DAGOBERTO GILB
Imagine a characteristic argument from a home like yours. You take the voice of the one who slams the door on the way out, describing what you see and where you go. (This piece will be used by those learning English and American culture.)

JULIA GLASS
Send a character, unwillingly and alone, into the woods. Rumor of buried treasure or a priceless rare orchid? A runaway child or spouse? A summons from an object of desire to meet at a hidden grotto? Dream up something irresistible. The character may encounter others in the forest but must come out the other side (or never leave) altered in some way.

MARY GORDON
Write a story that includes these three words: mother, murder, hair.

LAUREN GROFF
In *Six Memos for the Next Millennium*, Italo Calvino said, "Around the magic object there forms a kind of force field that is in fact the territory of the story itself. We might say that the magic object is

an outward and visible sign that reveals the connection between people or between events . . .We might even say that in a narrative any object is always magic."

For this exercise, think of a person you love, and then think of an object you most closely associate with that person. Take five minutes and try to describe the object in as much detail and dimension as you can, never once speaking of or referring the person you associate with it, but taking care to try to invest the object with your all of the complexity and nuance that exists in your relationship with that person.

JENNIFER HAIGH

Make a list of this character's regrets, large and small. Then tell the story of each regret: what happened, what the consequences were, what he wishes he had done differently.

JANE HAMILTON

Write an opening paragraph that speaks to an opening paragraph of a story that you love. See what happens . . . .

RON HANSEN

Insert a character into an extreme weather condition and note how the struggle with the elements reveals his or her personality and ways of coping.

PAUL HARDING

It wholly, factually can't be true, but as far as I can recall I've never written or assigned a writing exercise. I personally prefer to jump right into the fray, where everything is at stake, and take it from there. That's not advice, just a description of one approach. That said, one suggestion I make to my students is take a favorite passage from a favorite author and type it out for yourself. Doing so brings you deep into the archeology of language and meaning and the architecture of prose. Big, solid, uninterrupted blocks of writing are best, say, Faulkner, Proust, Woolf, but anything you admire will work.

ANN HOOD
Jamaica Kincaid's short story "Girl" brilliantly illuminates voice, syntax, place, and cultural details using brevity, economy, and point of view. Write a similar monologue in the voice of a mother from your ethnic or cultural background. Or reverse the story and write it in the voice of the daughter explaining to her mother.

PAM HOUSTON
Choose a POV/Tense combo that is not your go to choice (Second person present? First person future plural?), and write a scene that has been haunting you but that you haven't been able to get on paper yet.

GISH JEN
Write a scene in which the fact that two people are related—by blood or by circumstances—just heightens their differences.

CHARLES JOHNSON
Describe a character in a brief passage (one or two pages) using mostly long vowels and soft consonants (o as in "moan," e as in "see"; l, m, n, sh, etc); then describe the same character using mostly short vowels and hard consonants (i as in "sit"; k, t, p, gg, etc.).

The purpose of this exercise, Gardner wrote, is to help the student see that "describing a scene in mostly long vowels and soft consonants achieves an effect far different from that achieved by a passage mostly in short vowels and hard consonants."

PHIL KLAY
Write about a childhood memory that is important to you … from the perspective of a skeptical older sibling.

DENNIS LEHANE

Write a character who needs to leave her house to get something—whether it's a half gallon of milk or the dry cleaning or something she forgot at an ex-lover's place. Your choice of what that thing is and how your character goes about trying to get it will immediately inform who that character is. And the story will be set in motion the moment she walks out that door.

LOIS LOWRY

Write a page of dialogue between two people discussing a difficult situation, and one of the two people is concealing a piece of very painful information from the other.

COLUM MCCANN

Write a story about a writer who can't think of a writing prompt. Begin with the line, "He never liked writing prompts, but he hadn't written a word in four and a half years . . ."

SUE MILLER

Both of the stories I wrote about are structured in a way that suggests a possible prompt. In O'Brien, of course, there are lists, lists for each of his characters, lists that item by item suggest who they are, that accumulate to tell us something of what their personalities and histories are.

In Jones's story, the narrator provides those histories, some glancingly, others at greater lengths—but they too are lists, really. Lists of the possible versions of pain endured by black men in the narrator's world.

Lists about characters can lead to a deeper understanding on the part of the writer struggling to get at exactly who he's writing about, who he's creating. The novelist Carol Shields has, in fact, structured an entire book around lists—lists, and then the stories behind them. I sometimes look to the kinds of lists she works with in *Larry's Party* when I'm desperate. The favorite clothes of a character (what they look like, where they came from, who gave them to our character, when, what happened to our character's relationship to that person, how our character's taste in clothes changed as he/she did, what that says about him/her). What a character believes in. (In Shields, variably, "sterling silver," "a clean basement," "colonic irrigation," "guilt and salvation.") Houses someone has lived in, at what stage in her life, with whom, how she's felt about each of them. Cars he's bought or been given, on what occasion, what happened inside each one, what happened to each one. A character's health history. What crises, when, how they changed her/him. Shields even works with a list of words her main character looks up in the dictionary and why—and along the way, tells you a great deal about a particular period in his life.

I find it useful sometimes to make similar lists. For instance, let's say, a list of one of my character's strong opinions – on the greatest and the worst filmmakers of all time, and what makes them so; on what makes people interesting or boring; on the need for an awareness of evil in the world in order to move reasonably through it; on Michel Basquiat; on food sensitivities; on the Boston Red Sox; on mandated prison sentences; on pedigreed versus rescue dogs.

It's possible that none of the material you generate by making lists will make it into your story, but it will—well, okay, it *may*—help you understand who you're writing about. It may help you see why you've chosen this particular person, and what it is you can do—you want to do—with this choice.

ANTONYA NELSON

Exercise: Write with an eye on unconventional wisdom. As in: take a received truism—driving while drunk is bad; infidelity is immoral; running away is dangerous; hitchhiking is foolish; lying is sinful; killing an animal is cruel; abandoning a baby is actionable—and create a scenario in which the opposite is true. Under what circumstances might the conventional wisdom be the absolute wrong thing? And what character(s) would be involved in the inversion of such?

BICH MINH NGUYEN

Write about a song that now gives you pain. Listen to the song and write about someone listening to this song. When was it first heard? What does it bring back, and why? How many years have passed, and what has happened in that time?

STEWART O'NAN

Write a story about the thing your character wants and needs more than anything—the thing that will redeem him—or her—but they can never have.

JOYCE CAROL OATES

Write a dramatic monologue in which you take on the voice of an individual very different from yourself.

PETER ORNER

The poet Robert Creeley has a beautiful line where he says: Take a left where the old tree used to be. In this spirit, give someone detailed directions to a private place that only you, and perhaps a few select others, know how to get to. It might well be a place that no longer exists, and yet remains vivid in your mind.

ANN PATCHETT

Write a two-page scene about one of your parents in which they reveal so much about themselves through action that it could stand as their obituary. Then do the same exercise again about a character you've made up.

JAYNE ANNE PHILIPS

I prefer writing prompts based on literature because reading literary allies (we all have them) has been so important to me. I was about 22 when I first read "In Dreams Begin Responsibilities," and I wrote a one page fiction called "Wedding Picture" while reeling under its influence. "Wedding Picture" was included in *Black Tickets* (1979), my first book, but was published three years earlier in my first chapbook, *Sweethearts* (1976). The cover of *Sweethearts*, a letterpress publication by Truck Press of Carrboro, North Carolina, featured my parent's 1948 wedding picture—which is why my mother, long divorced, kept her copy in the piano bench. That piano, that house, my mother and father, are gone. Words can be immediate, defying death and time at every reading. I often pair "Wedding Picture" (one tight paragraph that describes an actual wedding picture, revealing a past and implying a future in few phrases) with "In Dreams Begin Responsibilities" as a writing prompt, asking students to bring in a photocopy of their parents' wedding picture, or if there was no wedding, an early image that represents their parents' beginning. One student brought in a photo of the orphanage in which he spent most of his childhood. I ask students to read and re-read "In Dreams Begin Responsibilities" until a first line comes to them. I ask them to imagine an early moment or meeting between their parents, post-commitment, pre-marriage, in a story that 'talks back' to Delmore Schwartz' fever dream, or to write a compressed, one-page response to their parent's wedding picture. Often we make a class anthology of the responses and the photographs, and celebrate that "limited edition" when we part.

KIRSTIN VALDEZ QUADE

Consider an adult outside your family who played an important role in your childhood: a teacher, a girl or boy scout leader, a coach. When did you get a glimpse of who this person was outside their role in your life? What complications do you imagine the adult's life held? From the point of view of the child you once were, write a scene in which your perception of the adult's role and his or her whole person come into conflict.

ANNA QUINDLEN

Write down these words: *Dewey Defeats Truman.* It's the wrongest headline in American newspaper history. From there there are a hundred ways for a narrator to go, a hundred places to have been or to travel towards.

RON RASH

Write a paragraph describing a place, and in the last line have a character enter that place and show some sort of reaction—positive, negative, curious, etc.

RICHARD RUSSO

Write about a time when you were confident in your opinion about something or someone and were dead wrong.

DANI SHAPIRO

Write the story of your parents' courtship. Even if you don't know it. Especially if you don't know it. Invent it. Turn them into characters. It's a story central to your very existence, but you can't ever really know what happened.

MONA SIMPSON

Read Grace Paley's "Mother" and "My Father Addresses Me on the Facts of Old Age" and then write a story about one of your parents, using bits of his or her own voice and idiom. Or: Read Leonard Michaels "Murderers" and write a story which touches extremes of darkness and comedy, carnality, and doom.

JESS WALTER

There is a prompt I sometimes give myself to get right into stories. I think of it as Start Later, or Act Two: Write a story that begins after the first action has already occurred: a one-night stand after the sex; a man returning to his desk after getting fired; two sisters in the Emergency Room after getting in a raucous holiday fight

TOBIAS WOLFF

Write a short piece in the voice of someone close to you—brother, coach, scoutmaster, teacher, friend—scolding you for your faults as they perceive them, and in so doing revealing something important about themselves. You're allowed to be funny.

MEG WOLITZER

Write a conversation between two people (just focus on dialogue) in which they never say explicitly what their relationship to each other is, but which we can understand anyway. And over the course of that same conversation, give us a little mini-story that we can follow. Essentially, the conversation should be a container for a great deal—just as a short story itself must be.

ABOUT THE AUTHORS

✦ ✦ ✦ ✦ ✦ ✦ ✦

COMPILED AND WRITTEN BY
Andre Dubus III

✦ ✦ ✦ ✦ ✦ ✦ ✦

RUSSELL BANKS was born in Newton, Massachusetts, on March 23, 1940, and was raised in Barnstead, New Hampshire. His father, a plumber, was an alcoholic and deserted the family when Russell was twelve years old, leaving him to help support his mother and three siblings. They lived in near poverty and moved from one apartment to another. In 1956, after three months on scholarship at Colgate University, Russell hitchhiked to Miami on an ultimately futile mission to join Fidel Castro in Cuba. He stayed in Miami, married, and in 1960 moved to Boston. Banks eventually found work in a bookstore and began socializing with people who read books and talked about them. Among them was the unpublished writer Leo Giroux Jr., who told Banks he needed to read more and gave him a list of writers Banks never would have known about. In 1962, at the Bread Loaf Writers' Conference, in Middlebury, Vermont, the novelist Nelson Algren read Banks's work and pointed out its strengths and weaknesses. Banks credits him with "validating me as a writer."

Russell Banks has become a major American author. He has published thirteen novels, six short story collections, two collections of poetry, and three books of nonfiction. His work has received numerous honors and awards, including twice being a finalist for the Pulitzer Prize for Fiction and three times a finalist for the PEN/Faulkner Award for Fiction. He is a 1976 Guggenheim Fellow and a member of the International Parliament of Writers and the American Academy of Arts and Letters, and in 1996 was elected a Fellow of the American Academy of Arts and Sciences. In addition to many other national and international prizes, in 2014 Banks was inducted into the New York State Writers Hall of Fame.

In a 1998 interview for the *Paris Review*, when asked about the first writer who clearly influenced him, Banks answered: "Whitman. It was in my late teens, and I suddenly realized that was the kind of writer I wanted to be. Not the kind of writing I wanted to do, but the kind of writer I wanted to be—a man of the people, but at the same time writing high art. It was the first time I had the sense that you could be a writer and it would be a lofty, noble position yet still connected to the reality around you. You didn't have to be Edgar Allan Poe, or Robert Lowell for that matter. Whitman was the first figure of that sort."

RICHARD BAUSCH was raised in a devout Catholic household: "At home," he said, "we said the rosary every night, and if the children were a little restless or distracted, we all sensed something of what it meant, and I believe we learned from that experience that words counted for everything."

Bausch was born on April 18, 1945, in Fort Benning, Georgia, and grew up in the Washington, D.C., area. He flunked out of college twice before joining the Air Force, in 1965. Four years later, after his discharge, Bausch drifted throughout the South and Midwest with the Luv'd Ones, a band for which he played the guitar and wrote songs. He also wrote poetry, got married, and attended Northern Virginia Community College before transferring to George Mason University. It was there that Bausch began to write stories and to take fiction-writing workshops. He graduated in 1974, then entered the famed Iowa Writers' Workshop as a teaching/writing fellow, studying with the novelists John Leggett, John Irving, and Vance Bourjaily.

Richard Bausch received his MFA in 1975 and has gone on to publish eleven novels and nine collections of stories, most recently, *Still Here, Still There* (2021) and *Living in the Weather of the World* (2017). His work has garnered major national awards, such as two National Magazine Awards, a 1984 Guggenheim Fellowship, a Lila Wallace–Reader's Digest Fund Writer's Award, and an American Academy of Arts and Letters Award. A widely acknowledged master of the short story form, Bausch has also received the 2004 PEN/Malamud Award for Excellence in the Short Story and the coveted Rea Award for the Short Story. Since 2002, he has been the sole editor of a prestigious collection, *The Norton Anthology of Short Fiction*.

Bausch describes his writing process: "I usually don't have a very clear idea of where I'm heading when I'm composing a first draft. I make it up as I go along, by feel. There's a certain aboutness that does determine some things, but it's never very clean-cut or cut-and-dried, either. I compose a draft, feeling my way through the territory, as it were, and then, having made all of it up and composed that first draft where, if it's going to be any good, there have been some surprises along the way, characters coming in that I didn't know would do so, things unfolding differently than I first vaguely imagined, et cetera—having done that, I start all over again, only this time I know the thing a little better. I'm educating myself as to what this one is, what it needs to work, on its own terms. Each time I sit down to this one, I'm a little smarter about it. I get smarter all the time with this one thing I'm trying to make perfect, and the smarter I get, the better I'm able to see it, the better I'm able to do to it what needs doing to make it right. For me, the process is discovery upon discovery, followed by increasingly shrewd heightening of what has been discovered, line by line."

When CHARLES BAXTER was fifteen months old, his father died of a heart attack. His mother eventually married a wealthy lawyer who moved them to an affluent suburb of Minneapolis and a forty-acre estate. "There often wasn't much for me to do except go out into these woods or fields or watch the sheep or read," Baxter says, "so I did a good deal of that."

Charles was born in Minneapolis on May 13, 1947. He graduated from Macalester College, in Saint Paul, and earned a PhD at SUNY Buffalo. The celebrated writers Donald Barthelme and John Barth were teaching there then, but Baxter chose not to study with them, or with anyone else for that matter. "I had a very thin skin and felt that it was very important for me, as a writer, not to be criticized," he says. "I think I felt that any criticism I got from these people would be lethal."

For the next fourteen years, Baxter taught at Wayne State University, in Detroit, his students coming from largely blue-collar homes, and spent a full year attempting to write poetry but failing at it. "It was as if the knowledge of how to do it had somehow left me, and I found myself ill-equipped to write," he says. "I was becoming more interested in sequences, characters, and characterizations, the rickrack of detail surrounding people."

He began to write fiction, and after an apprenticeship of many years, he began to publish his work, to high acclaim. He has since published six novels, six short story collections, three essay collections, and one collection of poetry. His work has won numerous awards and grants, among them from the National Endowment for the Arts, the Guggenheim Foundation, and the Lila Wallace–Reader's Digest Foundation. His novel *The Feast of Love* (2000) was a finalist for the 2001 National Book Award for Fiction.

"It's always seemed to me that a lot of my work has to do with somebody watching somebody else who is happy," Baxter says. "For me, stories begin with a kind of displacement; they're not about people who are happy, but about the people who are watching others be happy and trying to figure out how to get there or what it was that those other people did to arrive in that state. It's all over my writing."

Born in Washington, D.C., on September 8, 1947, **ANN BEATTIE** was an only child. She has described her childhood as normal and middle class. Her father was a grants management specialist within the Department of Health, Education, and Welfare. "It wasn't until I got to college," Beatty says, "that I began to take writing seriously—not my own, but literature. I took a course with Frank Turaj, and he taught me how to read. That was the beginning."

In 1969, after she graduated from American University with a BA in English, a personnel agency told Beattie she wouldn't get a job without cutting her nails. She had no intention of doing anything of the sort, so she enrolled in a PhD program. She was soon frustrated with the way literature was taught in graduate courses. "I never had a burning ambition to become a writer," Beattie has said. "I started writing because I was bored with graduate school—in some kind of attempt to care about literature again. . . . So I pushed my desk against the wall and started writing instead of reading criticism about writing all day."

Ann Beattie has become a major American author, publishing eleven short story collections, eight novels, an essay collection, a children's book, the 2011 novella *Walks With Men*, and her most recent novel (2019), *A Wonderful Stroke of Luck*. In 2000, she received the PEN/Malamud Award for Achievement in the Short Story. Four years later she was elected a Fellow of the American Academy of Arts and Sciences and in 2005 she received the prestigious Rea Award for the Short Story.

"It took me years and years to realize a very simple thing," she says, "which is that when you write fiction, you're raising questions, and a lot of people think you're playing a little game with them and that actually you know the answers to the questions. They read your question. They don't know how to answer correctly. And they think that if they could only meet you personally and look into your eyes, you could give them the answers."

MADISON SMARTT BELL was raised outside Nashville, Tennessee, on ninety-six acres of rural farmland. His household was a cultured one, however, and among his parents' friends were the novelist/dramatist Andrew Lytle and Poet Laureate Allen Tate. Bell, an only child, was born on August 1, 1957. Starting at a very young age, he endured chronic asthma and allergies; he began to seek refuge in reading, and rereading. (Bell estimates that he's read Robert Penn Warren's *All the King's Men* more than a hundred times.) He also began to imagine himself as a writer: "when I was not as tall as the table . . . By the time I was seven," he says, "I thought the writer was the most powerful person in the universe—that's what I wanted to be."

It was not until his senior year of high school, however, convalescing after suffering a collapsed lung, that he wrote his first story. In 1975 he entered Princeton University, because it had an undergraduate creative writing program, which was rare in the 1970s. "But you had to show them a body of work to get in," Bell says. "I didn't understand that the requirement was a paper tiger, so I left for a semester, moved back to Nashville, got a job, and wrote stories at night." The following semester, he returned with a book-length portfolio, "which was overkill," he says, "but I ended up in George Garrett's workshop and became one of the hundreds of people whose career he has started and fostered."

After graduating from Princeton, Bell moved to New York City. To support himself and his writing, he found work as a security guard, a production assistant, and a sound engineer for Radiotelevisione italiana. And even though he was competent at these jobs, he enrolled in Hollins College's master's program, where he won the Andrew James Purdy fiction award for his first novel, *The Washington Square Ensemble* (Viking, 1983). The inspiration for it, he says, came from the voices speaking in his head.

Bell has now published fifteen novels, two novellas, six books of nonfiction, and three collections of short stories. His work has earned him many honors, such as fellowships from the Guggenheim Foundation and the National Endowment for the Arts, and the 1989 Lillian Smith Award. In 1995 he was a Fiction finalist for the National Book Award and the 1996 PEN/Faulkner Award for his novel *All Souls' Rising*. He won the 1996 Anisfield-Wolf Book Award for the best book of the year dealing with matters of race and in that same year was named by *Granta* magazine one of the "Top American Novelists Under Forty." In 2008 he received the coveted Strauss Living Award from the American Academy of Arts and Letters.

"I try to spend the first three hours of the morning, Monday through Friday, writing on whatever project I have in hand," Bell says. "If it's fiction, I can often profit from a lucid dream state to fix the upcoming scene in my imagination before I get out of bed. There are a couple of religious observations I make first thing in the morning and ideally I move through those directly to composition." And, he says, "I figured out in the 1980s that the flow state is essentially a light hypnotic trance and that writers and artists intuitively figure out their own auto-induction methods of getting there. For me, it's easy. I'm a congenital daydreamer. My problem is more like being fully conscious of the 'real world' when I need to be."

ROBERT BOSWELL was born on December 8, 1953, the second of four children, in Sikeston, Missouri, but his early childhood was spent on a tobacco farm in Wickliffe, Kentucky, near the junction of the Mississippi and Ohio Rivers. This same place was of dramatic significance in Mark Twain's *The Adventures of Huckleberry Finn*, and Boswell says this novel changed his life and forever made him want to become a writer.

When Robert was eleven, his family moved to Yuma, Arizona, where his mother worked as a real estate agent and his father taught a high school class in government. During the 1960s, Robert was preoccupied with the looming draft and the Vietnam War and began to use drugs recreationally, a habit that lasted throughout the five and half years it took him to earn his bachelor's degree in psychology and English at the University of Arizona. "I finally made a conscious decision to quit doing drugs," he says. "I thought I'd never get through college otherwise, and I knew I wanted to accomplish something. But it took me years, really, to quit." He went on to acquire a master's in rehabilitation counseling and in 1979 found work as a job counselor in San Diego.

This path, however, didn't feel right. "For as long as I could remember," Boswell says, "I'd wanted to be a writer, but I'd been raised in a hardworking family (my parents grew up poor on Kentucky farms during the Great Depression) and the wish to be a writer simply hadn't seemed realistic to any of us. Reading John Cheever on the beach one weekend, I decided to give up being realistic and to study writing seriously. I decided I'd rather fail at writing than succeed at anything else. And so I turned my back on counseling."

Boswell has gone on to publish seven novels, three story collections, and two books of nonfiction. He has also had two plays produced. His work has received numerous awards: the 1985 Iowa School of Letters Award for Fiction, the PEN West Award for Fiction, and the John Gassner Prize for Playwriting, for example; and he has been granted two National Endowment for the Arts Fellowships, a 1989 Guggenheim Fellowship, and a Lila Wallace/Woodrow Wilson Fellowship.

As a young writer, Boswell says, "I wrote one bad thing after another, but after that my work got better. I think it had to do with finally understanding something writers were often saying: when you're writing fiction, what you pursue is truth. I managed to get ruthless, and hack away at the things that were dishonest in my stories. It's an attitude, a work ethic that has held true to this day. To write good fiction, typically I have to push it beyond any point I could have anticipated, and then be willing to give up on the story as *my* story and work back into it on its own terms . . . I have to write about thirty drafts of a book, or a story, or a letter, to get something I'm happy with."

Born on December 2, 1948, T. C. BOYLE grew up the son of alcoholic parents in Peekskill, New York. His father was a bus driver and his mother was a secretary; at fifteen Thomas began to rebel. He rejected Catholicism and started drinking and taking drugs and driving fast. He also became interested in the writing of J. D. Salinger, Aldous Huxley, and Jack Kerouac. At seventeen, he packed his saxophone and took off for SUNY Potsdam, where he intended to begin his life as a musician. He failed the audition, so he majored in history and English, the only subjects he did well in during high school. Boyle graduated in 1968, but he had acquired a weekend heroin habit that killed one of his friends and almost killed him. It was then that Boyle turned to writing: "Art bailed me out," he says. "It sounds corny but there's a power in it that I would never give up. There's a light that fills you when you're writing; there's a magic. I don't know what it is. It's a miracle and it's a rush and immediately on finishing you want to do it again. It's so utterly thrilling to me—it's all I want to do."

Boyle earned an MFA from the Iowa Writers' Workshop in 1974, then his doctorate in British literature from the University of Iowa in 1977. He has published twenty-nine books of fiction, most recently his 2021 novel, *Talk to Me*, and his work has earned many honors and awards, among them the 1988 PEN/Faulkner Award, a Guggenheim Fellowship, the 2014 Rea Award for the Short Story, and five O. Henry Awards. His novel *Drop City* was a 2003 National Book Award finalist for Fiction, and in 2009 Boyle was inducted into the American Academy of Arts and Letters.

"I've been teaching since I was twenty-one," Boyle says, "and I hope to keep on teaching as long as I can evade the zombies blocking the fast lane on the long, tortuous road to L.A. If I didn't teach—that is, get out of the house one day a week in order to discuss literature at the deepest level with young (and often not so young) geniuses whose fire burns every bit as brightly as mine, I would most likely be writing this from the subbasement of the old mental hospital in Camarillo, if my keepers had been so kind as to loosen the chains, that is."

RON CARLSON grew up in Salt Lake City. When he was in the fifth grade, he saw a classmate's notebook filled with hand-drawn pictures and writing and was astounded. "Marvin Wharton was writing a book," he says, "with illustrations and everything! It took the top of my head off. I remember it vividly. I thought to myself, 'That's right, you can write stories.' I guess I'm writing to catch up to Marvin, wherever he is."

But it wasn't until Ron was a teenager that he began to write regularly and more seriously. "I saw that it would be my way," he says. "It would be something I could go off and do without collaborating, and then bring it back. At first it was a curiosity and my teachers were befuddled by it, but along the way there were those who recognized something in my work and encouraged me."

Carlson was born in Logan, Utah, on September 15, 1947. His father was a welder and an engineer and his mother was a homemaker, "a farm girl from South Dakota," he says, who was also a writer. "My mother was a word person, a real quipster. She was famous in the 1950s for being a contestant in 'Utah: 25 words or less.' In 1959 she won $15,000 from Remington-Rand for writing about a shaver."

Carlson graduated from the University of Utah in 1970 with a BA in English. He worked for a time as an art-supply salesman, then entered the university's graduate program in English for his master's degree. To support himself and his writing, he joined the English faculty at a private boarding school in Connecticut, where he also coached hockey. In 1981, he moved back to Salt Lake City and his wife, Georgia Elaine Craig, became the primary breadwinner. Carlson wrote daily and found work modeling, parking cars, and selling Christmas trees. In 1975 he sent a handwritten letter and most of the manuscript of his first novel, *Betrayed by F. Scott Fitzgerald*, to the legendary W. W. Norton editor Carol Houck Smith. Carlson had found her name in *Literary Market Place* and chose her," he says, "because she wasn't a vice president. I thought, 'Well, she's an editor, so she won't be too busy.'" On returning from vacation, Carlson found a card from Smith that had been in his mailbox for two weeks. "Please call me," it said. "I'd like to make you an offer."

Ron Carlson has published six novels, five collections of short stories, one collection of poems, and one work of nonfiction, his critically acclaimed 2007 book on writing, *Ron Carlson Writes a Story*. His work has won numerous honors, such as the O. Henry Prize, inclusion in the *Pushcart Prize* and *Best American Short Stories* anthologies, an award from the National Society of Arts and Letters, a Fellowship in Fiction from the National Endowment for the Arts, and the 1993 Ploughshares Cohen Prize.

"What we're looking for at all times is honesty presented in language so that we can see the world again," Carlson says. "Can you surprise me again with something I already know? It's more important to be real than nice or bad." In discussing the habit of writing, Carlson says: "On the best days, I can get ninety minutes or seven hundred words. You use whatever ritual you can find. You push. . . . A lot of days I'd stop in the middle of a word. I'd know how to pick up because I knew how to spell. But during my busiest times at school, I have to keep myself alive with blips, maybe only two days a week. Ultimately, the goal is to be working more days of the week than not."

LAN SAMANTHA CHANG is the daughter of Chinese parents, both of whom endured the Japanese occupation of China and ultimately emigrated to the United States. Her father, a chemical engineer, found work in Appleton, Wisconsin, where Lan Samantha was born, on January 18, 1965. Her parents told her and her three sisters very little about what they suffered in China during World War II and its aftermath, and this only made Lan Samantha Chang more curious about her family history. "I think I became a writer because there was so much silence in the house on such basic issues that I was required not only to investigate to find out what happened, but then repeat to it myself and other people in order to understand the story," she says.

She was drawn to literature: "I've wanted to be a writer since I was four years old, which is when I understood that there could be realities that did not require me to be present in the world," Lan Samantha says. "Stories held a great solace and release for me, and I wished to make myself feel things, and to make others feel them as well."

She went to Yale University and told her parents she was a prelaw major, even though at the time there was no such thing at Yale. Instead, she followed her curiosity about her parents' heritage, and her own, and ended up graduating with a degree in East Asian studies. She got into law school, deferred entering, then borrowed money from her parents so she could take a year off. "My parents were terrified," she says. "They had come to this country so I could get an education and be well established and they had sacrificed an enormous amount. It's the old story. They wanted me to be a professional, so they were worried about my taking a year off. I went to work in New York. I was an editorial assistant at Vintage Books for two years, and at the end of the first year realized I had to think of something to do next, because my parents were so worried and because I knew I was rudderless."

"Even though I wanted to be a writer," she says, "I didn't know exactly how a person went about doing this. When I was at Vintage, I discovered in the library a copy of John Gardner's *The Art of Fiction* and read it over and over and over. So I began to educate myself. It's a very technical book. I think it's a wonderful book. He's kind of an opinionated coot. But I liked that. I like the authority."

Chang went on to study government at Harvard, then was accepted into the Iowa Writers' Workshop, and there she earned her MFA in creative writing. She now directs the University of Iowa Writers' Workshop, the first woman and the first Asian American to hold that position.

She has published four critically acclaimed books: the story collection *Hunger: A Novella and Stories*, and the novels *Inheritance, All Is Forgotten, Nothing Is Lost,* and 2022's *The Family Chao*.

Her work has earned a number of honors, including the California Book Award Silver Medal and the *Southern Review* Prize for her 1998 collection, *Hunger*, as well as Wallace Stegner and Truman Capote Fellowships at Stanford University, a literature grant from the National Endowment for the Arts, a PEN/ Open Book Award, a 2008 Guggenheim Fellowship, and a 2015 Fellowship at the American Library in Paris.

"Not all the time, but occasionally when I'm working on something, I get the sense that my characters are telling the truth. It's not necessarily the truth universally acknowledged; it's more of the truth to the circumstances that they're in, that which is usually not said. I suppose that's what I like about my writing, that it's an attempt to see human circumstances in an honest way, without bullshitting or putting on rose-colored glasses."

MICHAEL CUNNINGHAM describes his early years as "an embarrassingly ordinary childhood." He was born on November 6, 1952, in Cincinnati, but his family moved to Pasadena when he was ten. His mother was a homemaker and his father worked in advertising, "and I, of course, couldn't wait to get the hell out of there and live in a bigger and more dangerous and more interesting world," he says. "I couldn't wait. I was counting the days."

Cunningham was drawn to painting, but his early canvases in a local gallery were a series of religious tableaux, work he somehow believed painters were supposed to do—that is, he says, "bleeding Christs, ascensions into heaven." Soon enough, he realized he wasn't good enough to continue, but as a teenager he also enjoyed reading writers such as Virginia Woolf and T. S. Elliot. In 1976, he graduated from Stanford University with a degree in English, and was then accepted into the Iowa Writers' Workshop, where he worked closely with the novelist Hilma Wolitzer. In 1980, after he earned his MFA, Cunningham found work writing annual reports and press releases for the Carnegie Corporation. He also became more politically active and demonstrated for increased government funding for AIDS research. He even chained himself to one of the gates of the White House and was arrested for interrupting a speech by President George H. W. Bush.

But all along, Michael Cunningham was writing daily, and he has published seven novels, a collection of short stories, and a book of nonfiction, his 2002 *Land's End: A Walk in Provincetown*. Cunningham has received many awards, among them the 1995 Whiting Award; the 1999 Pulitzer Prize and PEN/Faulkner Award for his 1998 novel, *The Hours*; the 1999 Gay, Lesbian, Bisexual, and Transgender Book Award; and the 2011 Fernanda Pivano Award for American Literature.

"Place is enormously important to me," says Cunningham. "I think one of the things a novelist is doing is chronicling a place and a time, that we're in a certain sense a part of the historical record. I've been setting my novels in New York and describing New York in a fair amount of detail because I lived in New York. . . . I think it matters where one lives and the nature of the streets one walks down and the apartment in which you live. That's just very much part of the detail. It's a craft thing because what you're trying to do is seduce the reader into entering a parallel world. You're saying, 'Would you be interested in stepping through this interdimensional warp and inhabiting an inventive world?'"

When he teaches writing classes, Cunningham tells his students not to worry about what people they love will think of their work: "A certain slightly cruel disregard for the feelings of living people is simply part of the package," he says. "I think a writer, if he's any good, is not an entirely benign entity in the world."

JUNOT DÍAZ said this about his early years: "I grew up in this barrio where there's a ton of kids, where all we did was play all damn day. My experience in the Dominican Republic in those years was living in this wonderland."

He was the third child of five, born in Santo Domingo on December 31, 1968. His father worked in the United States and Junot lived with his grandparents and his mother until he was six years old, when the family moved to Parlin, New Jersey. They lived less than a mile from what Díaz calls "one of the largest landfills in New Jersey," but he was a passionate reader and would regularly walk four miles to borrow books from his library. "I wasn't a huge fan of the American experience for my first few years," he says. "It wasn't until I discovered books that I began to feel any fondness toward this adventure I was on, this adventure called immigration."

Junot graduated from Cedar Ridge High School in 1987. To earn his way through Rutgers University, he washed dishes, pumped gas, delivered pool tables, and worked at Raritan River Steel. "I can safely say I've seen the U.S. from the bottom up," he says.

"I may be a success story as an individual," he says, "but if you adjust the knob and just take it back one setting to the family unit, I would say my family tells a much more complicated story. It tells the story of two kids in prison. It tells the story of enormous poverty, of tremendous difficulty."

At Rutgers, Junot read the works of Alice Walker, Toni Morrison, Gloria Naylor, and Gloria Anzaldúa. "I came of age surrounded in college by these brilliant women of color and their radical epistemologies," he says. By his junior year, he began to spend at least two hours every night writing. "I was able to do that for a couple of years," he says. "It proved to me that there was more to this dream than just kind of a desire. There was something beneath it."

In 1995, Díaz earned an MFA in creative writing from Cornell University. "Too white," he says, "as in Cornell had almost no POC—no people of color—in it. Too white, as in the MFA had no faculty of color in the fiction program—like none—and neither the faculty nor the administration saw that lack of color as a big problem. (At least the students are diverse, they told us.)"

Díaz is the author of two collections of short stories and his widely acclaimed 2007 novel, *The Brief Wondrous Life of Oscar Wao*, winner of numerous major awards, including the 2007 Center for Fiction First Novel Prize, the National Book Critics Circle Award, and the 2008 Dayton Literary Peace Prize, the Anisfield-Wolf Book Award, and the Pulitzer Prize for Fiction; his 2012 short story collection, *This Is How You Lose Her*, was a Fiction Finalist for the National Book Award. His most recent work is the 2018 children's picture book *Islandborn*. Díaz has also been honored with a 2002 PEN/Malamud Award for Excellence in the Short Story, a Guggenheim Fellowship, and a MacArthur "Genius" Fellowship. In 2017 he was inducted into the American Academy of Arts and Letters.

"As artists" says Díaz, "we're not here to comfort anyone. If you want to have your back rubbed, you don't come to the arts for that. We're as artists here to point out the things we don't like to point out. We're the anti-politicians. We're actually trying to make the country better."

ANTHONY DOERR grew up in a house full of books and cites his earliest influence as C. S. Lewis:. "I remember my mother reading *The Chronicles of Narnia* to me and my brothers; I was probably eight. And I remember asking her: 'How did they make this book? How did they invent Narnia?' And she'd always say, 'It was just one person who wrote these books. And he's dead now.' Dead! What? Dead people could tell stories that still held power over the living? I had always had a sense that books were like oranges on a tree, that they pre-existed in the world, and humans came along and plucked them. But now my mother was saying people *made* them. One person, one book at a time. That was a revelation: One weird old guy could use language, the cheapest of materials, and conjure whole worlds with it? Then he could die and those worlds could still hold sway?"

Anthony Doerr was born in Cleveland on October 27, 1973, and was raised outside the city. isHis mother was an ecology teacher and his father ran a small printing business. Anthony graduated from the nearby University School in 1991, then went Bowdoin College, where he majored in history. "But I always had my eye on the English Department," he says. "I'd write long, lousy stories in notebooks about avalanches and keg parties and dogs that walked across Alaska and show them to nobody. It felt precocious and impertinent to say to my parents, 'I want to be a writer.' It was hard to even say that to myself. But that's what I wanted to do."

After earning an MFA in creative writing from Bowling Green State University, Doerr spent a few years drifting in and around Telluride, Colorado. He wrote his first published story then and sold it to *The Atlantic* in 2001. "I was paid maybe three thousand dollars for it," he says, "and the hourly wage on it was very small." It brought his work attention, though, and soon enough he had sold his first collection of short stories, to Scribner.

Doerr has published two collections of short stories, three novels, and a memoir. A Guggenheim Fellow, his work has received many accolades, such as the National Magazine Award for Fiction, three Pushcart Prizes, the Story Prize, and four O. Henry Prizes. His 2014 novel, *All the Light We Cannot See*, was a 2015 finalist for the National Book Award and the winner of the 2015 Pulitzer Prize for Fiction.

"I'm fumbling with ideas here that I can't fully articulate," Doerr says, "but that, I think, is the real responsibility for a literary writer: to strive toward complexity, toward questions, and away from certainty, away from stereotype."

"Maybe I'm a bit more comfortable with the fact that I never really know what I'm doing. I think it scared me at the beginning—I assumed all the 'real' writers out there knew exactly what they were setting out to write each time they sat down. I've been around long enough now," he says, "to know that most writers are like me, fumbling down hallways in the dark."

EMMA DONOGHUE's mother was a teacher and her father was the academic and literary critic Denis Donoghue. She was the youngest of eight children, born on October 24, 1969, in Dublin. "It was a house literally lined with books," she says, "so I spent most of my childhood mooching around, reading whatever I wanted . . . and this gave me the sense that this was something one could do: one could grow up and publish books with one's name on the spine."

From early childhood, Emma wrote poetry and at age twelve began to consume fairy tales. At nineteen she wrote her first novel "over and over," she says, the coming-of-age story of seventeen-year-old Maria Murphy and her sexual awakening as a university student in Dublin. *Publishers Weekly* called *Stir Fry* (1994) a "wry and tender debut."

"Pretty much everyone I knew was white, had two Irish parents, and was a practicing Catholic," she says. "I had no objection to all this until, at about fourteen, I realized I was a lesbian, and therefore, in my society's terms, a freak. This theme—not just homosexuality but also the clash between individual and community, norm and 'other'—has marked many of my published works."

Donoghue now lives in Canada and has published seventeen books, five of them short story collections, as well as the international bestselling 2010 novel *Room*, which was made into an award-winning film. She also writes literary history and drama for radio, stage, and screen, and her work has earned a number of awards, such as the 2016 AWB Vincent American Ireland Funds Literary Award and the 2011 National Lesbian and Gay Federation (Ireland) Person of the Year Award. *Room* was a finalist for the Man Booker Prize.

STUART DYBEK recalls growing up in the southwest side of Chicago as joyful: "playing baseball, hopping freights, and trespassing through factory grounds." His was a neighborhood of Hispanics, Czechs, and Poles. Dybek joined a gang and got into some minor trouble here and there, but says he saw little oppression or violence. He considers that period—the 1950s and '60s—as "a benevolent time." His father, however, a foreman for the International Harvester plant (Dybek's mother was a truck dispatcher), called Stuart "the Weed," a reference to his son's often untamed behavior.

Born in Chicago on April 10, 1942, Stuart was the oldest of three children, all of whom attended a Catholic school. He was a poor student there, as he would be in college—his classes just didn't interest him. His interest lay in music, especially the saxophone.

"I played saxophone for seven or eight years," he says, "and was in a group somewhat like the group you read about in 'Blight'—The No-Names. And I think the reason I began writing was that I had reached a point with music where my chops just weren't up to what I wanted. I just couldn't express the ideas I wanted to express technically. I just didn't feel I had enough talent to play the way I wanted to play, so at the same time I began writing. Even though the writing I was doing wasn't really very good, somehow it wasn't as frustrating. It seemed to offer more possibility for me than the music did. Possibly one aspect was that I was so in awe of music, I was so reverential toward music, that it might have been getting in the way a little bit."

"I didn't develop that kind of reverence for writing until later. Music was a real avenue out of the area I grew up in. It was an alternative to the prejudices you were surrounded by, and it was a legitimate way of thinking and feeling that wasn't necessarily academic. So if school had been problematic for you in some way, music was somehow an alternative that wasn't just being stupid. I mean, one alternative to school is to be rebellious by being dumb, whereas music is an alternative that doesn't insist on ignorance."

Creative writing didn't become his passion until one day when he was writing about Africa. He had been trying to describe how very tall the trees were, and this led him to the phrase "the tree scraped skies." He was so taken by it that he hurried to read it to his mother, who happened to be sick with a stomach flu; she threw up as he read it to her.

In 1964, Stuart graduated from Loyola University Chicago with a BA in English. He became active in the antiwar and civil rights movements, and for two years he was a caseworker for the Cook County Department of Public Aid. He also worked in advertising because he once read that the novelist William Styron did the same as a young writer. After receiving a master's degree in literature from Loyola, Dybek entered the Iowa Writers' Workshop, where he earned his MFA. He went on to teach for more than thirty years at Western Michigan University, and is now the Distinguished Writer in Residence at Northwestern University.

Stuart Dybek has published one novel, five collections of short stories, and two poetry collections. His work has won major national awards, such as the Lannan Prize, the PEN/Malamud Award for Excellence in the Short Story, an Arts and Letters Award from the American Academy of Arts and Letters, a Whiting Writers' Award, four O. Henry Awards, and the Rea Short Story Award, as well as fellowships from the Guggenheim Foundation and the National Endowment for the Arts. In 2007, Dybek received a MacArthur "Genius" Fellowship.

"It's the essential question, the ultimate test: one way you can always sort out the best stuff—yours or anybody else's—is by how alive it feels," Dybek says. "What often goes along with that feeling is that the story gets smarter than the writer, exceeds his initial conception, or starts making moves that the writer doesn't think of fast enough to make on his own. When stories start misbehaving like that, you suddenly reach the point where there's this overwhelming urge to digress from a nice, tidy narrative line and allow what might have been an easily written story to become far more chancy and complicated."

DAGOBERTO GILB's mother came across the border from Mexico illegally and his father, an industrial laundry worker, was born in Kentucky. Dagoberto was born in Los Angeles in 1950. His parents divorced when he was a small boy and he was raised by his mother. When she was young, she found work as a model before becoming a dental assistant. "I was always on my own," says Gilb. "I was the adult." She married an electrician when Gilb was a teenager. "She had to marry him," says Gilb. "She was essentially escaping. And I didn't like him, so I hit the road."

Dagoberto worked in factories, hung out with other troubled kids, and only occasionally returned home to sleep. After high school, he worked full time as a department store stock boy and a paper cutter, took courses at several area community colleges, and ultimately transferred to the University of California at Santa Barbara, where he double majored in philosophy and religious studies. "I was not a high school ace," he says, "but when I got to college, I loved it. It changed my life. I didn't know anything and every class I took was totally exciting to me. Books were like girls. I just went nuts over books."

He graduated in 1974 and was promptly admitted to the UCSB's master's program in religious studies. He earned his advanced degree in 1976 and began to go out on white-collar job interviews. No one hired him. "I remember applying to be a copy editor at an El Paso newspaper," he says. "I went in to see the editor, talking like I do, 'Yak, yak, yak.' And I sense he's interested in hiring me, thinks that I could be a good reporter. So we get into an elevator and he introduces me to this guy, but it's so I can deliver newspapers! I had credentials, man, they would still look at me and say, I'm not hiring you."

Gilb, a new father by then, ended up working in construction and eventually joined the United Brotherhood of Carpenters and Joiners in Los Angeles. But now he had dreams of becoming a novelist, and he stole time for his writing whenever he could. He moved to El Paso, where he met Raymond Carver, who was there to teach a course at the University of Texas. Gilb heard that Carver wrote exclusively about blue-collar people, but when he read some of Carver's work, he says, he thought, "'This isn't working class. They want working class, I'll give them working class.'" So he wrote his first short story, a tale of drifters and drug addicts called "Down in a West Texas Town." Carver read it, then told Gilb he would try to get him into Iowa's graduate writing program. But Gilb had never heard of it: "I was like, 'Why would I want to go to school?'" he says. "I was married. I had kids. I worked. I had a life. And I was writing. I didn't understand the meaning of what he was saying." Gilb was, however, encouraged, and he kept writing.

He went on to publish seven books of fiction, and his work has been honored with major awards, among them a 1992 National Endowment for the Arts Fellowship, a 1993 Whiting Award, the 1994 PEN/Hemingway Award, a 1994 Fiction finalist for the PEN/Faulkner Award, a 1995 Guggenheim Foundation Fellowship, and a 2003 Fiction finalist for the National Book Critics Circle Award. In 2008, his work earned the Pen Southwest Book Award.

"What truly provokes art is awe," Gilb says, "and that can be experienced as strongly in outrage and pain as in beauty. Some is unjust and caused by uncaring rulers; some is the random chance of birth and life's circumstance; often the two are one. Art unmasks, reveals the hidden, finds language or image and sound for the ignored, dismissed, the blinded, the muted. My art is fiction, and though I make things up, it—like all storytelling (excusing this Superman grandiosity!)—is for the sake of truth. Art and social justice often share the same demand and subject."

JULIA GLASS was born in Boston on March 23, 1956, and as a young girl growing up in Lincoln, Massachusetts, she loved to read and to draw. In the fifth grade, Julia started to volunteer at the local library, which she did all through college. Whereas her younger sister, Carolyn, loved animals and being outdoors, Julia preferred being indoors with her books and art supplies. "I was ridiculed in public school for being smart," she says, "a teacher's pet. I thought there must be some place I could go."

Julia talked her parents into letting her attend day school at Concord Academy, a private high school known for its strong art department. She thrived there, and went on to Yale, where she majored in art and was named Scholar of the House in Studio Art. Yale also granted her a travel fellowship to spend a year in Paris, and when she returned, she found work at Harvard University's Fogg Art Museum. In 1980, she moved to New York City. "I got a huge place in Carroll Gardens," she says, "and I eventually got a full-time copy-editing job at *Cosmopolitan*." She stayed with the magazine for two years: "The work didn't take much energy," she says. "I was painting and having this pleasantly austere life." She began to exhibit her work, but it became clear to her that she wouldn't be able to earn her living as an artist. She didn't start writing seriously until she was almost thirty, but she made more room for her freelance writing and the writing of short stories.

In 1992, Glass was diagnosed with breast cancer and just two weeks later she lost her sister to suicide. "I learned the meaning of *never*," she says. "I'd never see her again. If I had children, she'd never know them. . . . I came to feel that what I wanted to write, in essence, was a book about living beyond incurable heartbreak and irreparable loss."

That book was *Three Junes*. It was published in 2002 and won that year's National Book Award for Fiction. She has written seven more books, most recently her 2022 novel, *Vigil Harbor*. In addition to winning the National Book

Award, she has been a recipient of fellowships from the New York Foundation for the Arts, the Radcliffe Institute for Advanced Study, and the National Endowment for the Arts. Her work received the 1999 Tobias Wolff Award, three Nelson Algren Fiction Awards, and the 2009 Binghamton University John Gardner Fiction Book Award.

"What compels me is the resilience of human beings, period. As I've said before, all the most lasting fiction is about one thing: how we go on. Some writers tackle this in the context of war or poverty or tyranny; I tackle it through the intimate world of the family. We're all born into one," she says, "and most of us do our damnedest to form one. And, again, a certain innate voyeurism makes me want to 'know everything' about the messiness of making families work—or the heartbreak and the struggle when they don't."

It was a near miracle that **MARY GORDON** was born at all—her mother was in her early forties and had had polio, which caused limited use of her lower body. Nonetheless, Mary was born on December 8, 1949, in Far Rockaway, New York, and raised an only child in the blue-collar town of Valley Stream, on Long Island. Her mother, Anna Gagliano Gordon, was a legal secretary and the primary breadwinner. Mary was very close to her father, David, a Jewish convert to Catholicism who taught her to read before she was four years old, French and Latin by the age of six, and to hate the domestic role of women. Her father died of a heart attack when she was eight years old; Mary was taken three blocks away to her grandmother's home and not allowed to go back to their apartment. Her new home was a hostile one: her mother's family, deeply conservative Catholics, didn't approve of her Jewish heritage or her voracious reading.

Mary went to Mary Louis Academy, a Catholic high school, and excelled academically. When she applied to the secular Barnard College, however, her family objected and administrators at her high school balked at sending Mary's transcripts to Barnard. Mary ran away from home and lived in a friend's basement for three days, until she was able to turn things in her favor.

At Barnard she paid her tuition by working as a secretary and babysitting the children of her mentor in the English Department, Professor Janice Thaddeus. This was the 1960s, and Gordon became active in the feminist movement as well as the nationwide protests against the Vietnam War. She was reading the work of Virginia Woolf: "I was a poet then," she says, "and prose seemed to me a rather baggy and encumbered thing . . . I remember the phrase in *Mrs. Dalloway* that did it to me: 'trophies of nuts and roses.' There was a click like the snap of a broken bone, for something in me broke, broke apart. It was six years before I had the courage to try fiction."

Gordon graduated from Barnard in 1971 and received her master's degree from Syracuse University two years later. It was not until she began work on her MFA at Syracuse that Gordon began to write prose seriously. She has since published nine novels, four collections of short fiction, three memoirs, a collection of essays, a biography of Joan of Arc, and a book on religion, her 2009 *Reading Jesus*. Her work has been widely acclaimed and received national honors, such as a 1978 finalist for the National Book Critics Circle Award, the Janet Heidinger Kafka Prize for Best Novel Written by an American Woman, the

Literary Lion of the New York Public Library Award, a Lila Acheson Wallace–
Reader's Digest Writer's Award, an O. Henry Award, a Guggenheim Fellowship,
and the Edith Wharton Citation of Merit for Fiction. In 2007, she was awarded
the Story Prize for her collection *The Stories of Mary Gordon* and was also inducted into the American Academy of Arts and Letters. In 2010 she was inducted
into the New York Writers Hall of Fame.

"What's terribly important to me," she says, "deeply important—and this
is where I feel a sense of vocation—is to write about issues that are central
to women's lives, to write about them beautifully and in high style . . . [I]n all
honesty, I have to call myself a 'woman writer.' I won't call myself 'a Catholic
writer.' That's too limiting. I don't feel that was how I was formed. But I do
think I was formed as a writer by my femaleness."

When **LAUREN GROFF** was five or six years old, she discovered a copy of fairy
tales on her parents' bookshelf. "I read and loved the most savage and bloody
of the *Grimms' Fairy Tales*," she says. "Stories are the most powerful weapons we
have . . . fairy tales act as tiny inoculations against anxiety or terror: we are ex-
posed to the worst scenarios (parental death, abandonment, starvation, impris-
onment, and so on), and through the pluck and intelligence of the protagonist,
we're carried into a better life than before."

Groff describes herself as "pathologically shy as a kid." "Books," she says,
"were far more vivid to me than people." She went to the library almost every
day. "I really read everything, and I didn't understand most of it," she says.
"You read Jane Austen when you're eight, and you're not going to get the sort of
social niceties, but you're bathed in the precise language and the sensibility, and
that's what matters. I guess it's the tone that matters at that point."

Groff, born in Cooperstown, New York on July 23, 1978, was a competitive
swimmer, rowed at Amherst College, and graduated in 2001 with a degree in English and French. She moved to Philadelphia, found work as a bartender, and
wrote daily. "I was a writer long before I wrote anything interesting," she says.
"I went into college thinking I was a poet, but I'm a terrible poet! And yet I love
it. . . . I'm a terrible singer, and yet I love to sing. . . . I'm a really bad dancer, but
I love to dance. There are some things we do with glee because we're liberated
by being absolutely terrible at them. That said, I was quickly disabused of the
idea that I was a poet, and I started writing fiction and I spent three years out of
college trying to find a way to live and write at the same time."

Groff earned an MFA in creative writing from the University of Wiscon-
sin-Madison and has published six acclaimed books: two collections of short
stories and four novels, most recently 2021's *Matrix*. A three-time Fiction finalist for the National Book Award, Groff's work has also been a finalist for the
National Book Critics Circle Award, the Orange Award for New Writers, the
Southern Book Prize, the Kirkus Award (twice), and the Los Angeles Times
Book Prize. Groff also won an O. Henry Award and the Pushcart Prize, and
in 2017 she was named by *Granta Magazine* one of the "Best Young American
Novelists" of her generation.

"I think writing is intensely physical," she says. "Almost every good writer I
know is committed to being healthy. I love the discipline of training; at a certain

point, youthful zest gets spent and what you have left is the daily discipline of sitting down with it, no matter what. And there's nothing that gets me unstuck more than a very long run without music in the heat, because I stop thinking and my subconscious is left to wander its own way. If I sit down for three hours and can't do much more than read, I go for a run or walk or swim, and by the time I get back, I have some small glimmer of truth to use."

JENNIFER HAIGH was born in Barnesboro, Pennsylvania, a coal-mining town eighty-five miles northeast of Pittsburgh. The daughter of a high school English teacher and a librarian, she and her older brother grew up playing in "strippins"—land devastated by strip mining. When she was very young, she told her mother she "wanted to grow up to be a genie, a gas station attendant, or a writer." Haigh wrote in journals and for twelve years attended parochial schools. "I was raised in a Catholic family, spent twelve years in parochial schools, and had extremely fond memories of my interactions with Catholic clergy," she says. "It's no exaggeration to say that nuns and priests were the heroes of my childhood. . . . I had this very well-adjusted upbringing. My parents are still married to each other. They live in the same house I grew up in."

At Dickinson College, Jennifer majored in French and began to write fiction more seriously. "Very seriously and very badly," she says. "I look back at the stories I wrote as a very young writer, and they're exactly like everybody else's—the evil boyfriends, the tragic breakups, the fights with my parents . . . I grew up and had a job and worked a little bit, then came back to it when I had a bit more to say." In the meantime, she received a Fulbright Scholarship and studied in France. On her return she worked for Rodale Press, in Pennsylvania, then as an editor at *Self* magazine, in New York City. Around her thirtieth birthday, Haigh began to feel a stronger pull to her own writing, so she moved to Baltimore, where it was cheaper to live, found work as a yoga instructor, and began to write and publish her short stories. Haigh attempted to write two novels that she now refers to as "miscarriages."

In 2002, she entered the Iowa Writers' Workshop, where she finished what would become her first published novel, *Mrs. Kimble* (2003), winner of the 2004 PEN/Hemingway Award for Outstanding First Fiction. Since then, Haigh has published five more novels and a collection of short stories. Her work has been recognized with a 2002 James A. Michener Fellowship, the 2006 L.L. Winship/PEN Award for Outstanding Book by a New England Author for her second novel, *Baker Towers*, the Massachusetts Book Award, and the PEN New England Award in Fiction for her 2013 short story collection, *News from Heaven*, and her most recent novel, 2016's *Heat and Light*, was named Best Book of 2016 by the *New York Times*, the *Washington Post*, the *Wall Street Journal*, and *National Public Radio*.

"Each book is, to me, a unique engineering problem," Haigh says. "Unlike a poem, which can succeed or fail entirely on aesthetic terms, a novel is a machine—a one-of-a-kind contraption I'm designing, building, testing, and retesting, so that by the time it lands in a reader's hands, all he has to do is turn the key and the machine will come to life and start moving on its own. If I weren't a novelist, I might have been happy designing cars. Cars can be beautiful, but it's a car, not a poem. When you turn the key in the ignition, you want the thing to work."

And this: "I will say that the thing you're always trying for in writing fiction is to get at something truly universal. And I think we've all had this experience as readers where you read a passage in a book that articulates so perfectly a feeling you've had or an experience you've had and you really, literally, can't believe that somebody else knows exactly how that feels, these moments of deep recognition where you feel that this writer has understood something very personal to you. And that happens to me all the time as a reader and I guess that's what I'm shooting for as a writer as well."

JANE HAMILTON was born on July 13, 1957. Her father was an engineer for General Motors, her mother and grandmother were both writers; she believed she was meant to be the same. Jane grew up in Oak Park, Illinois, with four older brothers, and since she was very young, she'd been drawn to the written word. "We were also an intensely reading family," she says. "We didn't have a TV until I was twelve." In the first grade, she wrote her first short story and called it "Heather in the Wind," a title she still admires.

Throughout high school and college, Jane won prizes for her short stories and poetry, but she was also told that writing creatively was not a genuine career. In her sophomore year at Carleton College, in Minnesota, she overheard her poetry professor talking to someone and referring to her by name. He said that one day she would write a novel. "At the time, I had only written two short stories for his class," Hamilton says, "and the real potency of what he said was that it was not said to me. I had overheard it. It wouldn't have had the same power if he'd said it directly to me."

Another Carleton professor was also instrumental in helping to forge Hamilton as a writer, though this was not accomplished with professorial praise. "I must give him equal credit," Hamilton says. "He made all of us in the class feel stupid, so I sort of went underground and was smart to myself. I did my own writing and didn't show anyone, especially him. The lesson I learned from that teacher was that ultimately I really should write only for me."

In 1979, armed with a degree in English, Hamilton headed straight for New York City, where she'd gotten a job in a publishing house's children's fiction division. But on her drive east, she stopped in Wisconsin at an apple orchard owned by a friend's family and ended up staying there permanently. She never took that publishing job in New York, something for which she has no regrets; she became an apple farmer, working in her orchards spring, summer, and fall, then spending the winter inside where she focused on her writing.

Eventually, wanting more formal instruction, she applied to the Iowa Writers' Workshop, but—like thousands of other applicants—was denied acceptance into the program. She kept sending out her stories to various magazines and quarterlies, and when they were rejected, she'd send them out again.

In 1983, two of her short stories were accepted for publication in *Harper's* magazine, and more success soon followed.

Hamilton has published seven novels, two of which—*The Book of Ruth* (1988) and *A Map of the World* (1994)—were chosen for Oprah's Book Club. Her work has earned many other honors, among them the 1989 PEN/Hemingway Foundation Award for Best First Novel, the Great Lakes College Association New Writers Award, a 1993 National Endowment for the Arts Fellowship, a 1990 finalist for the National Magazine Award, and the 1998 *Publishers Weekly* "Best Book" and the Chicago Tribune Heartland Prize for her novel *The Short History of a Prince. Disobedience* (2000) was named to the *Library Journal*'s "Best Adult Books for High School Students," and in 2000 Hamilton was named Notable Wisconsin Author by the Wisconsin Library Association.

"The first draft of every book is never fun for me," she says. "That's when I try to give the story some sort of shape. I always have a certain fear that I won't get to the end of the story and after all that work there will be nothing to show of it." As a reader, she says, "I hold firm that fiction in the form of the printed word is still the most immediate and penetrating way to understand what it is to be another person. And reading a novel is still the loveliest way to both lose yourself and access your own best self."

"Writers who are serious will write because they have to. They will write because it's more difficult not to write than to write, because they have an urgent need to tell a story."

RON HANSEN, born on December 8, 1947, in Omaha, remembers that when he was a young boy, he felt that he was on the outside of things looking in. "Even as a kid I remember feeling like I was operating within a group and yet watching it from the outside at the same time," he says. "I think that's why people become writers. Most writers I know *did* fit in. They were athletes and student body presidents, yet they realized that they didn't truly belong." Ron grew up in a Catholic home with his twin brother and three sisters, and from early on he wanted to be a writer. "But it seemed like such a grand idea," he says, "that I wouldn't voice it to anybody. I thought maybe a lawyer."

Ron went to Creighton Preparatory School, a Jesuit high school. "Wow, in major, major ways I pretty much hated school," he says, "until I encountered Jesuit teaching in high school. I learned to love retreats with them." After graduating, Hansen entered Creighton University, where he took a course in modern British poetry and discovered the work of Gerard Manley Hopkins: "It occurred there in a class, and he's been a great influence on me and my writing ever since." Another early influence was Edgar Allan Poe. "His wild imagination captivated me," Hansen says. "In high school, I discovered John Updike, a very different writer and an impeccable stylist. The first great Westerns I read were Jack Schaefer's *Shane* and Walter Van Tilburg Clark's *The Ox-Bow Incident.*"

In 1970, he graduated with a bachelor's degree in English. He served in the US Army, then was accepted into the Iowa Writers' Workshop, where one of his teachers was the novelist John Irving, just thirty years old at the time, who became a mentor. "Many of his writing habits became mine," Hanson says. But after earning his MFA from Iowa in 1974, Hansen went on to a master's degree in spirituality from Santa Clara University, and in 2007 was ordained a permanent deacon of the Catholic Church.

Hansen has published ten novels, two collections of short stories, a book of essays, and a children's book. His work has garnered many honors and awards, among them fellowships from the Guggenheim Foundation and the National Endowment for the Arts, the Gold Medal for Excellence in Fiction from the Commonwealth Club of California, twice a Fiction Finalist for the PEN/Faulkner Award, a recipient of an Award in Literature from the American Academy of Arts and Letters, and a Fiction Finalist for the National Book Award for his 1996 novel, *Atticus*.

On faith and writing, Hansen says, "Yes, it's a witness to what God is doing in the world. We're supposed to worship and praise, and I can't think of a better way of worshiping and praising than to write poetry or fiction. Essentially fiction shows you how to live a moral life or how to avoid an immoral life and religion is trying to do that same thing, but fiction provides you models rather than lessons. . . . Authors ought to be truth tellers and frankly deal with the gritty realities of our world."

Born on December 19, 1967, **PAUL HARDING** grew up "knocking about in the woods," he says, on the north shore of Boston, in Wenham, Massachusetts. Summer, he'd go fly fishing in Maine and apprenticed repairing clocks under his grandfather. He had always read heavily, he says, and when he read Carlos Fuentes's *Terra Nostra*, he thought, "This is what I want to do."

But Paul was also a drummer, and after graduating from the University of Massachusetts Amherst with a degree in English, he traveled around the States and Europe playing drums in the rock band Cold Water Flat. Eventually the band broke up, and Harding found himself with some time on his hands. "I decided I'd take a crack at writing a story," he says, "because even though I hadn't really written anything, I was always an avid reader. I think that's a very common experience for a lot of people who end up being writers—you know, they start off their life as a reader."

In 1996, he took a writing course at Skidmore College with the Pulitzer Prize–winning novelist Marilynne Robinson. He so impressed her that she encouraged him to apply to the Iowa Writers' Workshop. Harding spent most of his time at Iowa working on a historical novel set in Mexico and told from the point of view of a twelve-year-old girl. When Harding earned his MFA, he knew the book was just not working, and he soon went back to a story he had begun about a fixer of clocks on his deathbed looking back in time. He expanded it into a novel and called it *Tinkers*. After three years of rejections, *Tinkers* was accepted by a small independent house and was published in 2009. *Tinkers* won that year's Pulitzer Prize for Fiction, the PEN/Robert W. Bingham Prize, and an American Booksellers Association "Indie Choice Honor Award." It was an International IMPAC Dublin Literary Award Longlist Selection, a *Los Angeles Times* Art Seidenbaum First Fiction Award Finalist, and a finalist for the Center for Fiction Flaherty-Dunnan First Novel Prize. It was also a *New York Times* bestseller and named "One of the Best Books of the Year" by the *New Yorker*, the *San Francisco Chronicle*, the *Christian Science Monitor*, the *Irish Times*, *Granta*, *Publishers Weekly*, the *Library Journal*, *Barnes and Noble*, Amazon.com, and National Public Radio. As a Guggenheim Fellow, Harding finished his acclaimed second novel, *Enon*, which was published by Random House in 2013. His most recent novel is 2023's *This Other Eden*.

"Fiction writing is all about telling the *truth*," he says. And "Not only do you need to read the best books, but you also need to read them *well*. I think it's true that generally speaking, your writing can only be as good as the best books you've read."

My creative process, he says, "is totally intuitive and fortuitous. It's improvisational. I write the way I used to drum. . . . I just start to do whatever comes over the wire. . . . I just kind of bop around the story. . . . I'm impatient—I want to know what the end of the story is and to move around the boundaries of it."

ANN HOOD was born on December 9, 1956, and grew up in West Warwick, Rhode Island. Her Italian immigrant family owned few, if any, books, but they had a rich tradition of storytelling. On Sundays and holidays, the household of nine, including her great-grandmother and grandmother, would tell stories around the cast-iron stove in the kitchen. "[M]y grandmother would tell stories about the supernatural." Hood says. "I was an observer, which gives you a different sense of how people tick—and which definitely informs my writing."

In the second grade, Ann discovered Louisa May Alcott's *Little Women* and fell under the spell of reading. Encouraged by a teacher, by the end of that school year Ann was reading books meant for fourth-graders. She says it gave her "an escape from my lonely school days." It also sparked in her curiosity about people and the world. Because her mother believed that buying books was a waste of money, Ann saved her allowance and began to buy the Nancy Drew series. "When I was about seven," Hood says, "I started to write my own books. I never thought of myself as wanting to be a writer—I just was one."

In 1974, she graduated from West Warwick High School and entered the University of Rhode Island, majoring in English. With her college degree, she immediately took a job as a flight attendant, and kept at it for eight years. "[I]n seventh grade, I read the book *How to Become an Airline Stewardess* and it fueled my desire to see the world. . . . I thought you needed adventures in order to be a writer. Of course, I know now that all you need, as Eudora Welty said, is to sit on your own front porch." But it was as a flight attendant that Hood began writing seriously, often in the galleys of passenger jets: "[D]uring that time, I would carry notebooks, and I would write stories. I began a novel called *The Betrayal of Sam Pepper*. It was the most dreadful thing ever written . . . I didn't know that's what I was doing; . . . I was teaching myself."

At twenty-five, Hood lost her only sibling, her brother Chip, to a freak domestic accident. "Chip's death is what really got me to pursue writing seriously," she says. "I write about families coping with loss, trying to regroup in a new configuration."

In 1985, Hood won a scholarship to the Bread Loaf Writers' Conference, where she studied under the writer Nicholas Delbanco and worked on stories that later became her first published novel, *Somewhere Off the Coast of Maine* (1987). Since then, Hood has published fourteen novels, a collection of short stories, and four books of nonfiction, among them her 2008 memoir dealing with the loss of her five-year-old daughter, Grace, called *Comfort: A Journey Through Grief*. It was a *New York Times* "Editor's Choice" and an *Entertainment Weekly* "Top Ten Nonfiction Book" of 2008. Hood's work has also received the

Paul Bowles Prize for Short Fiction, two Pushcart Prizes, two Best American Food Writing Awards, a Best American Spiritual Writing Award, and, in 2011, a Boston Public Library "Literary Light" Award.

"I write so that people will read what I write. I don't want to write a book that a thousand people read, or just privileged people read. I want to write a book whose emotional truth people can understand."

Reading is a component of her writing. "I always say it's so simple because it's: read and write," she says. "I still have books that I read and . . . and I still learn how to write from them. I also have notes. 'Start with action,' I remember writing once. I had noticed that all these books start with action."

PAM HOUSTON, born in Trenton, New Jersey, on January 9, 1962, learned to read at two and half and soon fell in love with her first book: Dr. Seuss's *On Beyond Zebra!* Her childhood, in Bethlehem, Pennsylvania, however, was a hard one. Houston remembers her father as a playboy who never hid his constant disappointment in her. It was a cold and abusive home, and early on Pam wanted to leave. "My fifth-grade teacher, the wonderful Mr. Kashner," she says, "looked me in the eye one day and said, 'You have the smarts to get the hell out of here.'"

Pam went to Denison University and graduated in 1983 with a BA in English with honors. She then got on her bicycle and rode with a girlfriend throughout New Brunswick, Nova Scotia, and Prince Edward Island. She traveled west, and in 1986 entered a PhD program at the University of Utah. There, she didn't care for the academic politics and left five months shy of earning her degree. In 1992, however, she went back to Utah and earned her master's. Shortly thereafter, she enrolled in the University of Utah's MFA in Creative Writing program. When her professors told her that she should do something else with her life, however, Houston quit and hit the road again. "My parents . . . gave their passion for travel to me," she says. "I'm happiest when I have one plane ticket in my hand and another in my underwear drawer."

A lover of the outdoors, Houston has been a horse trainer, a ski instructor, a hunting guide, and a licensed river guide. She has also published seven books: two novels, two short story collections, two books of essays, and, with cowriter Amy Irvine, 2020's *Air Mail: Letters of Politics, Pandemics, and Place.*

Her work has received national awards and honors, such as the Western States Book Award and a *New York Times* "Notable Book" selection for her 1993 story collection, *Cowboys Are My Weakness*; as well as the Evil Companions Literary Award, the 1998 Willa Cather Award for Contemporary Fiction, three Pushcart Prizes, an O. Henry Award, and inclusion in 1990's *Best American Short Stories*, for "How to Talk to a Hunter." In 1999 John Updike chose her "The Best Girlfriend You Never Had" as his only addition to *The Best American Short Stories of the Century.*

"My books always come from events, people, and places I have experienced or at least witnessed," Houston says, "but I also want to be free to mold and shape those events into the most meaningful story and the emotionally truest (as opposed to the most factually accurate) story, which sometimes means merging and shifting and tweaking reality to fit whatever demands the story begins to make on the material."

Houston says her taste in books has changed. "When I hear myself praising a book these days, the things I seem to be really appreciating is a fearlessness when it comes to compassion and sincerity, as well as a willingness to examine questions of faith (and by that I neither mean, nor exclude, questions of religion)," she says. "In other words, I've reached an age where I'm no longer at all impressed with the snide, the cold, the condescending, unless it's paired or mitigated by the opposite, the hopeful in the face of all odds, the reaching after the ineffable, the love."

Born on Long Island on August 12, 1955, **GISH JEN** grew up with her four siblings in a tough neighborhood in Yonkers, New York. "Well, I have to say that a lot went on in that suburb that was not so easy, and it was not funny. We were the only Chinese family in that area . . . so definitely people threw rocks at us. I mean, it was not pretty." As she got older, her parents—both immigrants from Shanghai—moved the family to the more affluent Jewish suburb of Scarsdale. "Certainly there were a lot of views about what a nice Chinese girl did and that didn't include becoming an author, I hardly need to point out. If I hadn't grown up in Scarsdale," she says, "in a culture where writing was this great thing, I don't know that I ever would've thought to pick up a pen."

Since she was very young, Gish was a voracious reader, but her family expected her to become a lawyer or a doctor or a successful businesswoman, so when she was accepted to Harvard, it was on a premed track. But then she took an English course taught by the celebrated poet and scholar Robert Fitzgerald, who said to her one day, "Why are you premed? . . . I suggest you consider doing something with words." Gish immediately switched her major to English. She remembers telling her roommate that she loved writing and wanted to do it for the rest of her life. "But I'm the daughter of immigrants," she says; "it never even crossed my mind for one minute that I might become a poet."

Jen graduated in 1977, then two years later studied business at Stanford before taking a leave to teach English to coal miners in China. Upon her return, she found a job in publishing in New York City but, she says, "I realized I had found myself in some middle ground. I was neither doing what I really wanted to do nor was I making any money."

She decided to pursue a master's in business administration, and applied only to universities that also had strong programs in creative writing. The study of business, however, just was not for her. "I think I overslept the first day of class," she says, "and then I overslept the second day. I overslept the third day. And by the end of the week it was clear to me that I was never going to class and I should just drop out. . . . And of course my parents would be very upset—very, very upset. My mother didn't talk to me for almost a year."

One morning, Jen woke up contemplating her own deathbed. "Someday," she thought, "I'd be lying there and my parents would be long dead. And I realized that if I hadn't even tried to become a writer, I'd be full of regret."

Jen applied to the Iowa Writers' Workshop and graduated with her MFA in 1983. She has published five novels, the acclaimed short story collection *Who's Irish?*, and two books of nonfiction, most recently 2017's *The Girl at the Baggage Claim: Explaining the East–West Culture Gap*. Her work has received

numerous awards, and she has earned fellowships from the National Endowment for the Arts and the Guggenheim Foundation, and she was awarded a
2003 Fulbright to the People's Republic of China. Her books have been recognized as a Fiction Finalist for the National Books Critics' Circle Award, a
1999 Lannan Award for Fiction, and a 2003 Strauss Living Award from the
America Academy for Arts and Letters, and in 2009 she was elected to the
American Academy of Arts and Sciences. In 1999, "Birthmates" was included
in *Best American Short Stories of the Century.*

"Things you wouldn't talk about in company," she says, "you're not supposed to write about either. But a writer is dedicated to truth—a writer's job is
to write about these things. So the naughtier you are, the better. The not-nicer
you are the better a writer you are. . . . My advice for young writers, minority
and otherwise: Write the book you were born to write—the book that only you
could write, that only you would dare write. Then pray."

The son of a homemaker and a security guard, **CHARLES JOHNSON** was born
on April 23, 1947, in Evanston, Illinois, and grew up near the campus of
Northwestern University. "My dad worked three jobs to, you know, to make
sure we never missed a meal," he says. "He was a very hardworking man. So
my mom didn't have to work. . . . But sometimes on the holidays, she would
take a part-time job at Northwestern . . . helping to clean up after the sorority
girls left . . . for Christmas break, for example. And they would throw out
their books . . . and my mom would bring them home." Charles's mother, an
art lover and ardent reader, shared these books with him, and he became a
reader. "I retreated into reading as a young person," he says, "the same way I
retreated into drawing. My passion was not to be a writer in the 1950s when I
was a kid and . . . in the 1960s when I was in my teens. My passion was to be
an artist—a visual artist and an illustrator and a cartoonist, and a political
cartoonist, right? So I would retreat into drawing . . . books and stories would
feed my imagination for visual art."

As a teenager, Charles would visit relatives in Brooklyn, then depart for
Manhattan, carrying his cartoon portfolio to show comic companies and cartoon editors. "I was passionate about becoming a professional cartoonist and
illustrator and sold my first several illustrations to Magic Company's catalog
in Chicago. I still have the dollar that I made," he says, "framed in my study,
because for me that was a transitional moment when I became a professional. I
got paid, finally, for doing art."

At Southern Illinois University Carbondale, Johnson majored in journalism, but by the time he graduated, in 1971, he'd already made a name for himself
as a political cartoonist. From 1965 to 1972, he created hundreds of illustrations
and comic strips for several publications, among them the *Chicago Tribune,* and
national African American publications such as *Black World* (formerly *Negro
Digest*), *Ebony,* and *Players.* By the time he began work on a PhD, in philosophy,
from the State University of New York at Stony Brook, he had already written
six of what he calls his "apprentice novels." He had also befriended novelist the
John Gardner, who became Johnson's mentor throughout the writing of his seventh novel—his first to be published—*Faith and the Good Thing,* released by Vi-

king in 1974. Since then, Johnson has published three more novels, three short story collections, two graphic novels, and twelve books of nonfiction, most recently 2016's *The Way of the Writer: Reflections on the Art and Craft of Storytelling*.

Throughout his career, Johnson's work has earned many honors: a Washington State Governor's Award for Literature, the International Prix Jeunesse Award, the Writers Guild Award, a Governor's Award for Literature, a Fiction Finalist for the PEN/Faulkner Award, the 1990 National Book Award for Fiction for his novel *Middle Passage*, and an Award in Literature from the American Academy of Arts and Letters. He has also received a MacArthur "Genius" Grant and fellowships from the Guggenheim Foundation and the National Endowment for the Arts.

"I've never liked being intellectually or creatively boxed in or pigeonholed," Johnson says. "I'm a trained philosopher (one of the few Black ones to earn a PhD in philosophy in American history), a professional cartoonist and illustrator since I was seventeen years old, and a storyteller in many genres, including screenplays and teleplays. I just love to create, that's all. And all the arts have in common one thing: They're simply about problem-solving and discovery. That process of discovery and problem-solving has been my greatest daily joy in life since childhood."

Born in 1983, **PHIL KLAY** grew up in White Plains, New York. His parents read to him and his brothers, "pretty much anything by Dahl," he says, "we just loved. That and Shel Silverstein's poetry. As a kid, I also used to sit in this clawfoot tub we had in our house and I'd read Edgar Allan Poe." He was always a reader: "You can only live one life," he says, "but books are a primary way for us to expand our understanding of how others live in the world."

Klay graduated from Regis High School, a free Jesuit high school in Manhattan, in 2001. There, he studied theology and was introduced to the works of Flannery O'Connor, Evelyn Waugh, Graham Greene, Walker Percy, Shūsaku Endō, and François Mauriac. Klay then went to Dartmouth College. In summer 2004, he entered Officer Candidate School. "I'd been in college studying English, creative writing, and history when I made the decision to join the Marines in the run-up to the Iraq War," he says. "I had a desire to serve my country, and I'm a physical guy—a boxer and rugby player. Notions of public service are valued in my family, but if we hadn't been at war, I doubt whether I would have joined the military. I was hopeful I could put myself in a position of responsibility, affect things for the better. It was a historic moment. I didn't want to sit on the sidelines. I joined in 2003, became a second lieutenant in 2005."

Klay was an officer in the Marines from 2005 to 2009, including thirteen months in Anbar Province, Iraq. He was a public affairs officer, which he calls "a very mild deployment."

"I didn't go with any clear sense I'd write about war, but Tom Sleigh—one of my tutors and a great American poet—made sure that before I went I'd read Tolstoy, Hemingway, Isaac Babel, and David Jones. He thought it important to study what the greatest minds had to say about war."

In 2011, Klay earned his MFA in creative writing from Hunter College and participated in NYU's Veterans Writing Workshop. "That's where I found a group of really smart and talented veteran writers . . . to share work and ideas with," he says. "It was a group of people who cared about the issues I did, and who'd argue them with me or recommend what to read or read my writing and tear it up with really smart, important edits. I couldn't get away with certain types of BS that civilian readers would let me slide on."

Klay's first book, a collection of short stories titled *Redeployment*, published in 2014, won that year's National Book Award for Fiction, the National Book Critics' Circle John Leonard Award for Best Debut Work in Any Genre, the American Library Association's W. Y. Boyd Literary Award for Excellence in Military Fiction, the Chautauqua Prize, and the Warwick Prize for Writing, and was a finalist for the Frank O'Connor International Short Story Award. It was also named one of the "Ten Best Books of 2014" by the *New York Times Book Review*. That year, Klay became a National Book Foundation 5 Under 35 honoree. His debut novel, *Missionaries*, was published in 2020.

"Putting the story on the page is a product of doubt, not a product of certainty," Klay says. "I write because I'm troubled or confused or fascinated by something in human experience I don't understand, and writing allows me a way to expose my own ignorance further. For me, a story begins with questions far more often than with answers. And even if I do have some very fixed notions at the outset of the story, writing usually complicates those notions or destroys them altogether."

DENNIS LEHANE was born on August 4, 1965, the youngest of five children in an Irish-immigrant family. He was raised in the Dorchester neighborhood of Boston: his mother worked in a public school cafeteria and his father was a foreman for Sears & Roebuck. When he was a boy, Dennis's mother gave him a library card. Almost every day, he would leave his home near Franklin Park and walk to the Uphams Corner branch of the Boston Public Library, which was in the heart of his blue-collar neighborhood. "We were working class," he says. "There were no books. There were some encyclopedias—I always say it was the day my father didn't see the salesman coming. And there was a Bible. I read the Bible from cover to cover when I was a kid. The Bible is an amazing piece of narrative storytelling."

"Whenever I think about that walk [to the library], I feel like that's where I came alive from an artistic standpoint. Questions about economics, questions about class, questions about race, they dominate my work."

Dennis went to the Jesuit prep school Boston College High School before entering Eckerd College, in St. Petersburg, Florida. While there, he wrote his first novel as "a goof, as a fluke," he says, "as something to do because I was bored. And to entertain myself." He graduated in 1988 and eventually entered Florida International University, in Miami, where he earned his MFA in creative writing. Before becoming a full-time writer, Lehane supported himself waiting tables, parking cars, driving limos, loading tractor-trailers, working in a bookstore, and counseling mentally handicapped and abused children. But since 1994 and the publication of his first novel, *A Drink Before the War*, Lehane has gone on to publish twelve more novels and two collections of short stories. His work was a finalist for the PEN/Winship Award and has won the 1995

Shamus Award for Best First PI Novel, the Anthony Award, the Barry Award for Best Novel, the Dilys Award from the Independent Mystery Booksellers Association, the Massachusetts Book Award in Fiction, France's Prix Mystère de la Critique, the Joseph E. Connor Award, the 2013 Edgar Award, and a Gold Medal for General Fiction, Florida Book Awards. Four of Lehane's novels have been made into feature films. He was a staff writer on the HBO series *The Wire* and a writer-producer on the fourth season of HBO's *Boardwalk Empire*. In 2007 he received an Edgar Award for Best Television Feature/Mini-Series Teleplay for *The Wire*, and in 2008 he was awarded the Writers Guild of America (WGA) Award for Best Dramatic Series for *The Wire*. He is the developer and writer for the 2022 miniseries *Blackbird*.

He has been writer in residence at Eckerd College: "I say to my students right off the bat, if there's not depth of language, if you don't bring some sort of music to your prose, if that isn't something you can put on the table, then please go do something else because it's the only thing that separates literature from any other art form. That's it."

And: "Writing a novel is like potato salad; everybody has a different recipe."

LOIS LOWRY was a middle child, which was just fine with her. "That left me in between," she says, "and exactly where I wanted most to be: on my own. I . . . lived in the world of books and my own vivid imagination." Born in Honolulu on March 20, 1937, Lowry grew up in a family of readers and at five or six years old began going regularly to the library. As she got older, there were few books written exclusively for young adults, so she went straight to adult books, drawn to those with a child protagonist, such as Betty Smith's *A Tree Grows in Brooklyn*. Lois was eight or nine years old when her mother read *The Yearling*, by Marjorie Kinnan Rawlings, to her. "She cried when she was reading it," Lowry says. "It wasn't embarrassing or frightening, it was that a story could do that. . . . [M]y mother was sharing words on a page that made you feel so deeply that she wept." It was then that Lois began to want to be a writer herself.

The daughter of a US Army dentist, Lowry moved frequently: to Brooklyn; to Carlisle, Pennsylvania; and to Tokyo, where she attended the Tokyo American School. She finished high school in New York City, then went to Pembroke College in Brown University in 1954. Two years later she left school and married, at age nineteen, Donald Grey Lowry, an officer in the Navy. The many moves of a military life followed. "California," she says. "Connecticut (a daughter born there). Florida (a son). South Carolina . . . Cambridge, Massachusetts (another daughter; another son), and then to Maine—by now with four children under the age of five in tow."

As her children got older, Lowry went back to college and in 1972 earned a BA in English from the University of Southern Maine. She then entered a graduate program at Brown, and was introduced to photography. Lowry began to work as a freelance journalist and took the pictures that accompanied her submissions to newspapers and magazines. *Redbook* magazine commissioned her to write a piece from a child's point of view, and the story was published. An editor at Houghton Mifflin then contacted Lowry and suggested she write a book for children. "[A]lthough I hadn't considered writing for young people," she says, "I did have kids of my own and had spent many years at that point reading to them what was available."

Lowry subsequently wrote her first book for young adults, *A Summer to Die*, published in 1977, when she was forty years old.

Lowry has published forty-five more novels and in 1998 her autobiography, *Looking Back*. Her work has garnered major awards: the Newbery Medal (1990 and 1994), the Margaret A. Edwards Award for Lifetime Contribution to Young Adult Literature, the Regina Medal, the National Jewish Book Award, the *Boston Globe*–Horn Book Award (1987 and 1993), the Sydney Taylor Book Award, the Hope S. Dean Award, the New England Book Award, and the *Chicago Tribune* Young Adult Fiction Prize. She was a finalist for the Hans Christian Andersen Award (United States) and won the Golden Kite Award.

"Reading is the best way to learn to write well," Lowry says. "Read as much as you can. Think about what you read: how the author made it interesting, or funny, or suspenseful. And write as much as you can, too. Keep a journal. Get together with friends who enjoy writing and read things aloud to each other and talk about them."

She describes her own writing process: "I sit at my desk every day. I do the *New York Times* crossword puzzle. I watch the park through my window. My CD player plays music, usually classical (at this moment, it's a violin concerto). I sip coffee. I type words into my computer. I retype them, rearrange them, and delete them, and retype them again and again. The phone rings. The dog woofs to go out. I get up and refill my coffee cup. Then I look at the words I've written and I rearrange them again. Eventually, somehow, a story is put together. There isn't anything magical. It's a lot of hard work, a lot of fun, and a lot of waiting for the words."

COLUM McCANN, born in Deansgrange, Ireland, on February 28, 1965, grew up with four siblings in a house filled with books. His mother was a homemaker; his father was a literary editor and journalist for the *Irish Press*. McCann recalls his childhood as a happy one, "non-traumatic and all that stuff," he says, and from when he was very young, he loved to read. The book he remembers enjoying the most was Mary Lavin's *The Second-Best Children in the World*. "The memory of it is like bread coming out of the oven," he says.

Colum excelled in sports and his studies, and after graduating from Clonkeen College, he was determined to become a journalist, something his father advised against. "I think maybe he told me not to be a journalist because he wanted me to become a fiction writer," McCann says, "and he was afraid that the world of journalism would swallow me asunder."

In 1982 McCann earned a degree in journalism from the College of Commerce Rathmines and began working as a reporter for the *Irish Press* group. By the time he was twenty-one, he had his own column in the *Evening Press*. "It was really awful," he says. "It was supposed to be for young people—what album came out, 'designer stubble'—all this sort of shit. . . . My friends and I had a good laugh. We got invited to all the great parties and stuff." McCann also wrote serious pieces, including one on Dublin's battered women, for which he was named Young Journalist of the Year.

In 1986, McCann moved to Cape Cod intending to write a novel: "There was a whole enchantment of traveling to America, a wanderlust, with no real intention to stay, but to become a writer. I bought a typewriter and had the same empty page in it for six months. I had nothing to write about." So he took a two-year bike trek across the United States and Mexico.

To pay for his food and lodging, he found work as a fence builder, house painter, ditch digger, bicycle mechanic, ranch hand, dishwasher, and journalist. "The road, for me, was a university . . . the greatest gift I was ever given," he says. "It was quite a trip for a middle-class Dublin kid. I went through all sorts of landscapes and met convicted murderers, crawfish fishermen, movie stars, models, firefighters, bicycle mechanics, you name it. Because I was transient, . . . they tended to tell me some of their most intimate secrets. They knew there would be no repercussions in their lives, since I was moving on. It was my education, and I think that in many ways it gave birth to me as a writer."

In 1990 McCann entered the University of Texas at Austin and he published, in Dublin's *Sunday Tribune*, his first short story, "Tresses." It won Ireland's Hennessy Award for "Best First Short Story" and "Overall Winner." McCann has been writing ever since. He has published three collections of short stories, seven novels (most recently, 2020's *Apeirogon*), and a work of nonfiction, 2017's *Letters to a Young Writer*. His writing has earned many honors and awards: the Rooney Prize for Irish Literature, a Pushcart Prize, 2002's First Recipient of the Princess Grace Memorial Literary Prize, and the 2003 *Irish Independent* Hughes and Hughes/*Sunday Independent* Novel of the Year, for example. He was a 2005 inductee into the Hennessy Literary Awards Hall of Fame, then won the 2009 National Book Award for Fiction, the Chevalier des Arts et Lettres, a Guggenheim Fellowship, an Award in Literature from the American Academy of Arts and Letters, and the International IMPAC Dublin Literary Award. In 2017, McCann was inducted into the American Academy of Arts and Letters.

Writing, McCann says, "is very much about the intuitive, the gut instinct, the shotgun leap into the unknown. Most of the time, I don't necessarily know where I'm going . . . Being too conscious of a journey brings a malady to it. . . . I think it's very much akin to being an adventurer or an explorer. . . . Most of the time you end up capsizing or catching the wrong current or, even worse, ship-wrecking. But every now and then—when the words are moving, and the sentences begin to align themselves, and the imaginative intent has caught fire with language—you strike new land."

SUE MILLER's mother was a homemaker and her father was an ordained minister who taught church history. "Listening to sermons Sunday after Sunday," she says, "I came to understand in my bones that writing has a form. Writing has a form and a structure and your job is to make it invisible." Born in Chicago on November 29, 1943, and raised in the neighborhood of Hyde Park, Sue preferred reading over most other activities. "*Jane Eyre* must have been something I read six or seven times as an early adolescent," she says, "and *Kristin Lavransdatter* and *Lorna Doone* when I was younger. My parents had a pretty rich library, no jackets on any of the books, so no descriptions. You just pulled something off the shelf and started to read it."

At sixteen, she skipped her senior year of high school and entered Radcliffe College. She felt overwhelmed and unprepared, however, and believed she was learning very little. This was in the 1950s, and the general societal norm, communicated directly to her from her own mother, was, she says, "you had to be neurotic to be a woman and want a career."

In 1964, Miller earned her BA in English literature and got married. To help put her husband through medical school, she worked as a model, waitress, high school teacher, and researcher in a lab pushing rats through a maze. At twenty-four, Miller gave birth to a son; three years later she and her husband divorced. A single mother now, she still managed to earn three master's degrees: one in early childhood education, from Harvard; another in English education, from Wesleyan University; and a degree in creative writing from Boston University. For eight years, she was a daycare worker. "When I was still working in daycare and my son was pretty young, I would read in the evenings," she says—"no television by choice, and no internet, period. Just long evenings, one after another, with a book. That was my education as a writer, my apprenticeship—reading closely, noticing how other writers were working. I was writing then, when I could, and eventually I began to feel that what I was writing was as good as at least some of what I was reading, and I started to send things out."

Miller published her first novel, *The Good Mother*, in 1986. It was critically acclaimed and spent six months on the *New York Times* Bestseller List. "The most important change that happened as a result of that book's success was simply that I had ample time to write," she says. "I didn't need to be hustling all the time, trying to line up the next adjunct appointment, and the next after that. I was forty-three when my first book came out. I felt set loose, set free, to write. I was certainly ready for that. I wrote a lot over the next few years."

Miller has gone on to publish ten more novels, a collection of short fiction, and her 2003 memoir, *The Story of My Father*. Her work has earned many awards and honors, such as a Creative Writing Fellowship at Boston University, fellowships from the Bunting Institute from Radcliffe College and the Guggenheim Foundation, as well as Fiction Finalist for the National Book Critics Circle Award.

"I try to work in the mornings," Miller says. "Usually, I write in my pajamas and slowly assemble myself. I don't get organized and sit down and get dressed. I do the laundry. I drift in and out of writing. I feel as though I'm using the time that I break away to stop and think about something, rather than sitting here and making it happen. I think I'm less disciplined than a lot of other people, I'm afraid, but on the other hand, I've written a lot of books."

RICK MOODY says his childhood in Fairfield County, Connecticut, was uneventful: "Nothing inherently interesting happened. I don't have a skeleton in the closet, anything like that. The only singular thing about me is that I read like a maniac." He says he read a lot of "nonsense" as a kid, but then, at age eleven, he discovered Ernest Hemingway. "[T]he breakthrough for me was reading *The Old Man and the Sea*. In sixth grade. In New Canaan. Even then, I had some epiphanic relationship to Hemingway's language. Even at that age it was revelatory. I just went and read everything else by this guy."

Moody was born in Manhattan on October 18, 1961. Both of his parents were avid readers, and his grandfather, who worked in the newspaper business, was a collector of hardcover, first-edition books. "He had a whole set of firsts of Faulkner and Salinger and all that kind of stuff," says Moody. "So this book reverence thing was really central to the people who raised me up, and that's what I did first. . . . I came to want to write because the first thing I loved was books, the texture of them, their physicality, and then also anything that was contained within."

Moody studied creative writing at Brown University with the writers Angela Carter, Robert Coover, and John Hawkes. "I wrote to please Angela Carter, and I wrote to please John Hawkes, and this may seem like a callow, naive motive for writing, especially since they were both astringent, complicated people. But the fact is," he says, "that I got better by writing in order to please them, and their responses made me excited to go back and work, and excited to learn more."

After graduating with a bachelor's degree in English, Moody took a year off and supported his writing by working at a series of nine-to-five jobs, including one selling recorded tours at a museum. But he didn't believe he was writing enough, so he decided to go to graduate school; he earned his MFA in creative writing from Columbia University. In 1986, Moody checked himself into a mental hospital for alcoholism. He ultimately became sober and turned himself fully to writing. He was an editorial assistant at Simon & Schuster, then took a job at Farrar, Straus and Giroux, "kind of as a line editor," he says, "manuscript trafficker guy." He was also writing what would become his first novel, *Garden State*, published in 1992. Moody has since published five more novels, three short story collections, and three works of nonfiction, most recently *The Long Accomplishment*. His work has been honored with major awards, such as the Pushcart Editor's Choice Award, the Aga Khan Award from the *Paris Review*, the Addison Metcalf Award from the American Academy of Arts and Letters, the Pushcart Prize, the PEN / Martha Albrand Award for the Art of the Memoir, the Mary Shelley Award from the Media Ecology Association for *The Diviner*, and Italy's Fernanda Pivano Award. He was also granted a Guggenheim Fellowship,

"The goal is to make the language express the great variety of human consciousness and how sort of multifarious consciousness is," he says, "but hopefully without ever being too abstract. . . . My idea of literature, as I've often said, is that it should save lives. My idea of literature is that it once *did* save lives, and was of consequence in that way. . . . There will always be readers and writers."

ANTONYA NELSON was born in Wichita, Kansas, on January 6, 1961. "I grew up reading to be involved in a world," Nelson says. "Often, I was more involved in fictional worlds than I was in what you'd call my real world. I was taught to read early (thanks, Mom) . . . I read everything. I still sorta do." Her mother and father encouraged her to write, but Antonya didn't believe she could ever make a living as a fiction writer, so she considered instead becoming a photojournalist or a special education teacher. "Then my mom sent me an entry form to a *Mademoiselle* magazine contest," she says, "and I just happened to have a story I had recently taken to a workshop, so I sent it off. It was kind of a fluke, but I won."

"My mom has been particularly influential because she wanted to write, and although she does, I was the first daughter and the one to live out her dream. My parents understand publishing more than other writers' families do because they're professors. My dad built a special shelf for my books in the dining room because he's interested in them in a way that goes beyond the average person. My parents think having a story in the *New Yorker* is the best thing that could happen."

Nelson graduated from the University of Kansas in 1983, then entered the University of Arizona's MFA program, where she met her future husband, the writer Robert Boswell, who was completing his degree just as she was starting hers. She graduated in 1986, and her first book, the short story collection *The Expendables*, was published four years later. Since then, Nelson has published six more collections of short stories and four novels. Her work has been honored with a number of awards, such as the Flannery O'Connor Award for Short Fiction, the Heartland Award in Fiction, the PEN Nelson Algren Award, the O. Henry Prize, a Pushcart Prize, and the 2003 Rea Award for the Short Story. She earned fellowships from the National Endowment for the Arts and the Guggenheim Foundation, and in 2009 was granted a United States Artist Fellowship.

"There's my central obsession, in a nutshell: family life. And the many ways that an unconventional understanding of it fascinates me," she says. Her advice: "If you have the impulse to write, trust it implicitly. If you don't succeed, it probably isn't an issue of your material, but the delivery and getting it captured on paper. Trust the impulse, and don't abandon the material. That's where a workshop can help: text is very malleable and elastic, so it's helpful to get input on revisions and to discuss your work with others. It helps shape your work and can lead you to the proper way to get the story told. . . . Report truthfully the world as you find it. Name it honestly, freshly, and put yourself on the line. A reader can tell if the work isn't revealing a genuine self behind it. It's the only kind of work that really matters."

BICH MINH NGUYEN was born in Saigon in 1974. Her father put the family on one of the last boats out before the city fell to the North Vietnamese. They continued on to refugee camps in Guam and Fort Chaffee, Arkansas, before they finally settled in Grand Rapids, Michigan, where she was raised. This was a predominantly white and conservative city filled with families of Irish, German, and Dutch descent, and whereas the grandmother tried to keep their Vietnamese traditions alive, all Bich and her sister wanted was to fit in. Bich was drawn to rock and roll, dances, and designer jeans. She also couldn't get over America's plethora of junk food, such as Twinkies and Ho-Hos.

Nguyen was a passionate reader, she says. "Like most writers, I dreamed of writing because I loved reading. I loved falling into someone else's imagined world and getting carried forward within his or her language and narrative. . . . Writing also felt like an enormous kind of freedom. In real life I was so shy I sometimes couldn't answer when someone asked me a question; in the imagined life I could speak through writing. I could be as close to fearless as I dared . . . was also intensely interested in language. Although I didn't know it consciously at the time, I'm sure that part of my obsession with reading, writing, spelling, and language was connected to my need to learn English—to master it."

For a long time, Bich kept her desire to be a writer secret. She was afraid that it was such a lofty goal that she'd be ridiculed for it. She also doubted whether anyone would be interested in what she had to say. "For years I wrote stories, poems, and 'novels' that basically mimicked whatever I was reading—often, British literature," she says. "I didn't discover books by Asian American writers (and it never occurred to me to write about being Vietnamese) until I got to college and read Maxine Hong Kingston's *The Woman Warrior*. Then, slowly, possibilities unfolded in my mind."

Bich Minh Nguyen earned her MFA in creative writing from the University of Michigan, and she has published two acclaimed novels and a memoir. Her work has been honored with major awards, among them the 2005 PEN/ Jerard Fund Award and *Chicago Tribune*'s "Best Book of the Year" for her memoir, *Stealing Buddha's Dinner*; the 2010 American Book Award for her 2009 novel, *Short Girls*, which was also named *Library Journal*'s Best Book of the Year. She was also granted a Bread Loaf Fellowship. Nguyen has also coedited three anthologies: *30/30: Thirty American Stories from the Last Thirty Years*; *Contemporary Creative Nonfiction: I & Eye*; and *The Contemporary American Short Story*.

"For me," Nguyen says, "writing is always about looking back and looking forward in the same moment. It's living within more than sphere, identity, and place, and trying to understand that—trying to find a few moments of stillness and clarity. . . . As soon as the kids go to sleep, I'm working. But I'm also learning to have a better relationship with time and trying not to fixate on how little there is of it."

"My advice for aspiring writers and poets is to read and write in equal measure. And once you're writing, stay there as long as possible."

Born the eldest of three children in Lockport, New York, on June 16, 1938, **JOYCE CAROL OATES** grew up in the nearby farming community of Millersport. She had daily chores but loved to read, a habit encouraged by her paternal grandmother, Blanche, who was the first to take Joyce to the public library. "As a young child I was a lover of books and of the spaces in which, as indeed in a sacred temple, books might safely reside," she says. "I was mesmerized by books and by what might be called 'the life of the mind': the life that was not manual labor, or housework, but seemed in its specialness to transcend these activities."

Joyce's grandmother gave her a copy of *Alice's Adventures in Wonderland*, by Lewis Carroll, a book Oates considers "the great treasure of my childhood, and the most profound literary influence of my life." She also inhaled the work of the Brontë sisters, Henry David Thoreau, William Faulkner, Dostoyevsky, and Hemingway. When she turned fourteen, her grandmother gave her a typewriter, and Joyce began to write. At Williamsville South High, she wrote for the school newspaper and in her senior year won the 1956 Scholastic Writing Award for her short story "A Dawn You'll Never See."

Oates earned a scholarship to Syracuse University, where she wrote "novel after novel," she says, "and always throwing them out when I completed them." There she read the works of Flannery O'Connor, D. H. Lawrence, Thomas

Mann, and Franz Kafka, and at nineteen won *Mademoiselle* magazine's national college short fiction contest. In 1960 she earned a bachelor's degree in English, then enrolled at the University of Wisconsin at Madison, where she received her master's. But it was not until she was a doctoral candidate at Rice University that she decided to make writing her life.

Oates has since published more than sixty novels (most recently, 2022's *Babysitter*), twenty-nine short story collections, over a half dozen plays, six collections of poetry, and seven books of nonfiction. Her work has garnered many national and international awards: among them five times a Fiction finalist for the Pulitzer Prize, five times a Fiction finalist for the National Book Award, three times a Fiction finalist for the National Book Critics Circle Award, winner of the 1970 National Book Award for Fiction, two O. Henry Awards, the M. L. Rosenthal Award from the National Institute of Arts and Letters, the Rea Award for the Short Story, the PEN/Malamud Award for Excellence in the Art of the Short Story, the F. Scott Fitzgerald Award for Achievement in American Literature, the 2010 National Humanities Medal, and the 2012 Norman Mailer Prize for Lifetime Achievement. among many others.

"Never be ashamed of your subject," Oates says, "and of your passion for your subject. . . . Your struggle with your buried self, or selves, yields your art; these emotions are the fuel that drives your writing and makes possible hours, days, weeks, months, and years of what will appear to others, at a distance, as 'work.' Without these ill-understood drives, you might be a superficially happy person, and a more involved citizen of your community, but it isn't likely that you will create anything of substance."

She goes on: "I have forced myself to begin writing when I've been utterly exhausted, when I've felt my soul as thin as a playing card, when nothing has seemed worth enduring for another five minutes . . . and somehow the activity of writing changes everything."

STEWART O'NAN, born on February 4, 1961, was raised in Pittsburgh, where his mother was an economist and his father was an engineer. From an early age, Stewart loved books. "The bookmobile and the library were the sources of my first outside reading," he says. "You could take out ten books at a time from the library. . . . I'd walk home with a healthy stack and plow through them so I could get another ten. Free books!"

He particularly liked anything by Ray Bradbury. "He was one of my first great loves. . . . One of my favorite books of all time is *Something Wicked This Way Comes*. I loved that book and for years I've said I'm going to try to write something like that."

But growing up in the 1960s and 1970s, Stewart was also captivated by the Apollo program and space flight and was quite good in math. So he went to Boston University, where in 1983 he earned a bachelor's degree in aerospace engineering. He married his high school girlfriend, then moved to Long Island and took a job working as a test engineer for the Grumman Aerospace Corporation. At night, though, he would try to write stories.

"Not sure why I started," he says. "I was married and we had a daughter, so the idea that I might ditch that lucrative profession, which I'd spent four years studying for, horrified my parents. My wife encouraged me, seeing that I spent most of my time reading and writing anyway." They soon moved to Ithaca, New York, where O'Nan entered Cornell's MFA in creative writing program. He received his degree in 1992.

O'Nan has published eighteen novels (most recently, 2022's *Ocean State*), the novella *A Face in the Crowd* with Stephen King, a collection of short stories, and two works of nonfiction, one of which was 2004's *Faithful: Two Diehard Boston Red Sox Fans Chronicle the Historic 2004 Season*, also with King. O'Nan has won numerous awards: the Ascent Fiction Prize, the Columbia Fiction Award, the Drue Heinz Literature Prize, the Pirate's Alley Faulkner Prize for the Novel, Fiction finalist for the *Los Angeles Times* Book Prize, the Oklahoma Book Award, two Connecticut Book Awards, the Martin Luther King Drum Major for Freedom Award, and an Award from the International Horror Guild. He was also a MacDowell Colony Fellow. In 1996, *Granta* magazine named him one of "America's Best Young Novelists," and in 2014 he was named a Boston Public Library "Literary Light."

"I'm primarily a realist and hope to show great empathy for my people without softening the difficult situations they find themselves in—yet my work inevitably veers into the cruel and the sentimental. My characters are lonely people," he says, "who have a real need to believe; the struggle between faith and doubt produces either heartening victories (Cheever) or horrifying defeats (Flannery O'Connor, Robert Stone). The work is often ugly and unsettling due to this extreme split between hope and despair . . . I hope it's generous, or, as Cheever said, 'humane' . . . I make a lot of false starts and stupid moves before I really learn anything. But that's what writing is for me—a learning process. I'm trying to understand what I don't understand. Love, hate, what it feels like to be you."

PETER ORNER was born in Chicago in 1968, and began reading at an early age. "I think of a book like *A Cricket in Times Square*, which was always my favorite book as a kid—I've carried that book around with me. I think I'm attracted again and again to writers who take what's very familiar and show that it has something without making a thing about it."

At his Chicago high school, Peter worked on the newspaper as a reporter, though he considers himself "a very bad journalist." And when at the University of Michigan, he says he "was nobody's definition of a model student. I remember being lost a lot, in more ways than one. . . . The novelist and UM professor Tish O'Dowd—who I can't thank enough—was my first and most generous teacher. I think what she instilled in me was don't take yourself so seriously. I think of how often she laughed in class. . . . That's a great teacher and writer who loves literature, right there."

After graduating from Michigan in 1990, Orner went on to Northeastern University School of Law. He then worked in North Carolina investigating conditions within the state's prison system: "One day I got a call from a mother whose son had killed himself. I couldn't do a thing to help her but listen. . . . I couldn't help but, years later I [wrote] a story about it."

Orner soon entered the University of Iowa Writers' Workshop, and earned his MFA in creative writing. He has published two novels, three short story collections, and 2016's essay collection, *Am I Alone Here?*, a finalist for the National Book Critics Circle Award. His work has received other major awards: the Rome Prize in Literature from the American Academy of Arts and Letters, the Bard Fiction Prize, Fiction finalist for the *Los Angeles Times* Book Prize, the Samuel Goldberg Award for Jewish Fiction, Fiction finalist for the PEN/Hemingway Award, two Pushcart Prizes, and finalist for the Young Lions Fiction Prize. He was also granted a Guggenheim Fellowship and a Lannan Literary Fellowship.

"No matter how much I revise the imperfections, the limitations are still there," Orner says. "We can't revise away our limitations, which is a good thing. You don't want stuff too perfect. . . . I revise and revise and revise. I'm not even sure *revise* is the right word. I work a story almost to death before it's done. And maybe this is it: I beat a story to within an inch of its life—that's when I know it's done. Not before, not after."

He continues: "Stories are a sacred thing. It's the only religion I've got. . . . Good writing leads to good—and by 'good,' I mean questioning—thinking."

Born on January 12, 1973, in Chicago, **ZZ PACKER** grew up in Atlanta and Louisville, but it was in Atlanta that her love affair with words began, on daily trips with her mother to the library. There she discovered Judy Blume's coming-of-age stories; *Harriet the Spy*, by Louise Fitzhugh; and the young adult novels of S. E. Hinton. In high school, she says, she read "whatever there was," including, at age sixteen Toni Morrison's *Beloved*. "I'd always loved writing because I'd loved reading," she says. "I think people who are readers are inevitably interested in how it's all put together, what literature is and how it works."

As a student at Seneca High School, in Louisville, she read one of her short stories to an audience of her teachers and classmates. She now believes the story was "melodramatic and overblown," but she could also sense that her young audience was responding to it and that she had the power to make people "feel something" with her writing. "I think that's the kind of thing that isn't emphasized enough when younger writers begin to write," she says.

In 1990 Packer began her freshman year at Yale. Although she had published her first short story, in *Seventeen* magazine, at age nineteen, Packer did not yet see this as her path: "I wasn't thinking that writing was something you could actually do. I kept thinking, 'I'm going to be an engineer.' That's what I was striving for: I was in college to get a job."

But while at Yale, Packer spent most of her spare time in a bookstore, poring over the shelves and reading as much as she could. She changed her major from engineering to literature, graduated with her BA in 1994, and entered the master's degree program at Johns Hopkins University, where one of her writing teachers was Francine Prose. "She obviously hated what we all had put forth," Packer remembers. "And it was this incredibly—not even humiliating—imagine you've have been selected to this program and this person who you have never met just basically says, en masse, she doesn't like our stuff. After she read what she liked and said why, I thought it was really great, this is the ultimate education. I went back and looked at my stuff in this completely different way. About a third—that would be about three people—looked at their writing but the others just rebelled and it was sad because she was right. That was one of the times that I realized that to be a writer, you have to have a certain humility; otherwise, you aren't going to improve."

After graduating from Johns Hopkins, Packer worked as a high school teacher; her goal was to teach and write daily. "I still wrote, but it was incredibly difficult. Teaching, the students really need you. You can't just say, 'No, I am going to do this really selfish thing, scribble.' So it was incredibly hard to write and teach public high school. I actually thought I was going to do it for a lot longer than I did. It really does take a long time to become a good master teacher. It wasn't working out, though I tried."

Packer was accepted into the Iowa Writers' Workshop and in 1999 earned her MFA in creative writing, then was named a Stegner Fellow in Fiction at Stanford University. In 2003, Packer published her acclaimed short story collection, *Drinking Coffee Elsewhere*. Her work has won a number of awards: a Rona Jaffe Foundation Writers' Award, a Whiting Award, the 1999 Bellingham Review Award, for the short story "Brownies," and Fiction finalist for the PEN/Faulkner Award. She was granted a Guggenheim Fellowship and a Hodder Fellowship at Princeton University, and in 2006, the National Book Foundation named her a recipient of the coveted "5 Under 35" Award.

"In a way, [writing] requires an obsessiveness that's not going to be taught," Packer says, "And that obsessiveness [is] trying to figure out how to be a better writer . . . writing and writing and writing and failing and failing multiple times."

Her current project is a novel: "I've been working on it for such a long time that I really want it to be something," she says. "I'm not coming into it every day thinking, 'I'm the greatest writer in the world.' Or, 'People are saying good things about me.' I come to it with, 'Okay, I have to try to make this work. And I will prepare for this to be a day on which it doesn't work.'"

The younger of two daughters, born on December 2, 1963, in Los Angeles, **ANN PATCHETT** fondly remembers her childhood: "The 1970s were a different time as far as parenting was concerned. . . .We were free-range children. We were put outside in the morning and gathered back in the night. . . . I loved the freedom of my childhood." Patchett's mother, a nurse and the future novelist Jeanne Ray, was married to Frank Patchett, a police captain. Her parents divorced, and when Patchett was six years old, her mother remarried and moved the family to Nashville, where she raised Ann and her sister as Roman Catholics; they were educated by nuns. Years later, Patchett said that a childhood spent dreaming of miracles and praying to statues was the perfect preparation for being a teller of stories.

Since she was very young, Ann knew she wanted to be a writer, something her mother encouraged. Ann was a voracious reader. "When I was growing up," she says, "Saul Bellow, Philip Roth, and John Updike were *it*. They had the biggest influence on me. They were the writers my parents read, the writers whose books we had around the house. I adore them. They never let me down."

Patchett went to Sarah Lawrence College, where her writing mentors were Grace Paley and Allan Gurganus. "Allan's lesson was how to work," Patchett says. "We had to write a story a week, and a revision didn't count. He said think of yourself as a pipe with a lot of muck in it, and you have to get it out. The only way you can find out what you're good at is to have written a ton of work. . . . Grace's lesson was the lesson of having a single voice and being one person, so you're the same person as a mother, a friend, a teacher, a writer, an activist, a citizen. That was an enormous lesson that I had a very, very hard time learning."

After graduating, Patchett entered the Iowa Writers' Workshop and earned her MFA in creative writing. She then moved back to Nashville and worked as a waitress while she wrote what would become her first published novel, 1992's *Patron Saint of Liars*. Since then, Patchett has published seven more novels and five books of nonfiction, as well as, most recently, her acclaimed 2021 essay collection, *These Precious Days*. Her work has won numerous honors and awards, such as the Janet Heidinger Kafka Prize in Fiction, a National Book Critics Circle Award Fiction finalist, the PEN/Faulkner Award, the Orange Prize for Fiction, the Peggy V. Helmerich Distinguished Author Award, the Harold D. Vursell Memorial Award from the American Academy of Arts and Letters, and the American Booksellers Association's Most Engaging Author Award. In 2012, Patchett was named one of the most influential people in the world by *Time* magazine.

"*Lolita* killed me when I was in college," she says. "It frightened me and offended me, and later on it became my favorite book because I could read it as a book about language and love and insanity and bravery and the hideousness and complexity of the human soul. . . . I believe literature takes place between the writer and the reader. You bring your imagination, they bring theirs, and together you make a book. It's a kind of literary chemistry, and what's great about this is that the book is going to be different for everyone who reads it."

The first book **EDITH PEARLMAN** remembers reading was the English children's book *Tales from Shakespeare*, by Charles and Mary Lamb, when she was eight years old. However, she says, she began writing when she was younger than that: "I started a book, I think, at the age of three. And it was called *All About Jews*. . . . I started to write the book at three, but I didn't get any further than the title. . . . When I was young, I wanted to publish a book simply to be buried with it, that's all I wanted. I had no ambition beyond that."

Edith was born in 1936 and raised in a middle-class neighborhood in Providence. Her Russian-born father, a doctor, died when she was a teenager. Her family were Jewish immigrants from Eastern Europe, and Edith's childhood was rich with Jewish culture. Her mother always had a stack of novels at her bedside, which Edith would borrow and read. "Before I was a writer, I was a reader," she says. "I like novels, essays, and biographies, but most of all I like the short story: narrative at its most confiding."

At Radcliffe College, Pearlman studied literature but focused on computer programming because she believed that would better help her earn a living. She ended up working in that field for ten years. "It had much in common with writing fiction," she says, "because of the various choices you had to make. Every word had a specific function and could not be misused or misplaced." But she did not consider herself a writer.

In 1967 she married Chester Pearlman, an amateur musician and psychiatrist. They had two children, and eventually Edith's husband believed they were financially stable enough that she should make writing her primary focus. "I wrote in the cellar for a number of years," she recalls. "I needed a private space and it had a furnace, so it was always warm." In 1969, she published her first short story. Since then, she has published more than two hundred and fifty, many of them collected in her five short story collections. She is considered a master of the form, and over the years her work has been honored with major awards, such as two Syndicated Fiction Awards, two Pushcart Prizes, three O. Henry Awards, four *Best American Short Stories* selections, the PEN/Malamud Award for the Art of Short Fiction, the National Book Critics Circle Award for Fiction, the Drue Heinz Prize for Literature, and the Mary McCarthy Prize in Short Fiction. Her 2011 *Binocular Vision: New and Selected Stories* was also a Fiction finalist for the National Book Award, the *Los Angeles Times* Book Prize, and the Story Prize.

"To me, a short story is a conversation between writer and reader," Pearlman says. "Since only the writer can speak, she must take care to respect the reader, to avoid telling him what to think, to say as little as possible and imply the rest with metaphor, ellipses, allusive dialogue, pauses. The reader then takes an active part in the conversation, supplying what the writer has only suggested."

Pearlman describes her writing process: "Each short story takes several weeks (five days a week, about four hours a day) to write, in many, many drafts, all on the typewriter. The draft then marinates in a drawer while I work on the next story or piece. The marinated story finally gets withdrawn, re-revised, typed at last into a word processor, and presented to my dear friend, colleague, and ruthless reader Rose Moss, who usually sends it back to the typewriter for another few weeks of revision. So each story takes about a month and a half in total time, two or three in elapsed time."

"Read. Read everything. Read all the time. Revise. Revise each story from beginning to end at least three times," is her advice. "When I say 'revise,'" she says, "I mean rewrite completely. Don't use the computer until the last few drafts."

JAYNE ANNE PHILLIPS was born on July 19, 1952, in the timber and coal-mining country of Buckhannon, West Virginia, where, she says, "everyone knew everyone's stories, but the stories were secret. As the writer in my family, I felt that I was the person who was charged with making sure all these stories and ideas survived, but at the same time you're not allowed to tell anyone. Writing is the telling of secrets. Secrets have to be told. It's terrible if they're not, but if you tell the secrets, they can transform and unite one moment with another and bridge the gulf among time, distance, difference."

Jayne Anne's father was a contractor and her mother taught first grade, and both came from Western Virginia families going back to the 1700s. "I grew up on a rural road in a ranch-style brick house that my father had designed and built," she says. "It had a big concrete porch in the back. Behind the porch was an acre of yard, then two or three fields, then a stream, and then the hills began. I remember sitting out on the porch alone, thinking, 'How far am I going to get from this exact place?' I was intricately bound to it, but I also had the feeling that I wanted to leave."

At age nine, Jayne Anne began to try her hand at creative writing, and by age fourteen she was writing poetry seriously, something she continued to do at

West Virginia University. She graduated with a degree in English in 1974, then moved to California and later to Colorado, supporting herself as a waitress while she worked on her "short fictions," eventually returning to West Virginia and working as a teacher for the Upshur County Board of Education. In 1976, her chapbook, *Sweethearts*, a twenty-four-page collection of flash fiction was published by Truck Press, and not long after this, she was accepted into the Iowa Writers' Workshop. She earned her MFA in creative writing in 1978. Since then, she has published five more short story collections and five novels. She has received two grants from the National Endowment for the Arts, three Pushcart Prizes, an O. Henry Award, the Sue Kaufman Prize for First Fiction by the American Academy and Institute of Arts and Letters, a Guggenheim Fellowship, and an Academy Award in Literature by the American Academy and Institute of Arts and Letters. Her 2008 novel, *Lark and Termite*, was a Fiction finalist for the Heartland Prize, the National Book Award, and the National Book Critic's Circle Award.

"I started writing as a poet," Phillips says, "which is why I'm still a language-oriented writer. I write very slowly. I sort of compose line by line, as a poet does. I never know what the final arc of a novel is. I'm really inside the material, descending deeper and deeper into it and leaving room for a kind of organic process to take place.

"I really don't 'draft' my novels, in the sense of planning them out," she says. "I begin with language itself, a line, a way into a voice, and find the story inside it. As for revision, I go over every line again and again, but I don't throw out a lot of material. I trust in the material itself and stay with it for as long as it takes. There are obvious disadvantages to this method—it's a slow, painstaking process. I call it the high anxiety method."

KIRSTIN VALDEZ QUADE can trace her ancestral line as far back as 1695 in northern New Mexico, and as a young child she enjoyed the stories of her large family. "I remember being a kid and looking through old family photos. I was fascinated with my grandparents' lives and I would pester them with questions. My desire to write started not with the sense that I necessarily had something to write about, but with a curiosity about what it's like to be other people."

Born on July 6, 1980, in Albuquerque, Valdez Quade attended thirteen schools throughout the Southwest as her father, a geochemist, moved the family from one field study site to the next. They often lived in tents or trailers, and their car rarely had a working radio. "I was such a reader," she says. "I spent a lot of time in the backseat of the car while we drove through those endless desert landscapes, and I read that whole time, voraciously and broadly, my reading determined pretty much by what was available in the library or bookstore wherever we were. . . . I read a lot of books and they stayed with me."

Valdez Quade graduated from Phillips Exeter Academy in 1998, then entered Stanford University, where she took her first creative writing classes. "We brought in work to entertain and move each other," she says, "and that was my first audience, fellow students sitting around the table." She began to work seriously on her short stories, something she continued while earning her MFA in creative writing at the University of Oregon. "I was out of college and living in Cape Breton, Nova Scotia, in 2005 when I started 'Nemecia,'" she says. "If I had known that it was going to take ten years, I don't know that I could have maintained that commitment. But if you only see one sentence into the future, then you can keep the faith."

Faith and hard work culminated in Valdez Quade's acclaimed 2015 short story collection, *Night at the Fiestas*, winner of the 2016 National Book Critics' Circle/John Leonard Prize for First Book. Valdez Quade's work has also won an O. Henry Award and been selected for inclusion in *The Best American Short Stories* anthology. She is also the recipient of a Rona Jaffe Foundation Writers' Award. In 2014 Valdez Quade was named one of the National Book Foundation's "5 under 35." Her debut novel, *The Five Wounds*, was published in 2021 and was awarded that year's Center for Fiction First Novel Prize as well as "One of the Best Books of the Year" by NPR and *Publishers Weekly.*

"A book that's very important to me is Graham Greene's *The Power and the Glory,*" she says, "which I first read in high school. I remember where I was when I encountered this passage, which appears once the priest has ended up in a packed jail cell, with men and women crying around him: 'When you visualized a man or a woman carefully, you could always begin to feel pity . . . that was a quality God's image carried with it . . . when you saw the lines at the corners of the eyes, the shape of the mouth, how the hair grew, it was impossible to hate. Hate was just a failure of imagination.' I think about this passage all the time when I'm writing. It's not pity. It's empathy. Greene there captures for me the project of fiction," she says.

"The process of writing for me is akin to archaeology, revising again and again to uncover layer after layer of a character's experience. The closer you look at a character," she says, "the more there is to see: Complications and contradictions are constantly revealing themselves."

Born in Philadelphia on July 8, 1952, **ANNA QUINDLEN** read fiction as a child, but she also read any biography she could find about accomplished women. "I was looking in books for a way to be," she says. "I spent an awful lot of time learning about Queen Elizabeth I, Florence Nightingale, and Eleanor Roosevelt. Some lovely librarian who recognized what a dissatisfied girl I was gave me a biography of Betsy Ross, but the entire time I kept thinking, 'She's famous for sewing!'"

The first novel Anna loved was Louisa May Alcott's *Little Women* because, she says, "Jo March wants to be a writer and then becomes one. Enough said." Similarly, from when she was very young, Quindlen wanted to become a writer, something her teachers encouraged. "The first person who ever told me I *was* a writer, as opposed to 'you should think about being a writer' or 'you might be a writer,' was a teacher," she says. "And that's a very, very powerful thing."

In 1970, after graduating from South Brunswick (New Jersey) High School, Anna found work as a copy girl for the *New York Times.* One year later, when she was a freshman at Barnard College, her mother died of ovarian cancer, and seemingly overnight Quindlen became a surrogate mother to her four younger siblings. Still, she earned her college degree in 1974, then for three years worked as a reporter for the *New York Post.* In 1977 she was hired as a general assignment reporter for the *New York Times*, partly due to a class-action lawsuit filed by seven women against that newspaper. "I'm an affirmative action hire," she says. "And that's only a problem if you don't cut the mustard. These women brought the suit; the *Times* settled it and said they would be hiring more women, promoting more women, and hiring women in parity with men. And there were a whole group of us who were hired in very short order, many of us quite young, and it was entirely because those women went out on that limb."

Quindlen was promoted to deputy metropolitan editor, and from 1981 to 1994 she became one of only three women in the history of the *New York Times* to write a regular op-ed column, "Public and Private," which won the Pulitzer Prize for Commentary in 1992. In 1995 Quindlen left the *New York Times* and has since published nine novels and thirteen books of nonfiction, most recently 2022's *Write for Your Life*. Her work has been recognized with numerous awards, including the Pulitzer Prize, induction as Fellow of the American Academy of Arts and Science, a Mothers at Home Media Award, the Clarion Award for Best Regular Opinion Column in a Magazine, the Clarion Award for Best Opinion Column from the Association for Women in Communications, the University Medal of Excellence from Columbia University, and the Amelia Earhart Award from Crittenton Women's Union, and in 2016 she was inducted into the New Jersey Hall of Fame.

"Some days I fear writing dreadfully, but I do it anyway," she says. "I've discovered that sometimes writing badly can eventually lead to something better. Not writing at all leads to nothing. . . ."

"It all comes down to the Nike slogan: Just do it. So many people tell me, well, I'm thinking of writing a book. Does anyone say I'm thinking of performing surgery, or I'm thinking of designing a building? Writing seems to be the only profession people imagine you can do by thinking about doing it. No. Put your butt in a chair and write. And never mind feeling blocked. Everyone feels blocked all the time."

Born in Chester, South Carolina, on September 25, 1953, **RON RASH** was raised in western North Carolina, where his ancestors had lived since the mid-1700s. "I did grow up with a lot of people who told stories," she says. "I would just listen to these stories and listen to the way these people talked. That was a great thing for somebody who wants to become a writer."

Both of Rash's parents were voracious readers, and every week Rash's mother would take him and his siblings to the library. When he was in the fifth grade, Rash discovered *The Jesse Stuart Reader*, which, over the next few years, he would read over and over again. It was "a moment of real revelation for me," he says, "because suddenly I saw the language I had grown up hearing, both in the higher mountains and in the foothills, on the page. And Stuart showed me that there was a beauty to that language, that it was something worthy of literature."

At fifteen, Rash read Dostoyevsky's *Crime and Punishment*. "It deeply affected me . . . it occurred to me then how wonderful it is that you can do this with mere splotches of ink."

A competitive track athlete in high school and college—he went to Gardner-Webb University, where his father taught—Rash didn't begin to write seriously until his late twenties. "The kind of obsessiveness I had in running and all that kind of stuff led into literature and the love of reading," he says. "I felt, 'If I don't give it a shot, a serious shot, I'll always be haunted by: What could I have done?'"

Rash earned a master's degree in English, then taught for two years at a small, rural high school in the South Carolina mountains before becoming a professor at Tri-County College, a technical school at which he stayed for seventeen years. "A lot of my students were lower middle class, middle-class first-generation [to go to college]," he says. "I taught classes for welders, and that was good because one thing I don't like is the novel about the middle-aged academic who has a nervous breakdown—to me that's tedious."

Rash has published seven novels, four collections of poetry, eight short story collections (most recently 2020's *In the Valley*), and a children's book. His work has been honored with major awards, such as the Sherwood Anderson Prize, the Novello Literary Award, the Appalachian Book of the Year, the Fiction Book of the Year by the Southern Book Critics Circle, the 2005 Southern Book Critics Circle Award Winner, Publishers Weekly Best Book of 2008, and two O. Henry Prizes. Twice he was a finalist for the PEN/Faulkner Award for Fiction and he was the winner of the 2010 Frank O'Connor International Short Story Award.

Rash is proud of his perseverance: "I didn't give up . . . I had enough faith in myself to keep writing when I was getting rejection slip after rejection slip. That's part of the deal," he says. "Too many writers who are good give up too quickly. . . . Learn your craft, be patient; if your work is good, somebody's going to notice. It may take a while. . . . The main energy has to go into becoming a better writer."

Rash has this to say about reading: "What I love about reading a really good writer is that it's an act of communion. . . . [Y]ou're communing with someone who's probably a lot smarter. I'm communing with say, Edna O'Brien or Stendhal . . . [a] good reader has imagination."

RICHARD RUSSO grew up in Gloversville, New York, in the 1950s—in that time a depressed and depressing place. Once the center of America's glove-making industry, when that declined, so did the town. Russo's father was a road construction worker who gambled and drank heavily, leaving Russo's mother to raise their son alone. Young Richard would frequently visit the town's library and read book after book. He has said that he's not sure if he would have become a writer without that experience: "The library was the tree I could climb up into to get a glimpse of the outside world," he said.

Russo was born on July 15, 1949, in Johnstown, New York (near Gloversville). Richard went to the University of Arizona, where he eventually earned a PhD in literature, which is when he began to try his hand at creative writing. He submitted his first attempt at a novel to the writer Robert C. S. Downs, who told Richard the work was essentially "inert." In an interview years later, Russo elaborated: "[Downs] said, 'You're setting it in a place you have a tourist's knowledge of and nothing is coming to life, with the exception of these forty pages of back story that takes place in this mill town in upstate New York. You had me there.'"

Richard Russo has gone on to publish two short story collections, a memoir, and eight acclaimed novels, most of which are set in blue-collar mill towns much like Gloversville. His 2001 novel, *Empire Falls*, won the 2002 Pulitzer Prize for Fiction.

Russo's characters tend to be from America's lower working class, and he writes about them with empathy, humor, and insight; they reveal our humanness, our lack of control, our self-consciousness. In an interview with Kathleen Drowne, Russo said, "From the beginning of my writing career, I've always been interested in ordinary people swept up in economic and political forces they can't begin to comprehend, as well as in the changing face of American labor. Becoming a writer has only deepened my sympathies for working people, who are always, it seems to me, the first to be sold out."

DANI SHAPIRO was raised in New Jersey by a strict, Orthodox Jewish father and a non-Orthodox mother. "I grew up in a house full of secrets," she says. "My parents kept the urgent and salient details of their histories from me—and somehow, I knew this. . . . [T]his need to know was the beginning of my becoming a writer."

Dani was born in New York City on April 10, 1962, and went to the Pingry School, a prep school in rural New Jersey. She wrote constantly in her journals and knew she wanted to be a writer, although she had no idea how. "I look back now at the girl I was," she says, "a voracious reader, the kind who reads beneath the covers with a flashlight, and an avid writer of letters that were full of fantasy and invention—at the time I wondered if there might be something very wrong with me. But in fact I was living in my imagination."

She attended Sarah Lawrence College, where one of her writing teachers was Grace Paley. "[J]ust watching her commute up from the city and teach her workshops and meet with students, who sat on pillows on her office floor . . . gave me my first window into the possibility of a different kind of life."

Still in college, Dani began to audition for modeling jobs, which led to advertising work for Scrabble, York Peppermint Patties, and Coca-Cola, so she dropped out of school. "I . . . had no talent beyond a certain photogenic quality—but I didn't know what else to do."

In 1986 her parents were in a terrible car accident, which killed her father and seriously injured her mother. Shapiro became her mother's caretaker. She returned to Sarah Lawrence and graduated in 1987, then earned her MFA there two years later. "My father's death made me a writer," Shapiro says. "Perhaps I would've become a writer anyway, but I don't know if I'd have had the drive, the courage, the awareness of life's fragility, and honestly, the power of the grief driving me, and the desire to put language to it. Nine books and all these years later, I'm aware that much of my work has been an elegy, a way of honoring him."

She has published five novels and five memoirs, most recently 2019's critically acclaimed *Inheritance: A Memoir of Genealogy, Paternity, and Love*.

"A writer who is overly confident," she says, "won't engage in the struggle to get it exactly right on the page—but rather, will assume that she's getting it right without the struggle. . . . I think it takes tremendous courage to write well—because a writer has to move past the epic fear we all face and *do it anyway.* . . . Writing is hard; on the other hand," she says, "the thought of not writing fills me with dread, because it's the sole instrument through which I come to know my own mind."

Shapiro believes that a writer has a responsibility: "to witness and shine a singular light. In the *Gnostic Gospels*, it's written that if we bring forth what is within us, it will save us. If we don't bring forth what is within us, it will destroy us."

MONA SIMPSON was born in Green Bay, Wisconsin, on June 14, 1957, to a Syrian father and a German American mother. Her parents divorced when Mona was very young, and at age thirteen she and her mother drove to Los Angeles to start a new life. In school, Mona was a good student but was also, she says, "a clown" and "a smart aleck who used to make jokes in class. I did get in trouble a lot when I was older and then I didn't like school so much anymore."

After graduating from Beverly Hills High School, she received a scholarship to attend the University of California at Berkeley, and there she found herself studying poetry with some fine teachers, most of whom also happened to be major poets. "I had amazing teachers," she says. "I had Leonard Michaels and Josephine Miles, Seamus Heaney. Raymond Oliver was great. Philip Levine. Thom Gunn. . . . I stuck with poetry as long as I could—as far as my talent would take me."

She received her bachelor's degree, then worked as a journalist nights and weekends. She enjoyed the job, she says, because she was getting paid to write, the thing she loved doing most. "I always knew it was what I wanted to do. For a short while," she says, "the first year of college I thought maybe I would become a doctor, but I changed my mind."

She then entered Columbia University's graduate writing program, and after earning her MFA, in 1979, Simpson found work as a temporary ticket taker at the Bleecker Street Cinema and as an acupuncturist, and then she worked for five years as an editor with the *Paris Review*. "It was a tiny office," she recalls. "Four of us worked there and it was really fun. We would read things that came from all over the country. It was George Plimpton's hobby; he got involved in editing the interviews, but other than that he pretty much let us run it." She also began to write and publish her own fiction, getting her short stories in the *Iowa Review*, *Ploughshares*, and the *North American Review*.

Simpson has published seven novels, most recently 2023's *The Commitment*. Her work has won numerous awards and earned her prestigious fellowships: a National Endowment for the Arts grant, a Whiting Award, a Princeton University Hodder Fellowship, a Guggenheim Fellowship, a Lila Wallace–Reader's Digest Fellowship, the *Chicago Tribune* Heartland Prize, Fiction finalist for the PEN/Faulkner Award, and an American Academy of Arts and Letters Award in Literature.

"I'm a big believer in creating a habit of writing and reading as much as possible," Simpson says. "I think most young writers wait until they're inspired to write a story, and then they stay up all night or write twelve hours straight to complete it and that's that. Then they wait till the next time they're inspired.

That has little in common with how most work gets made . . . So much of the work comes in revising and seeing something you did and looking at what it is and how it could be better. So I think it's a question of living in a structure, so that you're in your work all the time. To me, that's what helps."

JESS WALTER was raised in the working-class neighborhoods of Spokane, Washington, where his father worked at the Kaiser Aluminum plant. "When I was a kid, I wanted my dad to be a college professor, honestly. He was a gruff guy," Walter says. "*I* wanted to be more refined . . . I thought, *How did I get in this family?*"

He was born on July 20, 1965. When he was five years old, he was struck in the eye with a stick. "I can't see out of my left eye," he says, "but like any novelist, you have to take responsibility for the whole world and I see slivers of myself in everything and everyone in my books."

Jess graduated from East Valley High School, then entered Eastern Washington University, where he studied creative writing and journalism. At age nineteen he became a father. "Being a dad so young, put[ting] myself through college, and then work[ing] at a newspaper to support a child from the time I was nineteen until I was twenty-eight—that's the time you normally leave," he says. "I couldn't afford to. [I was] the first in my family to go to college. People tended to stick around and a get a job in the aluminum plant."

Walter spent the first eight years out of college as a reporter for a local newspaper, then left to write a book of nonfiction about the standoff at Ruby Ridge, Idaho, *Every Knee Shall Bow*, which was published in 1995. He then co-wrote and published a book on the O. J. Simpson murder case with prosecutor Christopher Darden. "I wanted to be a literary novelist," he says. "That was my dream. I thought, *You can't get there from where I am. You can't get there from Spokane.*"

But he kept working, and writing his 2012 novel, *Beautiful Ruin*. "It was the second novel I attempted," he says. "I was in Italy. My mom was dying of cancer. We went to Cinque Terra. I invented this little town, and in my mind it would be . . . a kind of magical realist story in which nobody could die of cancer there. . . . I wrote until I ran out of gas, as young writers often do. I set it down, I wrote another book. Picked it up and set it down and wrote another book. And this happened five times."

In addition to his two books of nonfiction, Jess Walter has published seven novels and two collections of short stories, most recently 2022's *The Angel of Rome: And Other Stories*. His work has won numerous awards. Among them are the Edgar Allan Poe Award, a Pushcart Prize, the Pacific Northwest Booksellers Award, the *Los Angeles Times* Book Prize, *Esquire* magazine's "Book of the Year," and National Public Radio's "Best Novel of 2012." He was a Fiction finalist for the National Book Award and three times a Fiction finalist for the Washington State Book Award. In addition, his short fiction has been selected three times for the *Best American Short Stories* anthology.

Walter has some advice for writers: "Trust your own instincts," he says. "Read. Read. Read. . . . Be patient. Be bold. Be humble. Be confident. Don't give in to the speed and surface banality of the culture. Don't give in to jealousy, commerce, or fear. Do charity work, or coach kids, or be a Big Brother or Sister, or something, whatever it takes to get out of your own head and avoid authorial narcissism. And whatever you do, don't ever take advice from authors."

TOBIAS WOLFF was born in Birmingham, Alabama, on June 19, 1945. His mother left his father when Wolff was five years old. "We moved when I was very young and kept moving, all over the country," Wolff says. "Camus has that great line about order being chaos grown accustomed to itself, and a child's life is like that, I think."

At age six, Tobias started to write stories. "I don't know exactly at what time the idea hardened in me to become a writer," he says, "but I certainly never wanted to be anything else." In Florida for a time, Tobias and his mother lived with her boyfriend, Roy; he was abusive, so she left him. She and her son drove to Utah, where she hoped to strike it rich picking uranium. Instead, she worked in an office, and when Roy showed up at their doorstep, Tobias and his mother again fled; they took a bus to Seattle.

They moved to Chinook, and his mother married a man with three children of his own and constantly harassed and humiliated young Tobias. He attended Concrete High School in Concrete, Washington, but in an effort to flee his domestic situation, he applied to a prestigious Pennsylvania boarding school with forged recommendation letters and transcripts. He was accepted but was later expelled. "I was not an academic success," Wolff says, "but I had a couple of great teachers and was encouraged to think I could take writing seriously."

He eventually joined the Army, became a member of Special Forces, and was sent to Vietnam as an adviser. It was there that he began work on a novel. "All of the writers I admired—Hemingway, Faulkner, Mailer—had had some kind of military experience, and had used it in their work, Hemingway in particular," Wolff says. "I somehow understood that his military experience, brief as it was, had validated his writing. In all honesty, it was something of a literary impulse that led me to go into the Army in the first place."

On completing his service, Wolff went to Oxford University and graduated in 1972 with a first-class honors degree. He worked briefly as a reporter for the *Washington Post*. "I had already formed the very firm intention of writing fiction," he says, "but I enjoyed being a reporter.... I was there during Watergate.... My desk was right next to Carl Bernstein's." In 1975, Wolff received a Wallace Stegner Fellowship at Stanford University, which brought him uninterrupted time to write. He earned a master's degree there, and has been writing ever since.

Wolff has published three novels, two memoirs, and five short story collections. He is considered a master of the short story form, and his work has won many major awards, including fellowships from the National Endowment for the Arts (twice) and the Guggenheim Foundation, the St. Lawrence Award for Fiction, the PEN/Faulkner Award for Fiction, the *Los Angeles Times* Book Award for Biography, the Rea Award for the Short Story, a Whiting Award for Fiction and Nonfiction, a Lila Wallace–Reader's Digest Award, the PEN/Malamud Award, the Story Prize, three O. Henry Awards, and the 2015 National Medal of Arts, presented by President Barack Obama.

"Stories are about problems," Wolff says, from somebody having a choice and having a problem with that choice and then the series of consequences that follow from making that choice. To portray that honestly is to show the way people parse out their choices, and self-interest naturally comes into play. It isn't so much a matter of wishing to be hard on people as wishing to be truthful," he says.

"After a while you begin to understand that writing well is not a promised reward for being virtuous. You can be faithful, work hard, not waste your talents in drink, and still not have it happen. That's what makes writers nervous," he says, "the sense of the thing being given, day by day."

MEG WOLITZER was born in Brooklyn, New York, on May 28, 1959, and was raised on Long Island by her novelist mother, Hilma Wolitzer, and her psychologist father, Morton. It was a house full of books, and the first time Meg felt the true power of reading came with E. B. White's *Charlotte's Web*: "I read sitting on my mother's lap," she says, "[it] was the most emotional experience: that was when I made the leap from seeing how to untangle words to realizing how books both contain and convey strong feelings."

When she was a teenager, Meg had an experience that ultimately steered her in the direction of the writing life. "I went to this camp in Stockbridge, Massachusetts," she says, "and I, for the first time, was taken seriously and started to think about the world and became probably a little pretentious. You know, I walked around carrying novels with the titles facing out so everyone would see what I was reading. I positioned myself on stone walls with a journal—a quilted journal. And at the end of the summer, you know, going back home, as in my novel, it was like a tragic thing."

Wolitzer studied creative writing at Smith College, then transferred to Brown University, from which she graduated in 1981. While still an undergraduate, she wrote her first novel, *Sleepwalking*, published in 1982. Since then, Wolitzer has published eight more novels for adults and two for young readers. She has been awarded a National Endowment for the Arts grant and a Pushcart Prize, and her work has appeared in *The Best American Short Stories* anthology.

"I do want to say the process of writing a novel is riddled with self-doubt and self-loathing," she says. "It was a happy and pleasurable experience in parts. But you know, you're so on your own, and there's so much to do. It can be like you're planning a big bar mitzvah. There are a lot of tables to take care of. . . . Some books feel like sorbets between courses: You weren't ready to write the next one, but you have to do something. Also, even if it doesn't come out in that book the way you wanted it to, you're just working away, you're thinking, you're getting better. I think it's very useful to think of your work as a whole big, imperfect thing. The novels you write at twenty-two versus those at fifty-three— if you can bear to look at the earlier ones, you'll see yourself. . . . I want to continue writing and publishing into my old age," she says.

"We all want to write the kind of book that we want to read," she says. "If you put in the things you're thinking about and create characters who feel like they could live—at least for me, that's the way I want to write."

ACKNOWLEDGMENTS

✦ ✦ ✦ ✦ ✦ ✦ ✦

"Sonny's Blues, James Baldwin & The Long-Distance Runner, Grace Paley" © 2023 by Ann Patchett

"I Stand Here Ironing, Tillie Olsen & Pale Horse, Pale Rider, Katherine Anne Porter" © 2023 by Mary Gordon

"King of the Mountain, George Garrett & Sredni Vashtar, Saki" © 2023 by Madison Smartt Bell

"Clay, James Joyce & Yours, Mary Robison" © 2023 by Meg Wolitzer

"The Circular Ruins, Jorge Luis Borges & Getting Closer, Steven Millhauser" © 2023 by Dani Shapiro

"Paper Lantern, Stuart Dybek & A Solo Song: For Doc, James Alan McPherson" © 2023 by ZZ Packer

"Bliss, Katherine Mansfield & The Prince, Craig Nova" © 2023 by Ann Beattie

"The Brother, Robert Coover & Sorrows of the Flesh, Isabel Huggan" © 2023 by T.C. Boyle

"The Garden of Forking Paths, Jorge Luis Borges & Continuity of Parks, Julio Cortázar" © 2023 by Anthony Doerr

"Barn Burning, William Faulkner & Bartleby, The Scrivener, Herman Melville" © 2023 by Gish Jen

"Winter Dreams, F. Scott Fitzgerald & Boys, Rick Moody" © 2023 by Stewart O'Nan

"Wakefield, Nathaniel Hawthorne & Where Are You Going, Where Have You Been? Joyce Carol Oates" © 2023 by Tobias Wolff

"The School, Donald Barthelme & Bullet in the Brain, Tobias Wolff" © 2023 by Jess Walter

"Love, William Maxwell & Dance of the Happy Shades, Alice Munro" © 2023 by Kirstin Valdez Quade

"The Lady with the Dog, Anton Chekhov & Good People, David Foster Wallace" © 2023 by Mona Simpson

"The Lottery, Shirley Jackson & Builders, Richard Yates" © 2023 by Richard Russo

"The Ice Wagon Going Down the Street, Mavis Gallant & Family Furnishings, Alice Munro" © 2023 by Jennifer Haigh

"The Overcoat, Nikolai Gogol & The Shawl, Cynthia Ozick" © 2023 by Lauren Groff

"Madagascar, Steven Schwartz & The Death of Ivan Ilych, Leo Tolstoy" © 2023 by Robert Boswell

"The Artificial Nigger, Flannery O'Connor & No Place for You My Love, Eudora Welty" © 2023 by Russell Banks

"A Father's Story, Andre Dubus & Young Goodman Brown, Nathaniel Hawthorne" © 2023 by Julia Glass

"La Noche Buena, Tomas Rivera & Paso del Norte, Juan Rulfo" © 2023 by Dagoberto Gilb

"The Grasshopper and Bell Cricket, Yasunari Kawabata & Birds, John O'Brien" © 2023 by Stuart Dybek

"An Attack of Hunger, Maeve Brennan & The Yellow Wallpaper, Charlotte Perkins Gilman" © 2023 by Emma Donoghue

"Bloodchild, Octavia Butler & Night Women, Edwidge Danticat" © 2023 by Junot Díaz

"Work, Denis Johnson & The Dead, James Joyce" © 2023 by Michael Cunningham

"French Lesson I: Le Meurtre, Lydia Davis & The Cask of Amontillado, Edgar Allan Poe" © 2023 by Lan Samantha Chang

"Babylon Revisited, F. Scott Fitzgerald & The Tell-Tale Heart, Edgar Allan Poe" © 2023 by Ron Carlson

"The Corn Planting, Sherwood Anderson & A Conversation with My Father, Grace Paley" © 2023 by Charles Baxter

"Hills Like White Elephants, Ernest Hemingway & The Real Thing, Henry James" © 2023 by Richard Bausch

---

I would like to thank Joseph Terry, Betsy Farrell, Aaron Keesbury, Cynthia Cox, Dea Barbieri, and Dr. Sue Trout for their invaluable help in bringing this anthology to full fruition. I would also like to thank my wonderful literary agent, Anne-Lise Spitzer, as well as Lukas Ortiz and Kim Lombardini. Lastly, this book would not be possible without the sure and steady hand of my old friend, Joshua Bodwell, and of my dear friend and tireless agent for over forty years, Philip G. Spitzer. —*Andre Dubus III*

A NOTE ABOUT THE AUTHOR

Andre Dubus III's seven books include the *New York Times* bestsellers *House of Sand and Fog*, *The Garden of Last Days*, and his memoir, *Townie*. His most recent novel, *Gone So Long*, has been named on many "Best Books" lists, including *The Boston Globe's* "Twenty Best Books of 2018." He has two new books forthcoming, his novel *Such Kindness*, due in summer 2023, and a collection of personal essays, *Ghost Dogs*, due in 2024.

Dubus has been a finalist for the National Book Award, and has been awarded a Guggenheim Fellowship, the National Magazine Award for Fiction, two Pushcart Prizes, and is a recipient of an American Academy of Arts and Letters Award in Literature. His books are published in more than twenty-five languages, and he teaches full-time at the University of Massachusetts Lowell.

A NOTE ON THE TYPE

Reaching Inside has been set in Goudy Old Style. Designed by Frederic W. Goudy for the American Type Founders in 1915, the old-style serif typeface takes inspiration from printing during the Italian Renaissance. The diamond shape of the dots of the i, j, and punctuation points give the sturdy typeface an eccentric touch. Goudy was perhaps the best-known and most prolific type designer of his era: by the time he passed away in 1947, he had designed 122 typefaces. The display type is Nobel.

Design & Composition by Tammy Ackerman